# THE ART AND POLITICS OF FILM

John Orr

Edinburgh University Press

For Hannah

© John Orr, 2000

Edinburgh University Press Ltd
22 George Square, Edinburgh

Typeset in Palatino Light
by Florence Production, Stoodleigh, Devon, and
printed and bound in Great Britain by
The Cromwell Press, Trowbridge

A CIP Record for this book is available from the
British Library

ISBN 0 7486 1199 1 (paperback)

# CONTENTS

# LIST OF ILLUSTRATIONS

—◁▷—

v

# ACKNOWLEDGEMENTS

Earlier versions of Chapters 4 & 5 have been published as:

'Paranoid Fictions: Conspiracy Theory, *JFK* and Nightmare on Elm Street Revisited' in Norman K. Denzin ed. *Cultural Studies: A Research Volume* Volume 2, Greenwich, CN: JAI Press Inc., 1997, 71–89
'Greenaway, Jarman and English National Identity' in Justine Ashby and Andrew Higson eds. *British Cinema: Past and Present*, London: Routledge, 2000

Stills are by permission of Gala Films, Artificial Eye, the British Film Institute, and the Theo Angelopoulos Production Company.

Special thanks to Vassiliki Kolocotroni for permission to quote from her 'Interview with Theo Angelopoulos' Athens, December, 1998.

# FOREWORD   THE UNCERTAINTY PRINCIPLE

—⊃⊂—

In any critique roving into the realms of abstraction, the formation of concepts must be based on an aura of certainty. We plot the history of anything against the changes we catalogue, the nature of structures against the essentials we uncover. There is both pattern and direction, coalescing as sure sign, hopefully, of intellectual firepower, but this is always something of a *trompe l'œil*. Partly we grope in the dark. Partly we invent and hope for the best. Cinema is a chameleon that can change shape at any moment, and move in any direction. As such it can defy any theory that purports to unlock its secret. Let us therefore take two names that are conspicuous by their absence in this book, since they illustrate the point. These are Abbas Kiarostami and Robert Bresson.

Bresson, the subject of a recent retrospective at the Edinburgh International Film Festival, defies most of the analysis in this book. His work has shown a remarkable consistency of tone, of style, of theme over a period of forty years. In Scotland, the legacy of his work has reverberated through the last twenty-five years of independent film-making, from the Bill Douglas trilogy, through the films of Bill Forsyth and Gillies MacKinnon on to the current work of Lynne Ramsay and Bernard Rudden. His work depends on many things but three always stand out: the expressive power of the static shot, the timing in the duration of the shot, and the muted delivery of the unknown figure, unadorned by actorly style. Film director Paul Schrader, who has written perceptively on Bresson, also claims his legacy. Yet Schrader makes American melodramas in a noir tradition, frequently uses crane shots and a moving camera and casts top professional actors. Though he may copy specific Bressonian sequences, the changes in tone and delivery are so great that his films stand out as part of a different world. Schrader may claim affinity between the prison visit finale of *Pickpocket* and the one featuring Susan Sarandon and Willem Dafoe in *Light Sleeper*. Yet no one would have thought about it unless he had mentioned it.

Influence or imitation may produce affinities. On the other hand they may not. Another Bressonian, Glaswegian Lynne Ramsay, has acknowledged the influence of *Mouchette* on her first feature, *Ratcatcher*. Yet she also claims Bresson's greatest impact on her came not from any one film but from his *Notes on the Cinematographer*, which she read at film school. Meanwhile out of the fêted film-makers at the turn of the century, some critics have regarded the Iranian Abbas Kiarostami as true, quintessential Bresson. Yet Kiarostami admits little enthusiasm for Bresson, let alone influence. Both, it is true, display an austere simplicity in their *mise-en-scène*. The static shot, the non-professional actor, the mute delivery, the timing of the cut are Bressonian signatures also present in the Iranian director. There, however, the resemblance ends. The cultures within which both directors have worked are very different. The complexities of existence they unveil move in very different ways.

It would be more accurate to locate the European roots of Iranian cinema in Italian neo-realism, which Iranian film-makers do admit to. Yet the haunting power of Kiarostami comes from something deeper than the neo-realist paradigm. It lies in his flair for probing behind the formation of the naturalistic image, for using his camera to inquire into the ontology of observing and thus open up an immense field of possibilities. In his 1990s films such as *Through the Olive Trees*, *Close-Up* and *Taste of Cherry*, his cinematic world is very different from that of Bresson. For it has that burning awareness of the presence of the camera Pasolini had seen in 1965 as part of the future of film. Yet he goes further, exploring the vexed relationship of cinematic fact and fiction in a second dimension, that of identity. How much of the figure we see on screen is an actor, and how much a person? In *Close-Up*, where Kiarostami films within his picture the actual trial of the impostor pretending to be film-maker Mohsen Makhmalbaf and integrates it into his own narrative, the circle is squared. We no longer have a grip on reality and encounter instead what Laura Mulvey has called the 'uncertainty principle'.[1]

The uncertainty is within the film itself. What does the observing figure in the film actually find out? Conversely, since we are linked to that figure by the common impulse of curiosity, what do we as spectators find out? This double layer of shared curiosity, never to be satisfied, becomes most apparent in *Taste of Cherry*, where Mr Badiei (Hamayan Irshadi) drives a white Range Rover around the quarried landscapes on the edge of Tehran in search of an accomplice in his transgressive quest to kill himself. In short he needs someone to fill in the grave he has dug for himself after the event. Irshadi, a middle-class professional in manner and appearance, encounters a number of working-class men in the course of his cruising, to whom he makes this bizarre proposition. In doing so he becomes a man of many parts: sociological observer, would-be suicide, possible sexual predator and casting film director. In a theocratic culture where personal identities are often moulded by religious obligation, Kiarostami pitches us into a sea of uncertainty by dissolving fixed labels and roles. The effect is more powerful through the evasion of any kind of melodrama and through the simple use of the location camera, which we would see, normally, as an establishing device rather than a destabilising one. It seems an apt style for the turn of the twentieth century and indeed has been salutary in the writing of this book.

For how, at the end of an uncertain prelude, is it possible for an informed spectator to understand any of Kiarostami's films when they are so deceptively simple and so profoundly enigmatic at the same time? And if we cannot do that, what chance do we have of analysing the last forty years of cinema as a whole, which makes up the subject of this book? The only answer is to mix total humility with complete arrogance. For the enigma is the challenge. If Iranian cinema had a simple and self-evident piety of the image, which some critics seem to think it has, it would be no challenge at all. We can proceed only on the basis of enigma: the enigma that cinematic curiosity must nourish itself in a film culture often starved by the dictates of global commerce. Out of that enigma, however, must spring new forms of certainty: a certainty that is always partial and incomplete, and sometimes no more than a moment of revelation soon to be forgotten. Yet certainty it is, and arrogant it is too. Now that we are at our prelude's end, let certainty begin.

'The Eavesdropper Investigated: Irene Jacob, Jean-Louis Trintignant.
*Three Colours: Red.'*

*Chapter 1*

# THE RISE OF HYPER-MODERN FILM

In a world where film and cultural theory are dominated by prefixes, this book forgoes the easy option of ignoring them by producing, somewhat perversely, its own. Against a prevailing rhetoric that bisects twentieth-century culture through the divide of the modernist and the 'post-modern' is posed an adjacent prefixing, hoping to stress a different set of meanings. This, for better or worse, is the transformation from the 'neo-modern' to the 'hyper-modern' in the cinemas of the West and the rise of the 'meta-modern' in the cinemas of the East. Film is an elusive form for any critic and the more one analyses it, the more elusive it often becomes. It has its own trajectory, its own history and its own perversity. At times it is more chameleon than form. All categories, therefore, are haunted by what they exclude or cannot encompass. Hounded by its caution in echoing previous arguments, this book none the less bites the bullet by searching for the core of something new. Its claim for Western cinema since 1960 runs roughly as follows. From the 1960s and 1970s when high modernist art was reinvented in film-making as *neo-modern*,[1] there were two directions which film took as it moved towards the end of century. In the East it assumed a *meta-modern* form, governed by a new aesthetic for illuminating the clash between tradition and modernity. In the West it intensified into *hyper-modern* form, governed by the problematic of technology and spectacle in the computer-driven information age. Here the distinctiveness of time and place as known parameters of the everyday world is ever under scrutiny.[2]

The key changes here are not those usually seen as 'post-modern', the reinventions of pastiche or nostalgia or the knowing celebration of

1

popular culture proposed by Jameson.[3] All these play their part, of course, but are largely ancillary. Film still engages with the predicaments of modernity. Cineastes the world over breach old taboos and break new ground, forge new forms, make new political challenges. The urgency of the new in fact defines the changing film/modernity relationship. Hollywood also has more, and less, to offer than Jameson's formula suggests. It remains the home of popular genre in which the excess of melodrama and its simplified division of good and evil prevail. In short it is still the home of the meta-narrative operating on a mythic level. True it is now looser in construction than before and because, globally speaking, it has to face more segmented audiences, its mythic play allows for more ambivalence and more contrary readings. Yet its big-budget spectacles are still prime movers in a game played for high financial stakes. They are *virtual spectacles* that go beyond classic melodrama in a number of ways. One of these, and one of the most essential, is to give a mythic gloss to the speed and movement of the information society. It is this fusion of new virtual technologies using special effects on the one hand, and the *mise-en-scène* of spectacle on the other, which makes the key difference to its current dimension and its immediate future.

Outside of Hollywood, film inhabits a similar world but confronts it differently. There are many maverick cineastes with their own artistic agendas yet even here post-modern readings become problematic. The cineaste, like the Hollywood director, must confront the bewildering complexities of the information society and the power of its electronic images. Critics in turn must rise to the challenge of analysing film in terms other than pastiche, irony, surface glitter or techno game-playing. In the 1980s and 1990s this confrontation of cinema as a technical form with the technologies which drive our world has been taken up in the films of Atom Egoyan, Martin Scorsese, David Lynch, David Cronenberg, Peter Greenaway, Krzysztof Kieślowski, Wim Wenders and Wong Kar-Wai, but also in the work of many others. Thus while Hollywood collectively celebrates the information age, the lone cineaste of the *fin de siècle* deconstructs it in new and fascinating ways. One celebrates while often pretending to be critical; the other probes and challenges at the edges of convention, innovating in form.

I

In the twenty years between 1958 and 1978 (notionally the 1960s and the 1970s), the time-lapse between the releases, say, of Welles's *Touch of Evil* and Malick's *Days of Heaven*, or Hitchcock's *Vertigo* and Resnais's *Providence*, a new film form swept to critical acclaim throughout Europe and North America, and also, crucially, in the national cinemas of Japan and Brazil.[4] The French New Wave and its transformation of American film, a daring shift appreciated by a new, enthusiastic graduate generation, spurred it initially. Yet it had been foreshadowed, perhaps, by the transformed filmic vision of veterans Luis Buñuel, now returned to Europe from Mexico, and Ingmar Bergman, who had startled audiences everywhere with his medieval fable of nuclear fear, *The Seventh Seal*. The French connection, in which Godard, Truffaut and the cineastes of *Cahiers du Cinéma* had reworked the classics of Welles, Hitchcock and Hawks, was quickly taken back again. *A Bout de souffle*, which can be seen as Godard's idiosyncratic fusion of *The Big Sleep* and *Gun Crazy*, became a model for Robert Benton's screenplay of gangster notoriety in the Great Depression. Modelled loosely on Edward Anderson's 1936 novel *Thieves like Us* and events of the time, Benton's script was turned by Arthur Penn into America's first New Wave masterpiece, *Bonnie and Clyde*. Where Godard's gangster film had started as a road movie and ended as a peripatetic fable of Parisian *flânerie* by a gangster on the run, Belmondo at loose in the city which he seemed to wear as a second skin, Penn's film went back into a recent history of small-town America which Hollywood had never shown. True, it had been touched upon by Fritz Lang and Nicholas Ray, but Penn's film was shot on location in the very kind of small town in East Texas where its Depression anti-heroes, Bonnie Parker and Clyde Barrow, had thrived, robbing banks with guns and getaway cars, wearing the latest fashions bought through mail order, posing for the camera in makeshift intimations of notoriety, folk legends rivalling Hollywood stars for local attention and getting it.

After overcoming Warner's initial antipathy to the film, the production team, headed by the charismatic producer–star Warren Beatty, were able to force the pace of distribution and witness great box-office acclaim for something written off as luridly violent and meretricious by its reviewers. It set in motion one great strand of American neo-modernism, the concern with the detail of recent American history that Hollywood had largely ignored. *Badlands* and *Chinatown* both follow in its footsteps as visionary films based on the detail of buried history, a poetic summation of actual events they turn into recognisable fictions. Malick based his dark Western film of the 1950s on the aborted history of Nebraska spree killer Charles Starkweather and his twelve-year-old girlfriend. Robert Towne, like Benton, had researched the history of notoriety, the political scandals over land and the control of the water supply in pre-war Los Angeles, for the exemplary screenplay of Polanski's *Chinatown*. The detail of contemporary American life surfaced with a new clarity and powers of observing in Rafelson's *Five Easy Pieces* and *The King of Marvin Gardens*, Pakula's *Klute* and Altman's *The Long Goodbye*. Just as Altman's genre picture invited us to see contemporary Los Angeles in a new light, Pakula's location thriller did the same for Manhattan. In *Five Easy Pieces* Rafelson showed a flair not only for dissecting the sexual and social mores of his generation but doing so through the different contours and landscapes of the West Coast in his 1970 picture and through the look of Atlantic City and the Jersey shoreline two years later. The new work is strikingly candid in its sexuality, but the candour extends to life in general, to the fragilities of individualism, to questions of loyalty and danger, to class and ambition, to the changing conflict between the sexes.

What is striking about innovation in all these films is the match of theme and style. The new candour is not a sign of Bazinian transparency of the image, or of the lyrical impressionism which Jacques Rivette has deemed the quintessence of the French New Wave and which finds its purest expression in the work of François Truffaut. Instead it adopts New Wave devices such as the jump-cut, the freeze-frame, the use of natural light, or the long location take with source sound, and absorbs them into a darker challenging vision of the probity of American life. The use of comic irony is still there, strongly so in Altman and Rafelson, but the prognosis is bleaker in the age of Vietnam and racial insurrection. The vision of recent history is shadowed by current events. In any film they are never far away. One sees quite starkly the ambience of narcotics, not only in the acid rock of *Easy Rider* or *Zabriskie Point* but also through Leonard Cohen's lyrics which usher in Altman's *McCabe and Mrs Miller* and in the ominous chords of The Doors over which booms the warning voice of Jim Morrison at the start of *Apocalypse Now*. All four movies evoke, directly or indirectly, the paranoia of the Vietnam period in American life.

We can see here how 1970s American film grooves into the transition from classical to modern film, from action-image to the time-image posed by Gilles Deleuze. In the classic narrative idiom action involves movement and constantly changing situation. In the modern idiom, however, it may change nothing at all. The French critic plays on the pun or semantic proximity of 'balade' (route) and 'ballade' (song) in French to claim that the composite lyrical trip, 'bal(l)ade', is central to the time-image of the new cinema which breaks down the organic integration of situation and action prevailing in the classic mould.[5] The road movie, one could argue, is its prime expression, not only in American features like *Bonnie and Clyde*, *Five Easy Pieces* and *Badlands* but also in Godard's *Pierrot le fou* and *Week-End* and in key films by Werner Herzog and Wim Wenders, *Stroszek*, *Alice in the Cities* and *Kings of the Road*. In 1976 *Kings of the Road* matched its border locations between the Federal and the Democratic Republics of a divided Germany to the American music driving its two male protagonists ever forwards on their meandering route.

The term *neo-modern* also signifies a return of the modernisms of the early cinema (Eisenstein, Murnau, Buñuel, Dreyer, Vigo) with more breadth of talent and opportunity, enhanced technologies, larger audiences and more freedom from censorship at its disposal. Although such work was often dismissed as 'arthouse' and 'obscure' in the 1960s, many cineastes scored major commercial hits with specific features. Fellini was consistently popular from *La Dolce Vita* onwards while Bergman had major successes with *The Silence* and *Cries and Whispers*, Antonioni with *Blow-Up*, Godard with *Pierrot le fou* and Bertolucci with *Last Tango in Paris*. Nowadays, Bergman and many others are viewed negatively for two key reasons: first, the contemplative nature of the image that defies current conventions of film speed and movement; and second, their introspective focus. Yet Bergman is at the centre, for our purposes, of a double movement, a Swedish director facing west and east at the same time, paving the way for Allen, Cassavetes, Lynch and Egoyan on the one hand, and Kieślowski, Tarkovsky and Angelopoulos on the other. Indeed many of the many variations on film's recent relationship with modernity seem rooted in the film form he developed from 1960 onwards.

Like Ibsen, Munch and Strindberg before him, Bergman worked in a Scandinavian vein which placed the difficulties of modernity upon an open landscape at once wild and seductive, dangerous and threatening. Here, it is the foreign city, the remote island or small community which provides the key setting for his films of contemporary life from *Through a Glass Darkly* onwards, in effect the absence of the familiar in which, however, close intimacies must try to survive yet often collapse. The strangeness of the setting was never supernatural but almost hyper-natural since Bergman and his cinematographer Sven Nykvist have always shown themselves adept at transfiguring seascapes and landscapes through the use of natural light. They are northern landscapes we find unusual and to which we are unaccustomed. *Persona* and *Through a Glass Darkly* were shot on the remote island of Faro in the Baltic. *The Silence* fabricates an imaginary Eastern European language and city. *The Shame* fabricates an imaginary armed invasion in the age of the Cold War. In all these films and many others, such as *Cries and Whispers* and *Autumn Sonata*, no Swedish city ever features. Yet Bergman's characters have the sensibilities of educated bourgeois city-dwellers with a cultivation of taste and knowledge, a pursuit of erotic pleasure, an ingrained sense of guilt and responsibility as rational persons. In the films he shows us, none of these qualities brings enduring happiness but rather solitude, or despair, or collapse.

Kieślowski and Tarkovsky inherit Bergman's tragic sense in the East but in New York Woody Allen inverts them quite remarkably into comic form on the streets of Manhattan. How is this schizoid response possible, let alone convincing? The unlikely link lies in Bergman's cinema of intimacy, where his placing of the camera and *mise-en-scène* bring us close to his characters not as icons or star figures, but as figures involved in the kinds of intimate transaction affecting us all. The full close-up used so often in his middle period is not just an instance of privileging the spectator's gaze. It is a way of drawing the audience into an intimate transaction between the figures on screen, an intimacy of the viewer hinging on the intimacy of the players. This is never the enticing transaction of erotic desire, however, but the jagged edge of uncertain propinquity where fear, distrust and hatred co-exist with the desire to be loved. This is in no way a prurience in which the spectator as invisible guest can luxuriate in the role of privileged voyeur. Rather, it is a form of discomfort at one level and empathy at another, a feeling of being both inside and outside the intimate circle at the same time. We do not identify with Bergman's characters but neither do we pity them. At one level we inhabit the same emotional universe that is open-ended, unresolved and often unsatisfying. We can, with the conscious effort of immersion in the image, recognise ourselves there. At another level, the opposite happens. We do not feel we inhabit the same social or physical world, and instead we are made to feel distant, estranged, even though at times we can admire the austere beauty of that world.

There is no doubt that in European terms, Bergman's legacy went east. In Tarkovsky, one of Bergman's greatest admirers, Bergman's sense of the relationship between figure and landscape is vital, the focus on the solitary setting, the face and figure which inhabit it. This of course brings the exiled Tarkovsky into Sweden late in life, to Gotland just south of Faro to make *The Sacrifice* with Sven Nykvist and produce a film to which Bergman gave unstinted praise. In Kieślowski we find the one cineaste who has been able to rival Bergman's vision of intimacy as an imaging of inner truth in the midst of despair and adversity, and also, in his *mise-en-scène*, as a unique fusion of the voice and the look. The Kieślowski close-up also depends upon the intimate dyad of characters for its visual power, as in *A Short Film about Killing*, and expands in its way into a triangle between the spectator and the two screen protagonists who dominate the frame.

In Woody Allen, on the other hand, there is the adoption of a different canvas and a different panorama for intimate feeling, that of the city and the social network. Bergman's intimacies, which are so unbearable they at times become inarticulate with rage or shame or else lapse into silence, are naturalised by Allen as forms of discourse in a therapeutic culture where you would also tell your best friend what you have told your analyst and vice versa. The melange of broken relation-ships is more profuse in Allen, but less damaging. The network and the milieu help to break the emotional fall and offer a way out. There is too his own variation on classic Hollywood genre, Cavell's metaphorical (or literal) 'comedy of remarriage',[6] like *Hannah and her Sisters* or *Husbands and Wives*, where partners swap or exchange and resurface, twinned to their new intimate. The healing of wounds uncertainly prevails, the past overcome, the future anticipated. In *Annie Hall*, Allen's most popular

film, the homage to Bergman was overt. Posters for *Face to Face* stare
down at us from behind Alvy (Allen) and Annie (Diane Keaton), while
at the start Alvy is framed in Bergmanesque close-up, confessional-
style, talking to camera. Later Allen turns dark tragedy into pure comedy by echoing Bibi Andersson's repeated monologue in *Persona*.
Where Andersson's fateful speech was first framed from Liv Ullmann's
point of view (POV) and then repeated from her own, Allen has Alvy
rehearsing a play in New York where two actors repeat word for word
a key conversation he has had with Annie in California.[7]

This triumphant transition to comedy would be unthinkable without
the cityscape of Manhattan. Allen on his home patch innovates
through the look of the city, the location setting that is often familiar
but made distinctive through the cinematography of Gordon Willis or
Carlo di Palma. He seems unerringly to put his characters in the right
place at the right time and to naturalise time and place, to make them
as familiar as Bergman makes them strange. The comic proceeds both
from the conventions of the natural – this is how people do talk or
confess and so on – but also from the frailty of their aspirations which
may be foiled at any time or made to look socially embarrassing. For
Allen's middle-class professionals, the social and the city are the cush-
ioning effects that turn the potentially tragic into the perennially comic.
Allen is thus at his best in *Annie Hall, Manhattan* and *Hannah and her
Sisters* when he gives these conventions their full imaginative force
and at his weakest in *September* or *Interiors* when he isolates his characters and tries to make them sombre: in other words, when he
self-consciously imitates Bergman.

Cassavetes is a more distant figure here. Like Allen, he grew up in
the culture of New York City and adapted strong feeling for the city
location aided by the improvisational jazz feel so marked in his famous
first picture, *Shadows*. We could say that he takes the place in American
cinema that Bergman had in European cinema, but without obvious
direct influence or transcription of *mise-en-scène*. What is the same in
both directors is the unrelenting intimacy, the use of close-up, the
privileging of the close witness who is neither voyeur nor detached
observer. In part it may lie in their common debt to Carl Theodor
Dreyer and his framing of the human face. Yet like Bergman,
Cassavetes also has his roots in theatre and uses equally the same
cast of actors as a theatrical troupe. In Bergman the familiar faces are

Harriet Andersson, Bibi Andersson, Ingrid Thulin, Liv Ullmann, Max von Sydow and Gunnar Björnstrand while Cassavetes constantly uses Gena Rowlands, Katherine Cassavetes, Peter Falk and Ben Gazzara. It was however, a different kind of theatre that inspired them. Bergman had taken from Ibsen and Strindberg the problem of the psyche under the shadow of modernity, the dilemma of how individual finds true self-expression in a civilising, and constraining, ambience. From Ibsen in particular, whom he directed with great success on stage, he had converted the problematic of female identity, witness *Persona*, from a dramaturgy into a new film form. Cassavetes, on the other hand, had come up through the Actor's Studio and inherited the more performative nature of American theatre in which the figure of O'Neill had been the undisputed giant. In playwright and cineaste we find a common American denominator, a stress on the acting out of the roles of daily life as theatrical performance, the turning of encounter into drama and dilemma into event. Here the dilemmas of the civilising impulse take a new turn in the arena of exclusion. We witness vulnerability among the characters of Cassavetes like Mabel Longhetti and Cosmo Vitelli, which comes from living at the edge and wishing for something intangibly more that can seldom be spoken.

To the audience within the cinema, Cassavetes adds the audience within the film. In *A Woman under the Influence* Gena Rowlands constantly acts out the role of hostess to her husband Peter Falk's working buddies with a degree of hyperbole which borders on social disaster. In *The Killing of a Chinese Bookie*, the master of ceremonies in Ben Gazzara's strange basement cabaret, Mr Sophisticated, belies his name at every opportunity, forcing a reluctant audience into acts of unwanted attention. Yet the hysteria of 'acting out' emits a sense of desperate solitude that converts antagonism into sympathy, both among the audience on screen and in the cinema. The figures Cassavetes shows us are Pirandellian characters less in search of an author than an audience, their eagerness to please varying inversely with their capacity to do so. As Margulies has noted, the performance of Mabel (Gena Rowlands) is one in which the more she performs, the more her sense of self disappears by becoming too visible and too theatrical.[8] She is constantly on the verge of the kind of breakdown that had shattered professional actress Elizabet Vogler (Liv Ullmann) into muteness at the start of *Persona*.

While Bergman's austere *mise-en-scène* gives the viewer an intimacy with his characters that is seldom obstructed by external factors, Cassavetes does the opposite. Like Welles, that other great American transformer of theatre into film, he stresses the simultaneity of the event, the cross-talk full of interruptions, the constant movement of characters in modes of inattention. Unlike Bergman's plotted camera positions, his hand-held camera chases moving actors around the set while a second unit frames a telephoto or long-lens shot of the acting ensemble from the viewpoint of a peering and baffled intruder, seeing things from the outside, from in the doorway, or the other end of the room, or across the other side of the street. The view is obstructed, while the words are often indistinct.

Another comparison Cassavetes provokes is with New Wave director Jacques Rivette who also tried to forge a filmic theatricality and also made long films with extended sequences of improvisation. Indeed not only were his films longer, so were the improvisations. Whereas Cassavetes consigned much of what he had shot to the cutting room floor in editing down to between two and three hours, Rivette opted to be outrageously extensive, with the result that films like *Out One* and *L'Amour fou* are seldom shown to English-speaking audiences. The filmic practice of both directors highlights the artificiality of cinematic duration, of the conventions of running time. Since both were fascinated by duration, the time in which it takes human encounter to unfold is an epiphany which normal forms of editing sacrifice in denying the real time of encounter. Both cineastes also stress the tactile quality of acting in the use of long takes, so that intimacy here is more with the figure than the face. More Bazinian than Bergman or Cassavetes, Rivette eschews the close-up for the eye-level medium shot, but the Parisian bar scene in *Out One* with the prolonged struggle between the biker and the girl who tries to rob him, shot in no more than three takes, compares in its texturing of the moving body with the scenes in *Woman under the Influence* of Peter Falk endlessly running up and down stairs to reclaim his fleeing children, who flee from him again and again. In both *Céline and Julie Go Boating* and *Chinese Bookie* we have the creation of a spectral city, Paris or Los Angeles, where the deeper the film explores, the greater our sense of illusion, the more the real is supplanted by the imaginary.

In *mise-en-scène*, the neo-modern turn gave birth to a new poetics, which sprang from its key reinventors of film language – Welles, Antonioni and Godard. In many ways they can be seen as forming three points on an equidistant triangle, all feeding different elements into the recreation of film form. Their films, with odd exceptions, are distinctly unalike, so it is perhaps extraordinary that Bertolucci's most acclaimed picture, *The Conformist*, metaphorically joins all three points on the triangle and forges a single form. Yet it never actually does so. The lines remain incomplete, for Bertolucci has his own style and his own voice, necessary escape valves from the anxiety of influence. The most we can say is that neo-modern film is a series of styles of which these three signatures are the most distinctive and enduring signs of transformation.

Let us first take Welles. In his two great films of the period, *Touch of Evil* and *The Trial*, Welles forged a mobile technology of enhanced speed and virtuoso image making through wide-angle and deep-focus shots. His dynamic *mise-en-scène* and long takes were matched by overlapping sound and razor-edge montage, where sudden switches of time and place are bewildering, exhilarating, claustrophobic and agoraphobic all at once. This narrative leap is not merely stylistic ellipsis, a disassociation of sound and image or the sharp, unexpected cut which disorients the viewer. It is also a pure visceral displacement of the image from its traditional function of comforting or seducing the spectator. Its force field has since charged the kinetic energies of Truffaut, Bertolucci, Kubrick, Coppola, Scorsese, De Palma, Spielberg and Stone, all of them profoundly indebted to him. Moreover, his challenge to film language was inseparable from his concern with the burning injustices of the modern world. His work is an aesthetic of shock on two levels. It combines impact with disorientation. The more immediate the image, the more dislocating it becomes. Welles's aesthetic thus inverts Hollywood's tried and tested formula. Instead of the seductions of shock, the greater the impact of the Wellesian image, the less alluring it becomes.

Antonioni and Godard work in different directions, Godard with frantic urgency, Antonioni with reflective languor. Yet both shared a sense of the screen's limits, its fragility, its failures to show us the events in offscreen space or probe to the full the mysteries of the modern soul. Both explored stylistic devices for decentring their subjects, removing them from the centre of the frame or where in any particular montage the audience might expect them to be. This process, referred to by Pascal Bonitzer as 'deframing' (*décadrage*),[9] thus throws doubt upon the domination by their subjects of their own life-world. Whether these are the dislocations of landscape, modernist architecture or the sheer weight of consumer detritus, deframing throws subjects out of kilter and threatens their ontological status. Both directors also use colour as a form of painting with light, which has parallels with developments in modern art. In Antonioni's *The Red Desert* there is a level of abstraction in the coloration of the industrial landscape which echoes Mark Rothko's painting of intangible objects, while Godard's use of saturated colour with a hard surface sheen for the Riviera sequences in *Pierrot le fou* shows the clear influence of Roy Lichtenstein's cartoon-strip paintings and Pop Art.[10]

While Godard was infatuated with its trivia of everyday life and the bewildering speed of its incessant distractions, Antonioni's film language demands a contemplative stance, a viewing mode that became unfashionable in the impatient 1990s where the cult of speed and motion has flooded the field of contemplation. Compared to Kieślowski's Three Colours trilogy, Antonioni's 1995 collaboration with Wenders, *Beyond the Clouds*, seems to belong a previous era, to echo his greatness only to show us how far the nature of film form has changed. What his great narratives had shared with Godard is a discrete set of linear epiphanies, defining episodes loosely connected, which take events along the roundabout routes of the time-image. Often in Godard the epiphanies are done in contrasting styles, as in *Week-End* where each of the road movie's separate sequences has a different style of *mise-en-scène*. Not only does narrative leapfrog errat- ically through time and space, where speed after all is the film's subject, it does so in a set of styles so varied we might well be watching a compilation of film shorts on the same theme. The defining films of the 1960s such as *Vivre sa vie* or *L'Eclisse* are city epiphanies, each of which has its own weight and rhythm, irrespective of speed, with a defining figure, Anna Karina or Monica Vitti, and a unifying style. Vitti's plane trip to Verona, for instance, which succeeds her break- up with Francisco Rabal and precedes the encounter with Alain Delon, is a Deleuzian 'bal(l)ade' in which she relaxes and marks time between affairs. There is nothing of note at Verona airfield except the casual presence of a few American airmen, which may be arbitrary or on the other hand may be a signifier of the film's deeper theme linking Western financial crisis to the threat of nuclear war.

II

We might want to compare these epiphanies with the art of hyper-modern narrative in key films of the mid-1980s, such as *After Hours*, *The Belly of an Architect* and *Wings of Desire*. All these are city films, Manhattan, Rome and Berlin respectively, yet something more is at play. For a start there is in all three a narrative density and a speed of viewing which break with the neo-modern aesthetic. The earlier form is episodic and neo-Brechtian in its dissociation of the image (Godard), or contemplative and defamiliarising (Antonioni). In both forms there is an inherent critique of European bourgeois civilisation, the system as malaise. In the later films that critique starts to break down. What succeeds it is an aesthetic of the audiovisual densities of urban experience where the cultural accretion of signs, in which the hero is immersed, drives him to breaking point. It is not just a question of the audiovisual stimuli of the city and the way it is addressed, the question that had earlier preoccupied Simmel and Benjamin. It is the sense too of a configuring of speed, movement and information upon which there appear to be no finite limits.

Following Welles, especially in *The Trial*, Scorsese's *After Hours* turns Griffin Dunne's nocturnal traversing of Manhattan into a middle-class nightmare of irreversible motion. It is as if Dunne, like Moira Shearer in the Michael Powell film Scorsese so reveres, had on a pair of manic red shoes, here invisible, which danced away with him until he had all but expired. Estrangement, detachment, alienation effect, all tropes of the neo-modern, are replaced by the immersion of the subject in an overloaded world where Simmel's blasé attitude can no longer be sustained. The speed of the camera matches the speed of the journey from place to place so that all settings become non-places in Augé's sense, the complete opposite of Allen's 'familiar' Manhattan. The time-image turns into a continuous trip into the unfamiliar. Yet this is not to defamiliarise us in the formalist sense, since the unfamiliar is absorbed into the speed and momentum of the montage. It is to immerse us in the overload of the information age and its audio-visual signs.

Greenaway's style is somewhat different. In Rome, his American architect Stourley Kracklite (Brian Dennehy) undergoes a different form of involuntary immersion in the texture of the city, anticipating one kind of experience of professional success and enduring something tragically different. Scorsese's kinetic camera always moves us on so that although we may not jump literally through space and time, we still seem to move with each cut into a different world. Greenaway's visual density, on the other hand, comes from within the *mise-en-scène* itself. The supreme architectural city with its impacted archaeology piles layer upon layer of its past on the present torment of the dying, and cuckolded, architect. Its rich feast of spectatorship, in which Greenaway stages sumptuous images of famous sites in deep-focus photography and changes them out of all recognition, is also a set of variations on the tragic scene that is Rome. It is a city Dennehy cannot conquer in any way at all, either through passion or profession. His exhibition of Boullée's designs for the city, which never came to fruition, are an abortive simulation of an aborted simulation of a city which is too vast and too formidable for either of them. Its nature and history cannot be simultaneously captured, a dilemma exacerbated and not alleviated by all the forms of knowledge we have in the late twentieth century. The more we know about the history and the politics of the city, the more its actual nature seems to disappear.

*Wings of Desire* combines stylistic elements of both pictures. Like Scorsese, constant movement within the sequence fascinates Wenders, so that we traverse Berlin using aerial panoramas with elegant speed and complexity. At the same time his camera, like that of Greenaway, accretes detail of buried histories in the city so that it stores as it moves. In a way his two city angels, Damiel and Cassiel, are signs both of a metaphysical predicament and of narrative devices to forge an angelic mindscreen.[11] They see and hear what ordinary mortals cannot, the voices of countless city-dwellers floating in and out of the soundtrack as the angelic camera swoops over their apartment and crosses them in the street. *The Trial* serves as a template here for all three city films since they forge an agoraphobia which comes from their vertigo of the infinite. The infinite is not theological, but social.

At one level, for sure, the multiple antennae of experience overwhelm Simmel's blasé attitude. There is too much too quickly everywhere for either the subject or the viewer to absorb. We share that vertiginous mindscreen which I want to call the *coeval dislocation of experience*, or *coeval disconnection.* Here alienation is replaced by immersion, and defamiliarisation by the pathos of recognition. Above all, subjects are, as Cronenberg said of his characters in *Crash*, 'disconnected'.[12]

In Hollywood, the response to the crisis in the neo-modern runs on a parallel track. It attempts to mythologise and transcend disconnection through the technological sublime,[13] our fear and fascination with technologies of time present and time future, and above all with their visceral impact. One of the first effects of this change can be seen in political narratives, where the politics of investigation changes dramatically. Films like *The Long Goodbye, Night Moves, The Conversation, The Passenger* and *Chinatown* were all 1970s models of the investigator investigated, robbed of heroic status and turned inside out. Starting with *All the President's Men*, Hollywood sets the process in reverse. The investigators are still rough-edged diamonds in risky situations, down on their luck and faced by the forbidding complexities of the modern world, but you can identify with them. Whereas Pakula's film refines the time-image to represent investigating as open-ended duration, the new figures thereafter are more impatient and more hyperactive. John Travolta in *Blow-Out*, Nick Nolte in *Under Fire* or James Woods in *Salvador* are all flawed and unlikely heroes stumbling on to events of great political importance which have been suppressed, a trope which reaches its most complete expression in the squeaky-clean Jim Garrison played by Kevin Costner in Stone's *JFK*. Other films fit all too easily into the frame – *The China Syndrome, Missing, The Year of Living Dangerously* and *Mississippi Burning*. The audience get behind damaged heroes pursuing worthy causes in their uneven quest for justice. For after the crises of racial unrest, Vietnam and counter-culture revolt in the West, they reinvigorate common liberal causes by melodramatic means. Thus the heroic bourgeois subject is recuperated by building on the neo-modern legacy and then crucially altering course. The hyper-modern template we have noted in Scorsese, Greenaway and Wenders is then altered. It is embodied directly in the hyperactive investigator who stumbles upon the double standards of liberalism, home and abroad, risking Establishment opprobrium in doing so. Stylistic devices change. Action is speeded up so the time-image, which questions how much we can absorb of a dislocated present, is mythically transcended by a hyperactive troubleshooter, who matches the speed of film to the speed of the world. In a sense, if we take this a step further we leave politics altogether. Beyond liberal melodrama there always lurked a pseudo-politics of spectacle happy to stray from actual worlds into the virtual worlds of science fiction. Here were the experimental forms of spectacle that ushered the new age of hyper-modern film. For they paved the way to a new mythology, a mythic reinvention of virtual computer worlds, of the information society destined to work at every level of existence – military, scientific, commercial, artistic, intimate.

According to Virilio, such worlds involve a derealisation of sense experience, which a buoyant Hollywood makes mythic through science fiction and hi-tech action movies as an exciting and dangerous virtual reality ride.[14] Here the physical increases in speed, movement and density of the information society are fused with the new forms of electronic telepresence and instant communication to create a virtual world on screen and then reinvent it as a *natural* world. In hyper-modern Hollywood the heroic icon has a central place. New heroes are maverick figures who work within the auspices of the techno-scientific machine. Here there are echoes of earlier genres, the Westerner, the private eye, the undercover cop, but now the professionalism is techno-scientific. Sigourney Weaver is the new female executive mythologised as astronaut captain in *Alien*; Harrison Ford is the private eye-become-blade runner who has the scientific know how in 2019 to use the Esper and the Voight-Kampff test in his hunting down of replicants; FBI agent Jodie Foster in *The Silence of the Lambs* is locked in not only to her profession but also to its electronic and computerised surveillance, where serial programming is seen as the effective antidote to serial killing. Elsewhere the action-hero is already biotechnical, the maverick enforcer with a steroid-chemical body locked into new technologies of speed and violence and framed by the new technologies of special effects. If the cyborg is the new heroic – or demonic – figure of the contemporary gloss on a future world, of which James Cameron's *Terminator 2* is the supreme example, this is because the Hollywood star has become a cipher of special effects, an image in the machine, a well-paid victim of techno-entrapment. In hyper-modern Hollywood the narrative passage of the cyber-icon cues in the perpetual risks and malfunctions of the information society, which are mythologised as the force field of fate in the age of digital interaction and the personal computer.

Where Hollywood glorifies technology-in-general because its success depends upon the addiction to technology-in-particular, upon the empire of special effects and the strategies of simultaneous global transmission, film aesthetics moves in a different direction outside the borders of the empire. Offworld, to use the idiom of *Blade Runner*, is now a different place to what it was. The simultaneous glossing and experimenting with electronic technology in Cronenberg, Egoyan, Wenders, Greenaway and many others yields to us as viewers a critical fix on its domination in our life-worlds. Yet it does more. As opposed to the spectacular horrors of Hollywood hyper-modern, it chronicles the unspoken terrors of a technical life-world in which speed and motion have generated fragmentation and solitude. The neo-modern 'subject investigated' becomes the hyper-modern subject deconstructed through the ubiquity of technologies, which reflexively form the conditions for daily living. This links the key films of the 1980s to the key narratives of the 1990s. Five keynote films of the 1990s search in very different ways the core of the hyper-modern predicament. These are Kieślowski's *Red*, Egoyan's *Exotica*, Lynch's *Lost Highway*, Cronenberg's *Naked Lunch* and Wong Kar-Wai's *Chung-King Express*.

Let us take them in outline one by one. *Red* is the story of a fashion model who meets literally by accident a retired judge perfecting telephone voyeurism, monitoring all the calls in his neighbourhood, including her own, and now passing judgement on others by proxy where once he had done it in court.[15] Through the motif of phone-tapping Kieślowski deconstructs the wider voyeurism inherent in daily technologies of communing. In *Exotica* Egoyan explores the way new technologies lure us into recreating the banalities of everyday life as 'exotic' performance and his lap-dancing emporium is a transparent hyper-real locale where sexuality is reinvented as a set of disconnected relationships. In *Lost Highway* Lynch takes video surveillance as means and metaphor for the violation of domestic space. The anonymous videotape delivered through the letterbox by an unseen hand with its video images of intrusion through the skylight, visually 'rapes' the intimacy of Bill Pullman and Patricia Arquette, the distraught couple festering in their desolate suburban home. In Cronenberg's film of Burroughs' notorious novel, Peter Weller's narcotic hallucinations of Mugwumps and typewriters turning into beetles suggest for a biotechnical age the nightmare vision of transverse crossover between the organic and the mechanical world. Technical objects become living forms and humans are frozen into the posture of machines. In Wong Kar-Wai's pyrotechnic version of compressed living in Kowloon, urban space becomes phantasmagoric, as couples traverse the same locations without meeting and then meet knowing nothing of their adjacency and then finding out even less, or else they traverse the same spaces at different times in relations of amorous disconnection where neither body nor soul will meet. The speed of time passing and camera moving dizzily in hand-held motion only exacerbate and never expiate the predicament of distended solitude.[16]

Let us focus in once more on *Red*. Kieślowski starts with two stunning shot-sequences. In the first a male hand dials a phone number and the camera tracks with a series of disguised cuts the speed of the call through the cable via the exchange and undersea to its receiver in another country where the engaged tone repeats and the engaged buzzer flashes. An intermediate shot shows a man (later known as law student Auguste) walking his dog out of his Geneva apartment to a nearby café. As he enters the café in high-angle long shot the camera pans and tilts upwards before tracking forwards into the apartment window of Valentine (Irène Jacob) to catch the moment at which her phone rings in an empty room. She appears out of nowhere to answer and move around the flat with the cordless instrument, still in the same shot, answering her boyfriend who has called her from London. As Valentine sits motionless by her bed, Kieślowski finally cuts to facial close-up. We return to the man coming out of the café and making a phone call from his own flat to a weather report call voice. He kisses the female voice down the phone and replaces the receiver, later getting into his jeep before driving off just as Jacob enters the shot and then enters the same café from which he has just departed. While Kieślowski uses offscreen space in ways akin to Antonioni or Godard, the whole sequence intensifies the film experience through its perpetual adjacency. Auguste and Valentine live in adjacent apartments, phone their respective lovers at almost identical times, and use the same local café consecutively. Yet their paths never truly cross even though it seems from the imprint of the montage on the viewing eye that they are in fact phoning *each other*. This, if you like, is a montage of *coeval disconnection*.

We might want to call this the heretical route to the hyper-modern. While Hollywood cinema makes mythic the hyper-modern as virtual spectacle, the cineastic alternative presents it as coeval disconnection. The concern with the reflexive nature of the image, the filmic use of other forms of imaging remains as *visual* as ever, making nonsense of Jameson's claim that in the post-modern the optical gives way to the purely sonic.[17] Rather the fusion of sonic and optical is made more intense by a technical life-world of simultaneous presence, where different technologies, the car, fax, telephone, computer, camera, run in parallel but never in tandem. This is both speed and implosion, the acceleration of which Giddens speaks when he sees late modernity as a juggernaut in danger of careering out of control, the implosions of telepresence which define for Virilio the invisibility of instantaneous information and for Negroponte increasing domination of the global network of bits over the tangible world of atoms.[18] Yet the key departure from the neo-modern does not lie in the triumph of the city of bits over the city of atoms. It lies in the accretion of another form of vital layering which alters the atomic city upon which it is superimposed. The new cinematic city is both city of atoms and city of bits. In Kieślowski's trilogy, both *Blue* and *Red* are triggered by the fate of the car accident, the technical rendering of a daily fusion of a daily fate, the equation of motorised speed and random encounter. In Egoyan's films, the bourgeois subject lacks definition unless it centres itself amidst screens and cameras (*Family Viewing*), or translates daily fate into stylised performance (*Exotica*), or perversely does both (*The Adjuster*). In *Lost Highway* the electronic instrument as video camera or mobile phone is turned into a Gothic monstrosity violating human privacy and presence, a harbinger of hyper-modern rape. It is a metaphor that the brutal hard-core movie screened towards the end of the film makes distressingly literal. In all these films, coeval disconnection creates an implosive density where the coordination of the senses is stretched to an almost impossible pitch. It gives a new, at times frightening meaning to the old cliché that everything happens at once.

*Chapter 2*

# HOLLYWOOD AND THE POLITICS
# OF VIRTUAL SPECTACLE

In the age of the PlayStation let us play with names instead. Our fable of Western cinema so far has been a tall tale, a tale of two siblings, the Cain and Abel of information culture on celluloid, Esau and Jacob competing unfairly in the global village. The biblical names are interchangeable. If the hyper-modern is divided beneath its carapace, how better to mark it out than by mythic precedent and invent a sibling rivalry that is purely metaphorical? We have after all two unequal contenders for the prize of box-office glory. Vision or metaphor, it matters not. This dual offspring of advanced technologies proffers alternate visions of the hyper-modern, one as spectacle, and the other as art. You pay your money and you take your choice. In *Lost Highway* Bill Pullman and Robert Loggia are signifiers, respectively, of psychic derangement and the ubiquity of evil in the fabric of American life. Yet mass audiences know them better for their acting in *Independence Day*, where as the US President and his military Chief of Staff, they resolve to save what is left of the civilised world from genocidal aliens. Lynch's film is a disturbing meditation on derangement, corruption and death. *Independence Day* is a holocaust fantasy posing as a feel-good movie, complete with conspiracy in-jokes about Roswell and Dr Strangelove, and scenarios of virtual war. In *Lost Highway* there are three terrifying murders. *Independence Day* wipes out millions, but no one really dies at all.[1]

This takes our tale one stage further. The power-hungry sibling resorts to spectacle and the sublime to sell the power of technology and emerges as Hollywood's cyborg victor. The maverick offspring narrates the solitude and terror at the heart of the information machine, though that machine is so dispersed, so diffuse, so everywhere it has no heart at all. If this sounds like a fable of the orthodox and the heretical tangling over the mantle of the sacred, then in part it is, but with one proviso. The orthodox must constantly mutate in the electronic age since their mandate comes not from heaven but from the box-office, which despite much survey research and great vigilance, is never totally their own invention. The orthodox are consequently unorthodox and their lust for commerce depends upon a modicum of art. Meanwhile the heretics of the hyper-modern must gain enough audiences on different screens of varied sizes to continue on their modest way, financially out of the loop but full of poetic surprises in their consecration of form. Their lust for art depends, to say the least, on a modicum of commerce.

Auteurism is a code name for a movement that no longer exists. The hyper-modern is now so dispersed around the globe that there is no core, no centre, no country which truly defines it. Indeed it is no longer purely 'Western' at all. For auteurism now has no hiding-place in the tangible movement or the network. There is no longer a French New Wave, a New German cinema or a maverick alliance of Easy Riders and Raging Bulls which enables us to nail a label to a collectivity. The nearest is the Danish Dogme '95, a group so tiny in a country so small it has simply become an effective way of getting noticed for its innovation and code of low-budget filming. Even the renaissance of the British cinema in the 1980s had no central core or manifesto, no common theme linking its disparate parts. In America itself the Sundance Institute has provided a forum for independent film-making but is not the source of any cinematic movement, at best a clearing-house and catalyst. While Cain is cruelly coherent, Abel is a persona with no centre. We are left with a set of global names, of dispersed cineastes with no place in Hollywood. When money talks, they are always somewhere else.

When money does talk, we know the regular story. As commercial traffic, hyper-modern Hollywood is launched from techno-financial encounters of the global kind. Its film reality is also virtual. For the centre of Hollywood is little more than a slum, a set of tourist shrines set amid dilapidated buildings now housing mainly poor Latino immigrants. Meanwhile the virtual image of Golden Age Hollywood, as

Mike Davis notes, has eloped to Florida theme parks, courtesy of MCA and Disneyland.[2] Hollywood the legend has become purely notional, in other words 'Hollywood'. Movie deals are done nearby in the LA area while many features have migrated north to Seattle for their shoots or over the border to Vancouver with its cheaper labour costs. The industry power-mode has also changed. No longer the preserve of mogul patriarchs as in classical mode, it has become something very different, a set of shifting and fluid corporate enterprises with high-risk profiles for its frangible élites and a vast range of economic and media interests outside of film. Thus Warner Brothers duly became Warner Communications and, in time, Time–Warner, then Time Warner Turner, then merging with AOL and EMI, a vast corporate audiovisual and communications empire spanning the world. It was a deal soon to be imitated by other companies.[3] By 1990, Paramount Pictures had become Paramount Communications Incorporated (PCI), drawing in music, video, cable, publishing and basketball under its vast corporate umbrella. Disney took over ABC/Capital Cities, launched profit-gorging theme parks and devolved power to executives at in-house ancillaries such as Touchstone and Miramax. Fox, once prefixed by the Twentieth Century, is now the appropriate in-house studio of Rupert Murdoch's growing media empire.

Yet the lure of the name 'Hollywood' is hard to extinguish. Even though its technical hardware often originates in the Far East, 'Hollywood' remains American to the core. It can be bought into but never bought out, as Sony found to its cost in its takeover of Columbia pictures. Noted directors like Ridley and Tony Scott, John Woo, Hector Babenco, Barbet Schroeder, Wolfgang Petersen or Paul Verhoeven move in from other countries and continents, but few move out unless they are cast out, like the maverick Orson Welles making *The Trial* and *Mr Arkadin* in Europe in the mid-1950s and early 1960s. With actors and cinematographers the volume of traffic is even higher, and invariably one-way. 'Hollywood' now stands at the electronic summit of world culture while the most fascinating cineastes in the world remain, with a handful of exceptions, those who never go there. It is a feat concentrated in the last twenty years. In the 1980s, and in tandem with the presidency of a former B movie star whose best-known gambit in politics was to dream up a nuclear defence system called 'Stars Wars' after his favourite sci-fi movie, Hollywood's rebirth as a studio system became a prelude to global domination of the box-office by the end of the century. The cultural buoyancy of Bollywood in Bombay and the resurgence of Islam in the Middle East have been more than offset by the end of the Cold War, the triumphalist culture wars of the General Agreement on Tariffs and Trade (GATT) accords and the opening up of China. When James Cameron proclaimed himself 'King of the World' as *Titanic* swept the board at the 1998 Oscars, he may have been vain but he was also right. Indeed as a virtual city Hollywood now seems the apt place for its most powerful invention of the late twentieth century, the cinema of virtual spectacle, which *Titanic* embodied to awesome perfection.

I

Where do we make a start with all this? An epilogue is needed before we make the crucial cut, the incision into the fabric of recent history to find the origins of virtual spectacle. The 'legend' of Los Angeles, the city, has recently been affirmed by two box-office films, *Heat* and *LA Confidential*. The latter is Hollywood's version of James Ellroy's 1950s *policier*, the former a cop thriller for the 1990s which charts the monumental disasters of a bank heist gone wrong. Both see LA through the magic looking glass of cinematographer Dante Spinotti, who gives us the most striking architectural images of the city in recent film, no mean feat after it has been done to death by endless TV shoots. Ellroy has said that he chose not to write about the present city because it is too dispersed, too socially disparate to form a common core for his narrative structure and his take on police and politics.[4] Instead, like Walter Moseley, he creates the legend of the post-war city as a coherent corrupt metropolis. In trying to give LA a core and structure in his 1995 thriller Michael Mann gives us a virtual city instead. True, there have been reports of '*Heat* heists', alarming city shootouts between cops and bank robbers, which could almost be modelled on the film itself. Yet the film's monumentalism is both thematic and stylistic, using a fabulist *mise-en-scène* to key into what Davis has called Southern California's 'ecology of fear'.[5] For we somehow feel that the heist is so explosive in its eruption and so vast in its consequences that it bears the freight of both social and natural

calamity, those disasters of riot, city-wide gang wars, earthquake, flood
and fire which have ravaged a whole region. Yet actual references to
any of them in the movie are non-existent. The cops-and-robbers
feud, which mimics the cult of 'honour' in the classical Western, is
anti-mimetic, and largely white-on-white in a city of supreme ethnic
contrast. There are of course safe token gestures, such as the mourning
of the young black hooker brutally murdered by the crew's one (white)
psychopath who thus violates the crew's 'honour'. The rest of them
are, after all, good white family men. Yet this is a passing sequence
to pull at the heartstrings. What matters is something else. The fore-
grounding of the heist as a spectacle of immense visual power makes
us feel that the whole city is shaking to its foundations. Indeed the
full frontal force of the heist is inexplicable, unless we consider something the film does not even mention, the Rodney King riots which
a few years earlier had torn whole areas of Los Angeles apart in one
of America's worst civil disturbances of the century.

While, no doubt, screen treatments of the King scenario were
pitched frantically around Hollywood in the days after violence
subsided, such brutal rending of the social fabric has never been the
stuff of which big-budget features are made. In *Heat* they are conspicuous by their absence, but perhaps something more pernicious is
afoot. By now, police corruption has been standard fare for TV movies,
but seldom broached with any intelligence in features unless
embedded deep in the past, like *The Godfather* or *LA Confidential*. An
exception might be made for the odd LA film like *Internal Affairs* but
the kind of perception and acuity to be found in the critical commen-
taries on the LA Police Department (LAPD) by Davis, Joan Didion
and John Gregory Dunne seldom finds its way into the shooting
script.[6] Indeed *Heat* goes quite remarkably in the opposite direction.
After the Rodney King débâcle, the LAPD is rescued mythically from
its shredded reputation. With Al Pacino's charisma as unerring guide,
it becomes an epicentre of male bonding, honour and relentless devotion to duty.[7] Yet the bombastic narrative openly excuses the police
blunders and ineptitude which allow the heist to go ahead and many
of the crew to escape afterwards. This spectacular contrast of the
rational and the absurd is fascinating as part of the stuff of legend.
The investigation is fully staffed, hi-tech, with round-the-clock surveillance yet somehow helpless before the robber's simple cunning and

the invisible hand of fate. This hapless contradiction only makes sense if we take into account the racial unconscious of the city's topography. What is truly signified is absent from the film. What we have is far from actual, historical disaster. It is, instead, a monument to virtual spectacle.

It may well be a symbolic midpoint in the rise of Hollywood hyper-modern which can be traced back to three key films made in the late 1970s/early 1980s, films which are still cult pictures and, by now, household names – Spielberg's *Close Encounters of the Third Kind*, Coppola's *Apocalypse Now* and Ridley Scott's *Blade Runner*. These, in a way, are the founding narratives, acronym CLEANBLADE, genre narratives in the best American sense of the word, the first new science fiction, the second transformed war film, the third triumphant hybrid of sci-fi, private eye and film noir. All subvert and transform their own genres but to call them 'post-modern' for doing so because they contain superior elements of pastiche or reflexivity is to miss the point. They are all authorly works, singular visions and deadly serious, honing in on the changing face of the information age and yet, paradoxically, providing it with that mythic underlay which Hollywood has since taken to its heart. Initially their fates varied. Spielberg's film was a blockbuster hit, Coppola eventually broke even on a major budget which threatened at one point to bankrupt United Artists, and *Blade Runner*, panned in previews and feeble in box-office on first release, has since become a global cult movie. On its re-release in 1991 with a new director's cut it was already a return to the future because by then it had become a defining influence on science fiction everywhere. In its time CLEANBLADE reinvented cinematic spectacle as a new form of fear and fascination, probing disquiet about present and future worlds alike, insinuating our seduction by Promethean technologies which, in the zone of perpetual danger prophesied by Martin Heidegger, define our daily fate. To this sacred trinity we might add a fourth name, since it acts by default, by the very absence of the techno-world the others unveil. It is of course Stanley Kubrick's *The Shining*, whose Overlook Hotel is completely cut off in mid-winter from the outside world, and where the horror of family solitude as absence from the technical life-world 'out there' signifies a deeper horror, the horror of civilisation's void, of the nothingness at the centre of connection.

CLEANBLADE is a primal sonic and optical triangle, a first footing
of time and speed in a world of electronic communications called by
Castells, as we have seen, the information age or the network society.[8]
A more precise and limiting term might be the *networked society*. Here
human relations revolve more and more around instant transfers of
discourse, technology, money and information. Social privilege increasingly becomes a matter of inclusion or exclusion from such discourse.
The technologies of the information age are both the implicit subject
of CLEANBLADE and the essence of its composite form. The technologies they portray as objective features of war, space, the city and
the future are inseparable from the technical innovations they use as
film, but how, given its dry and very general description, does the 'networked society' ever become a fertile ground for cinematic myth? The
first sign of its potential lies of course in its instant global reach across
nations and continents. Yet that brings us back to the paradox which
CLEANBLADE foregrounds as myth. Information as *content* of the
message in the computer age is inseparable from the *forms* of communication by which it is transmitted. For McLuhan the medium would
become the message in the new global village. This is not so much the
reduction of content to form as a final and triumphant fusion of both
in favour of the latter. From the interactive computer to the mobile
phone, content, invariably, is absorbed into form. For film, as we have
seen, the paradox is reflexive since its technologies are part of the
symbiosis of new technologies in general. As Baudrillard pointed out,
*Apocalypse Now* was not only a high-budget screen simulation of the
Vietnam War, but also a self-dramatising repeat of its impossible logistics and perceptual derealisation shot in the Philippine jungle ten years
on.[9] Both the war and the defining film of that war were operational
nightmares. The US could leave Vietnam to consolidate elsewhere.
Coppola could leave the Philippines to edit his footage in LA. By the
time the picture ends, Kurtz's alien hideaway in its hallucinatory jungle
could just as well be set on another planet. Thus if Coppola reinvented
geopolitical reality as the virtual spectacle of war he also reinvented the
war movie as science fiction.

As the information age was gathering pace or better still was
imploding towards the century's end as a more intense form of
computer socialising, its nature was becoming more elusive. For its
imploding force is characterised, as Paul Virilio has recently noted, by

two key elements: *speed* and *invisibility*.[10] Time is virtually shortened to zero by simultaneous transmission and a perpetual telepresence, which is beyond the horizon of the naked eye. Yet the vanguard of this movement into a global infoworld is not initially the mass media. It is two-pronged, a legacy of the nuclear Cold War since 1948. Driven by American imperatives, its politics is both military and scientific, the intermeshed Research and Development with billion-dollar budgets where space exploration, a goldmine for hyper-modern myth, has been locked from the start into the geopolitics of military defence systems. During the Reagan era of the 1980s, this dyadic force field expanded to what Paul Edwards has termed the new phase of the Cold War, the 'closed world' of Cold War II.[11] Here the SDI (Strategic Defense Initiative) is combined with the SCI (Strategic Computer Initiative) to produce a closed world of computerised political discourse in which nuclear defence, reliant on centralised computer control, is aligned with the uses of artificial military intelligence, an integrated R&D plan to create a closed world, and also create, according to Edwards, false defence alerts during the eighteen months in which NORAD (The North American Defense Organization) installed new computers for military defence systems.[12] This policy spearheaded an upswing in the mass production of computers and their related technologies of which film technologies are a key beneficiary. Not only did Hollywood's reinvention of science fiction run parallel to the intensification of the nuclear arms race, the making of big-budget spectaculars was an indirect spinoff of technologies at play.[13] The cyborg is Hollywood's imaginary rendering of the destructive potential of artificial intelligence. Yet the link is clear. Science fiction films have mythologised their military benefactors, indeed ever since the computer-controlled cameras with their Dykstra lenses first used on *Star Wars*. At one level Hollywood narratives of the future have provided mythic solutions to the open-ended anxieties of the arms race. At another, Hollywood is locked into the networked society as a whole through computerised special effects, miniature remote-controlled cameras, computer-animated mattes and digital morphing. In Tony Scott's film, *Enemy of the State*, Will Smith is being hounded by the Image-and-Signal Intelligence Operations of a rogue National Security Agency (NSA) chief (Jon Voight), whose desktop surveillance specialists are not men in black but Microsoft slackers in T-shirts and sneakers. They would seem just as much at home working for Bill Gates or for a special effects team editing a big-budget spectacular.

While the NSA slackers of Scott's film make the actual virtual, and turn the fugitive body into an abstract digital figure, Hollywood editing breaks down the borders between the actual and virtual altogether. It is no longer possible for discriminating viewers to tell the difference between a pure location shot and a studio matte, to tell in effect where the studio ends and the location begins. The single screen image is often a computerised re-assembly of fragments of different filmed images, a virtual mosaic made seamless to the naked eye by digital means. Film is, more than ever before, the advanced technical product of the world of science which it seeks through its box-office narratives to portray as pure fiction. Amidst Virilio's overblown rhetoric, which celebrates the hyper-modern image rather than deconstructing it, one thing does become clear. The image does simulate the invisible and provides the core of Hollywood's politics of virtual spectacle.

CLEANBLADE is now a cult composite, which can be reread in the light of its progeny. Viewers can worship it in film, disc or tape copies of the original or in film feature derivatives made under its influence and in its shadow. Its triadic fix was to inject into the viewing sensorium the visceral impact of technology as pure spectacle. Crucial to this, however, was the transformation of location into spectacle. The films of Coppola and Spielberg were both extensive location shoots while *Blade Runner*, though a Warner's back-lot movie, integrated key LA landmarks such as the Bradley Building, Central Station and the Second Street tunnel into its futuristic studio vision. In *Apocalypse Now*, the logistical nightmare of filming came out of climatic extremes, the heat and the monsoons, plus the military demands made by President Marcos for counter-insurgency operations on that part of his air force in use as vital extras. Yet the technical forms were precise and spellbinding, so much so that people still admire and study in great detail the cinematography of Vittorio Storaro, the sound editing of Walter Murch and the production design of Dean Tavoularis.[14] In all three pictures spectacle has a quality of 'thereness' which some have tried to copy, others have preferred to ignore, but none has ever been able to emulate.

Let us look more closely at some of the clinching scenarios of spectacle. In *Close Encounters* the radio and radar tracking of the alien spacecraft by experts is matched by the naive perception of its bewitching translucency by awed amateurs, the empire of light which finally induces in them with the landing of the Mothership a submissive rapture and for expert and amateur alike a shared scientific ec-stase. In *Apocalypse Now* the nightmare of Willard's trip upriver to 'terminate with extreme prejudice' insane rebel officer Kurtz, turns into nightmare in the narrative sense and is a bad trip in the new chemical sense, a form of narcotic hallucination which goes seriously wrong. Coppola's narrative linked three distinct forms of narcosis in producing its eerie spectacle of sacrificial destruction. The increasing resort to drugs by the disgruntled grunts on their one-year tour of the war-zone was matched by the resort to speed and acid among some of Coppola's actors, as the insane logistics of filming war in the Philippine jungle matched the insane logistics of fighting it in the jungles of Vietnam. This in turn is echoed in the narcotic temptations for the hip spectator anticipating its viewing or re-viewing, of turning its onscreen nightmare into an armchair trip. Being spaced out is now a double-edged sword. It is the narcotic watching of the virtual spectacle, which might as well be set in outer space. The information age runs both an official and an unofficial curriculum. There is being wired and being wired. In *Blade Runner* the horrors of the future city are twofold: the viewer's horror of the underclass on Animoid Row as the future of all cities but equally the implosive horror of the biotechnical, the genetic engineering of the Tyrell Corporation turning out replicants indistinguishable at first sight from humans, just as the studio-manufactured 'naturalness' of the authentic shot is almost indistinguishable from the shooting of raw footage without filters or artificial lighting.

In the middle of this flashback to 1980, let us insert another and go even further back in time, to 1969. CLEANBLADE's break with the neo-modern was made possible only by Stanley Kubrick's *2001*. As we have seen, the European neo-moderns had earlier enhanced the mimetic image precisely in order to challenge its validity through the delirium of form.[15] While CLEANBLADE inherits that delirium of form, it subordinates it in Kubrick mode to the *mise-en-scène* of the sublime spectacle. Yet paradoxically, *2001* remains on the other side of the divide. Its formal, abstract design for a post-historic, and pre-historic, world was crucially *neo-modern*. For the first time in the history of movie science fiction, Kubrick had created space-age spectacle through a *mise-en-scène* of intense and abstract beauty, which cues in the technological sublime, that mixture of fear and fascination we feel towards the object of our perception which overpowers us.[16] The spectator watches *2001*, however, in a state of awesome detachment, an oxymoron built into the very structure of the *mise-en-scène*. The difference with later science fiction is crucial. In Kubrick there is a clinical detachment, which breaks down our empathy with the main characters in the spaceship. We see them as a distant species, human as we are but culturally other, literally distanced in space and time by the dystopian effects of the future world towards which we are moving. The Kubrick alienation effect lies in the creation of an invisible barrier between the spectator and the sublime image.

A decade later, the barrier has gone. CLEANBLADE takes abstraction back into the realm of the empathic quest and narrative overdrive. We are made to share the paranoia of Sheen, Dreyfuss and Ford as a desperate quest for buried truths, unlikely truths withheld through silence and conspiracy. The pathos is enticing and a generation later CLEANBLADE's siblings gave up on abstract aesthetics altogether. The location is secondary and functional to the post-production manipulation of the image. Increasingly they made this manipulation of the virtual image a means of *endorsing* the validity of the image. If there is any art here at all it lies in James Cameron's 'impact aesthetics'.[17] Only science fiction or disaster movies could force upon us the consequent paradox with such myopia. In film culture we now face greater ontological uncertainty when the image is representational, less uncertainty when it is virtual. The box-office audience unwittingly takes Barthes's cool ideology maxim to its ontological limit. They deem virtual cultures 'natural' and actual cultures 'unnatural'. It becomes 'unnatural' to watch documentaries at the cinema and boring to watch most things shot in realist format. Critics conditioned to condemning Hollywood as an assembly line of unthinking realism and invisible narrative are now at a loss to define its new box-office world of virtual spectacle in which only the spectacle seems real.[18] Indeed the post-Marxist embrace of Hollywood has been filtered through celebrations of cyborg utopia, where it becomes a cult 'postmodern' idiom to discourse analytically on dystopian films. The movie industry has moved smartly to restore its cultural pedigree and act up to this mythic elision of high and low cultures. True to form, the new box-office villains of the age have a pseudo-scientific pedigree, a biotechnical cachet as malfunctions of the information age. Aliens, replicants and serial killers, the *fin de siècle* money monsters all have one thing in common. Not only are they the nightmare products of the new age in an update of, to use Sontag's classic term, 'the imagination of disaster'; the demons themselves embody the reflexive codings of the information culture that has produced them. They are knowing demons, hi-tech monsters, perverse and malformed subjectivities at the heart of the machine. If they are monstrously evil in the old sense of the term, they are, like Hannibal Lecter or the scientific serial killer of *Copycat*, reflexively evil in the new.

A new ball game emerges. The spectator's sense of the compelling and the authentic remains; there is no bad faith here. For the validity of the image is in part a user-friendly matter of suspending disbelief. On top of that, however, a more active principle is at work. The attraction of virtual spectacle lies in its fix on the *technical* derealisation of the perceptual field, the going-beyond-normal-perception as a viewer's adventure, which is also simulated as a *scientific* journey into the unknown. It is a roller-coaster ride to test the best and no coincidence that Douglas Trumbull, brilliant special effects innovator on *2001* and *Blade Runner*, should move on to the IMAX rides of the new virtual amusement parks.[19] Moreover, the sci-fi hyper-modern offers a way to bypass the puzzle of the limit of the camera's vision. Scott Bukatman suggests it transforms offscreen space by eliminating it, by a metaphorical 'zooming out' in its evocation of the technological sublime.[20] Awestruck, the camera in films such as *Contact* tries to capture the essence of the cosmos in its awesome magnitude, hoping the audience will be awestruck too, but the sting in the tail comes from the conditions under which this takes place. It does so increasingly through confrontation with the world of the invisible, of virtual telepresence, of what Virilio has called the 'sightless vision' of the information age where he sees time displacing space as the prime mover of the technical life-world. What he overlooks is the way in which the moving image, which multiplies in this virtual world, converts time back into space again. This ubiquity of the recorded image is part of the techno-revolution that enhances the powers of simulation and virtual space. Here Hollywood sets Virilio's argument into reverse as American know how triumphs over Gallic discourse. It triumphs through the mythic framing of the electronically invisible by a new spatial imaginary. By converting the invisible back into the visible, the contemporary film converts 'time' back into 'space'. The viewer's pure addiction to virtual spectacle, whether framed as military jungle, galactic journey, alien visitation, genetic malfunction or dystopian city, all points in one direction. The technical side of filming becomes an unconscious quest to search out novel means of visualising the invisible. The mythic equation of hyper-modern Hollywood with the workings of the information age, on which by now we are all hooked in a banal yet addictive dependency, reveals itself above all in the return of science fiction. Cyberspace (internal, banal) equals Outer Space (spectacular) plus Future Space (awesome, dangerous). The banality of telepresence is duly converted into the virtual sublime.

On the face of it, the computer screen can be dreary and lack dimension, like the grey screen on which this text is being written. The cinematic wide screen, by contrast, is tactile and sensory, and draws the viewer into its spectacle. In the near future the two may well draw together as the enhanced PC becomes a composite vessel for all forms of digital imaging; but a sense of uncertainty lingers. Here we can return to Bukatman's prescient maxim and note his precise definition of the end of offscreen space. 'If the anxiety provoked by electronic culture is a function of its nonvisibility', he comments, 'then an overemphasis on visibility and immersion is only to be expected.'[21] Virtual spectacle is a film experience one inhabits rather than merely watching. There is nothing outside of its imaginary world, no lingering absences, residues or alternate worlds. If literal cyberspace film is commercially unsuccessful – one thinks of *The Net*, *Hackers*, *Johnny Mnemonic* and *The Lawnmower Man*, it is because audiences do not, on the whole, want to watch screens within screens within screens. Rather they want to feel *inside* the screen, as the box-office success of *The Matrix* has demonstrated, and film-makers in turn want to convince audiences they are missing nothing by their guaranteed inclusion. In virtual spectacle, narrative is both explicit and depthless at the same time. It is a closed world of discourse in which images may repeat with a visceral intensity in their after-effect but meaning evaporates almost immediately.

Here CLEANBLADE can be claimed a primal source, but a source which Hollywood has betrayed. It offers up narrative scenarios of depth, inner and outer, internal and external, which verge on the zone of invisibility through the derealising spectacle. In *Close Encounters* the vision of alien presence cues in the hallucinatory visions of waking sleep where sleepers, still dreaming but on the verge of waking, believe themselves fully awake. The circuit is ironically closed by the film's cultural aftermath in the zone of unspoken hysterias, the increasing accounts of alien abduction detailed by Elaine Showalter, narrative tales of the abducted which seem to rely heavily on the format of Spielberg's film or its imitators.[22] Life, we might say, now imitates spectacle more than it imitates art. In *Apocalypse Now* the inner trip of chemical narcotics corresponds to the actual trip upriver in an absurd war which for Willard's platoon is increasingly played out on a virtual battlefield filmed an as Expressionist fireworks display. The arena of war is both actual and hallucinated at the same time, a duality merging in the composite image Coppola creates for his audience. Perceptually speaking, he creates, or at least tries to, suspension of suspension of disbelief. In *Blade Runner* future Los Angeles is thematically and visu-ally a closed world, its montage an elliptical cutting between diverse highly designed spaces of enclosure matching the claustrophobic look of classic noir – night and neon, smog and rain – to a dystopian city. Desolate and dehumanised, it is, to paraphrase Elias Canetti, a cross between the world in the head and a headless world. Harrison Ford's Deckard is an investigator at once bemused by the spatial labyrinths of his own city, in other words by Scott's elaborate sets, which he is forced by duty to explore but from which nature seems to have vanished. At the same time he appears to be chasing down his own nightmare. He is inside of a dream that will not end. We could see Scott's film as a vision of the closed computer discourse of simulating nuclear war emerging in the latter stages of the Cold War. The hyper-functioning of the Tyrell Corporation produces replicants through genetic engineering. In a trope that has been copied for nearly two decades now, the malfunctioning of the replicants, the loss of control over them produces the threat of catastrophe.

Coppola's Vietnam was followed nine years later by Kubrick's Vietnam, *Full Metal Jacket*, also scripted by Michael Herr. If Coppola turned apposite location into dream world, Kubrick dispenses with Asia altogether and creates a virtual Vietnam in two southern English set-tings, a military barracks in Cambridgeshire and the industrial 1980s dereliction on the Isle of Dogs. This virtual Vietnam is a stylistic *coup de grâce*. The first setting is in fact American, a Marines training camp where future combat is simulated under the tyrannical eye of a bulldog sergeant. The second is a derelict Vietnamese town where the sergeant's most insolent marine joins a platoon under fire on a search-and-destroy mission. Kubrick frames both settings through extreme recessional lines using depth of field. Inside the barracks rows of endless bunk beds, outside rows of parading marines generate parallel lines almost to vanishing point. In the desolate theatre of war, the same tunnel vision prevails, the platoon's forward movement through desolate streets towards an invisible enemy in a blinkered advance. In training and combat, Kubrick's constant use of track and deep focus enlarge our sense of tunnel vision, of a war fought within a forced frame from which all wider perspectives have been eliminated. Thus his response to those who claim his camera keeps unnaturally low to avoid showing the London skyline, which in one shot it inadvertently does, might well have been that any sense of the wider world of Vietnam is excluded from the military mission to 'save' it. In any event the curse of combat repeats the curse of training for combat, but with a difference. The myth of complete certainty is replaced by the experience of complete uncertainty, and Kubrick is looking for its filmic correlative. The logistics of war and perception on screen become identical.

Let us now time-travel and go back again to the age of *Dr Strangelove*. As Thomas Disch notes, the popularity of science fiction in the 1960s rocketed after the great crises of the Cold War, Cuba and the Berlin Wall.[23] This upsurge can be seen, he suggests, as a vast mythic exorcising in film and text of the fear of nuclear holocaust, a means of going all the more easily the way of *Dr Strangelove*'s subtitle, in which we stop worrying and learn to love the Bomb. If we play out our horrors as future scenario or extra-terrestrial foreboding, we deflect this-worldly angst about collective human folly. Thus the nuclear arms race of the great powers has been matched by the rise of 'scientific' fantasies of text and screen. The actual space race centred on Cape Canaveral has been matched by the virtual race within cyberspace and the imaginary race into outer space where fiction has the ultimate poetic licence. It can, like most aliens of unexplored galaxies, travel faster than light. This is a far cry from the different rockets and their astronauts that Tom Wolfe described in *The*

*Right Stuff*, who for the most part possess the mobility during flight of patients on a surgeon's operating table and are seen by their deadly rivals of the stratosphere, ace jet pilots like Chuck Yeager, as no better than the chimpanzees who took part in the same simulation trials. No coincidence perhaps that in *2001* the virtually upright chimp 'Moonwatcher', who throws his dinosaur's bone heavenwards, is turned by time ellipsis into an astronaut of the twenty-first century. Philip Kaufman's film of *The Right Stuff* also captured the tongue-in-cheek quality of Wolfe's narrative but significantly changed the ending. While Wolfe celebrates Yeager's heroism and the miracle of an escape from his damaged jet as a form of pioneering in the stratosphere, Kaufman's film sees it being superseded by the success of the space programme, juxtaposing Yeager's solitary flight against the communal success of the Mercury space programme. Yet it took Hollywood over twenty-five years to catch up with the space programme and turn it into truly bankable melodrama. This it duly did in the 1996 *Apollo 13*, which recapitulated the misdeeds of the 1970s for the big screen with big stars. Even here, both in the spacecraft and down at Mission Control, the filming is largely composed of static shots, astronauts up there in front of control buttons barely moving, intercut with controllers down here in front of control panels barely moving. Is Tom Hanks a stand-in for a chimp? It was never like this on the space-ship *Nostromo*, where the *Alien* series was launched with a hyperactive flair for the screening of disaster. While safety and lack of gravity tied down the real astronauts in their mini-shuttle through a tiny segment of the solar system, science fiction gave *carte blanche* to upwardly mobile cyborgs – strictly Northern Hemisphere types – travelling through galaxies faster than light, but always 'up' and never 'down', since such galaxies in the popular imagination are always 'above' the earth. Yet there was a salutary point to the Apollo movie, a reminder that in the era of Vietnam and Watergate no one much was bothered about the launch at all until the circuit around the dark side of the moon nearly turned into disaster. In a way Hollywood was doing penance – but profitable penance – for its own failure to feature the actual over the virtual. At the end of the day simulation of the flight is also more heroic than the flight itself. The film here performs a melodramatic embroidering of the complex situation in space history. In the film the astronaut left behind (Gary Sinise) insists on conducting simulation trials for his buddies where he will not, if he presses the wrong button, be stranded in space along with obsolete satellites. This simulation, where pressing the wrong button does not mean certain death, results in the space crew pressing the right button to avoid certain death.

Let us now move to futuristic earth. The cyborg is a dystopian variation on biotechnical progress. Hence pictures like *RoboCop* or *Demolition Man,* where the cyborg is a dehumanised machine made necessary by the failure of the metropolis. This extrapolation of worsening trends in the social fabric, where reason must catch up with urban anarchy, pitches the precision of the machine against the random chaos of an amoral civilisation. What we have is a civility in regress, spiralling backwards or forwards towards the primitive. Thus Spielberg's *Jurassic Park* is the last word in hyper-real theme parks, the biotechnical simulation of the prehistoric for the hyper-modern spectacle. In a decade where the 'dinosaurs of rock' are still going strong, Spielberg's dinosaurs of virtual spectacle go even stronger. The prehistoric monster reborn out of extinction is a novel variant on the futuristic replicant rebelling through malfunction. Inventors (and investors) play with fire and get burnt. This spectacular regress, an example of the 'sadistic sublime' as Wollen calls it,[24] is something beyond the capacity of a purely industrial studio system with projects being shunted along the sound stage assembly line. Each big-budget movie is its own special empire, its Babelsberg of special effects. The uncertain future, which preys on the sci-fi imagination, ironically glosses the new chronology of film-making. The camera is secondary to the editing machine. Raw footage is now cast as hostage to the fortunes of post-production, the audiovisual blending of film images from everywhere and nowhere.

## II

Well before *Reservoir Dogs* and *Pulp Fiction,* hyper-modern Hollywood had reversed the time-image of the neo-moderns. *Blade Runner* and the *Terminator* diptych are films that loop around themselves, invoking space as future metaphor only to end its offscreen presence. We have instead a novel product – offscreen time. It is almost as if the time-image of Bergsonian philosopher Gilles Deleuze had been taken over by cyborg actor Arnold Schwarzenegger. Perceptual complexity, still baffling to most film critics, is displaced by ingenious but awesome spectacle. The thought is not flippant at all. Deleuze had seen in Kubrick's *2001* the metamorphosis of the time-image into a new form of 'electronic automatism'.[25] For Deleuze the great directors of the time-image, and here Welles and Resnais stand out, had produced narratives of pure sonic and optical signs in which the connections between cause and effect, past and present, intention and movement, had all been scrambled and broken down, effectively ending the rules of organic narrative promoted by the Hollywood studio system. The new cinematic image was dominated by 'the powers of the false': unreliable memory, unreliable narration, hallucination, fantasy, temporal disconnection, the continuous image perpetually ship-wrecked by the power of the cut to short-circuit time in any direction. Through virtual spectacle Hollywood reclaims narrative, however, by producing its own gloss on the seriality of time. The time-image, which absorbed and replaced the Hollywood movement-image, in turn appears to have been replaced by the spectacle-image, which absorbs it. Yet forms of the time-image continue to flourish outside Hollywood. The appearance of absorption, of time by spectacle, remains an illusion. Yet for Hollywood it is a necessary illusion, for in science fiction time is at the hub of spectacle.

A fascinating link is provided here, as Deleuze noted, between the films of Alain Resnais and the new science fiction.[26] Resnais's early cinema had been predicated on ruin and catastrophe as time past – Auschwitz in *Night and Fog*, Hiroshima in *Hiroshima mon amour*, the Algerian war in *Muriel*, the Spanish Civil War in *La Guerre est finie*. At times the mannequins of *Last Year at Marienbad* act as if insulated inside the world's last living château. These are all films of aftermath, of revisiting the scene of the crime through images posing as documents or memories. Here Antonioni's haunting absences of offscreen space are rivalled and replaced by the haunting absences of times past, but sharing equally the depopulation of the image, the loss of the human figure where it was or where one might expect it to be. At the time of CLEANBLADE, however, Resnais reinvented his time-image, moving in *Providence* from present to future instead of present to past. John Gielgud's drunken narration appears at first sight to be an ageing writer's unreliable reverie. Instead Resnais stands Proustian narration on its head and with the aid of David Mercer's exemplary script gives us a remembrance of things to come. Like Truffaut in *Fahrenheit 451*, Resnais goes for metonymic dystopia. Its subtext is the Gallic gloss on Anglo-American culture. Truffaut had shot Bradbury's fiction just outside London's suburbs while Resnais placed sequences from Mercer's screenplay on location in American East Coast cities.

This contrasts with those speculative visions of post-war Europe plunged back into war during the Cold War, visions very different yet very precise, Bergman's *The Shame* and Buñuel's *The Discreet Charm of the Bourgeoisie*. In both films, nameless warriors had terrorised the European bourgeoisie, invading their intimacies, occupying their living space, turning alienation into a luxury they can no longer afford. Resnais goes one step forwards, bridging the neo-modern and hyper-modern divide. *Providence* was released in 1978 and we could cast it, along with *Mon Oncle d'Amérique* as a cineaste's pre-emptive strike against virtual spectacle, running parallel to CLEANBLADE but on a miniature circuit. The mindscreen of ageing writer John Gielgud, which incriminates his family in a fictional scenario of the near future, has a visual template echoing that of Welles and Hitchcock. The ghostly deserted streets of the city are heavily filtered amid bright sunlight rather like the fog filters in *Vertigo*. The court scenes and the prisons echo *The Trial* while 'Providence', the writer's decaying pile in the country, echoes the derelict 'Xanadu' of the dying Kane. This is a form of free indirect subjectivity in which Gielgud's drunken fictions become a fragmented chronicle moving forwards, backwards and sideways in time, where each sequence is a series of discontinuity cuts between sets which are not contiguous, where in a couple of reverse-angle cuts the balcony will change from dark mahogany pillars overlooking the city to a bright white veranda overlooking the sea. This is science fiction without the science, present here only in the shape of the astrophysicist son by an absent mother. In one of Gielgud's fantasies, he turns up as a feeble hippie who claims to be a lost astronaut. This indeed is the doubled journey into inner and outer space.

Gielgud's mindscreen is a pivotal moment in the life of the time-image. It is still the cool apocalypse of *Marienbad*, *L'Eclisse* and *2001*, somewhat ironised but a chilling out, momentarily, from the hot apocalypse of CLEANBLADE: and the hot apocalypse is soon to be on a roll as the lure of science fiction converts the fear of nuclear war into the fascination with other worlds. The border jungle at the end of Coppola's film has gone the same way. It is a Jurassic Park of the war-torn imagination, a mannered regress into the primitive, which is already science fiction. It reminds us too that much sci-fi apocalypse from *Mad Max* onwards begins with a new world arising from the ashes of destruction. Future-tense science fiction finds its favourite trope in the dawn of the post-holocaust world, the new beginnings which bring forth the new man who is no longer man but cyborg. Resnais's lost astronaut of the bourgeoisie gives way to the replicant and the terminator. Here the terrors of time take a new turning which is really an old one, back towards melodrama. Where Resnais frames the killings of *Providence* as a form of circular terror invented reflexively by a malicious but declining imagination, – the ageing writer's, science fiction goes with the illusion for its global audience. The imagination of disaster is more real than the disaster of the imagination.

Here another perverse equation suggests itself. Two great sci-fi movies gloss the height of Cold War I. Two equally defining movies mark the start of Cold War II. Yet each pairing is decisively split by the Cold War divide. Soon after *2001*, Andrei Tarkovsky made *Solaris*. A decade later the order was reversed. Soon after *Stalker*, Ridley Scott made *Blade Runner*. The art race perversely mirrored the arms race. For many sci-fi buffs, Tarkovsky's films were an affront to the genre, but perhaps that is the point. It has simply been taken for granted that the genre is Western and *au fond* American, but Stanislaw Lem and the Strugatsky brothers, who wrote the books Tarkovsky adapted, were as much within the Soviet orbit as Arthur C. Clarke and Philip K. Dick were in the Anglo-American. While *2001* and *Blade Runner* allow us to forget nuclear war by moving catastrophe sideways, in Tarkovsky it is somehow still there, still lodged within our sacrificial unconscious, stubbornly refusing to be exorcised by the imagination of other disasters. The shift also points up a wider shift in film form which becomes more pointed the more we move away from the Western ambit. While virtual spectacle smothers the relationship of the actual and the eternal, elsewhere it is crucial. While the West becomes hyper-modern, the East, as we shall see, becomes meta-modern, a shift of prefixes which illuminates a divide of worlds.

After Resnais a key divide defines the encounter between film's rival siblings of the hyper-modern, one predicated on the time-image, the other on the spectacle-image. Hollywood converts the hidden terrors of the technical life-world in the former into the open horrors of narrative spectacle, inverting the term's usage in ordinary language. We often say, 'I was horrified by X,' meaning the event whose impact is indirect; we seldom say 'I was terrorised by X,' because then X becomes the direct source of our terror. Being horrified suggests a distance, a balance between reason and emotion, between visceral reaction and mental judgement. Screen horrors pretend to eliminate the distance and extinguish the power of judgement, making reaction vicarious. The audience is not directly threatened but act out the 'as if' of the melodrama. The spectator goes with a horror which is at once more awesome because mythologised as spectacular image, but more harmless because it is an ocular illusion of the big screen. In virtual spectacle the hidden terror is converted into partial horror offset by the fascination with the sublime, which usually accompanies fear. The hidden terror of time-travel as a cosmic imaginary is not so much the abyss of a world without end as the fear of a world without chronology. *Blade Runner* and its many successors turn that hidden terror of time into the horrific spectre of the cyborg, whose mechanical fascination vitiates the fear of the unknown. The hyper-modern cineaste resources the information age differently, searching out hidden terror but seldom converting it into overt terror, chronicling instead the hyper-modern endeavour to overcome the non-identity of meaning and image. For much of the time the viewer is kept at a disquieting distance. This may be a gloss on the technical life-world as a place of risk in which the everyday is fraught with the anxieties of malfunction and disconnection, the diurnal dangers of speed and motion, the predicament of solitude. What the art film lacks is precisely what Hollywood sci-fi reassuringly gives, the fascinating sublime produced at the cutting edge of production design and special effect. Meanwhile the cyborg transcends the human monster, giving a human face to our fear of monstrous invention.

The cineaste's speciality is the diffusion of terror sprung by anxiety; in virtual spectacle it is the diffusion of horror shaded by fear and fascination. Paraphrasing Freud's classic formula, we might say our anxiety at intangible threat in the real world is converted by Hollywood into fear at tangible threat in the imaginary world. In standard horror format, diffuse anxieties are transformed into instant fear. The locus classicus is *Psycho*. The lingering, perverse charm of Hitchcock's movie, at the time a calculated risk, was that it takes so long for mayhem to strike. The fleeing Janet Leigh's anxieties over her minor fraud, which take up half an hour of running time, are displaced by the sixty-second eruption of the Gothic mother as her flashing blade rips through the shower curtain. The essence of dramatic suspense here is inherited by the new horror genre from John Carpenter and Wes Craven right through to *I Know what you did Last Summer*. The genre has little truck with academic distinctions. It is impossible to separate out, as Carroll has claimed, the natural from the supernatural in any philosophy of horror.[27] The real test of genre efficacy is to be able to move quickly and seamlessly from one to the other, from the natural-as-banal to the supernatural-as-horrendous in one fell swoop. For Carpenter and Craven the suburban American home, cosily naturalistic, is the perfect setting for their own distinctive eruptions of American Gothic.

The change from Hitchcock to hyper-modern Hollywood becomes clearer. It lies in the absence of guilt and ambiguity, or of moral conscience about the taking of life. Carpenter's teenage victims in *Halloween* set the pattern: typically amoral brats into minor violations, who are more cute than wrong. The audience cares less about the violation than its use as a sign. They know brattishness will soon result in vicious comeuppance, and the sooner the better. That is, the sooner they get to the sequences at which they 'cannot bear to look', the better for the movie. Even a sophisticated movie like *Copycat*, which bypasses the supernatural, is a prisoner to the demands of screen time. Audiences get impatient if they have to wait too long for their vicarious fix. Thus for Doctor Sigourney Weaver, scientific expert on serial killing, horror starts straight at the end of her self-confident lecture on profiling which opens the film. Leaving the lecture theatre for the washroom she is stalked and threatened by one of her former profile victims, now vowing to get even. Yet his brutal cornering of her also gives the game away. He is sadistic but not scientific, not smart and reflexive enough to play her at her own game like the real copycat killer, who builds up his own profiles on all the big serial killers preceding him and kills serially according to the customary method of each killer in turn.

The key for audience attention is not only the first five minutes, now enshrined as sacred necessity in the high-concept picture. It is also repetition. In James Cameron's *Terminator* films repetition horror is mechanised into the figure of the invincible cyborg. The Terminator, after all, 'keeps on coming'. The horror genre generally thrives on the promise–threat of this cyclical eruption. The return of the irrepressible is the genre's impact substitute for Freud's return of the repressed, the secret drive of the psyche replaced by the virus of the body-machine. Here, as if to make content subordinate to format, Cameron happily casts Schwarzenegger as bad cyborg in the original *Terminator* and as good cyborg in the sequel. It matters little. In Cameron and Verhoeven the body is more explicitly an organic extension of mechanical power, a European trope permeating militaristic war memoirs and fascist writing in the 1920s, and here returns in futuristic form. Several critics have made the cyborg link to the Freikorps mentality of Weimar Germany, most notably Klaus Thewelheit.[28] The post-war mindset was forged out of a new brutalism and quickly erected into an intellectual cult. With his anti-humanist quest for a permanent fusion of military discipline and destructive chaos, fascist philosopher Ernst Jünger had paved the way in the 1920s for a vision of the military-industrial future where technology was a source of the endless quest for global domination by superpowers thrusting legions of worker-soldiers into endless conflict. This form of struggle was by its nature collectivist. Individualism is to be exterminated or rather technology ensures that it falls away. In its post-Nazi reincarnation as filmic myth, the anarcho-fascism of the terminating cyborg is by contrast hyper-individualist, a fusion of the American Dream with retro-Teutonic myth. It reassures its mass audience that the body in the machine belongs to someone in particular and not just anybody. The duel of the cyborgs in *Terminator 2* is thus a conflict of advanced prototypes in which the morphing iconography of the singular face and shape and figure is crucial. The cyborg is an individuated fetish and in the case of Schwarzenegger a crucial sign of stardom. Meanwhile the film is manufactured for its global audience through a form of segmented marketing whereby it has an attraction for neo-Nazis and liberals alike. The programmed amoralism of the Aryan Schwarzenegger gives the audience a cybernetic take on the motor force of the mechanical body, and the freefall conspiracy theorising of Linda Hamilton a paranoid take on the malfunctioning human brain. It is a marriage made in the laboratory. In the sequel, chance would have it that her paranoia is vindicated by time-travel while his automatism creates acceptable victims, mainly vicious rednecks who get in his way. The innocents may be threatened, terrorised and forced into collective panic but happily fail to get themselves killed. The movie can delight feminists by allowing Hamilton a sadistic pleasure in the violence of the gun (normally male), which has no meaning for the male cyborg, now a neutered killing machine. Hamilton's plan of killing a black nuclear scientist and his family with great relish can give pleasure to racists everywhere. Her last-minute change of heart and laboured wringing of conscience can equally bring pleasure to guilty liberals, who believe she is only killing people in order to save the world from nuclear catastrophe.

From morphing cyborgs to morphing ocean liners, Cameron has shown himself to be at the cutting edge of digital technology in the realm of special effects. Impact aesthetics is not his invention but something implicit in CLEANBLADE's earlier template, which he inherits. Despite the cultural interlock of sci-fi film and fiction, ranging all the way from popular comics to Burroughs, Pynchon and Gibson, that template holds. Its filmic imaginary also contains the kernel of that psychedelic crossover between acid and cyberspace, the symbolic linking of the 1960s generation and the 1990s generation, which we also find outside of film in the chequered careers of Timothy Leary or Jaron Lanier. For both claim to have found salvation twice over, the first time in LSD, the second time in cyberspace, and then framed them rhetorically as part of a New Age continuum.[29] We might note too that the Ken Kesey acid-bus and Apple/Microsoft garage culture, Californian first and last, came in different generations out of the same area of Silicon Valley near Stanford University.[30]

At its best science fiction is a dystopian turnaround of utopian euphoria. The future shows what the present cannot, the promises of science perverted and betrayed. CLEANBLADE's filmic imaginary is also a paranoid imaginary, embodied in the desperate quest for truths concealed. Investigating the hidden malfunctions of the heartless machine is anything but euphoric. In their wide-screen successors the details become more complex, spectacular, ingenious and breath-taking, but the fascination remains the same. The system of discovery is fascinating for the half-outlaw immersed within it but feeling out of it, ever seeking the imaginary vantage point in order to move outside the matrix, the biosphere, the virtual world posing as the real one. In that sense *The Truman Show, Dark City* and *The Matrix* are all *fin de siècle* films updating the paranoid techno-myth. The hero finds that his conception of the natural world is chimerical, an ingenious invention concealed from him by its diabolic perpetrators. Heroism and its attraction for the audience take on a new form. Beyond chaos the system incorporates all, but I am I, outside of it for that brief ecstatic moment in which I make the fateful discovery, which is all eternity.

## III

To be outside is to assume a cast of ambivalence. It is the fate of hero and monster alike, insane visionary and conniving demon. The dark side of the good brother, the deranged visionary who uncovers the pernicious and conspiratorial system is the bad brother, the serial killer who escapes the carapace of the human altogether. In one genre the visionary outsider is good and society bad; in another, society is besieged and the killer-outlaw diabolical. To take the serial killer film as a subgenre of crime is to misread it, for it is much more. In the 1990s it takes its place firmly within the politics of virtual spectacle. True, much of it revolves around factual information and relates to the actual patterns of the networked society. It is indeed a response to a disturbing criminal pattern, which has emerged in the United States since 1965 but that pattern is also to be seen in other societies undergoing vast upheaval such as Russia or South Africa. Mythically speaking, however, film has made it an American phenomenon and its mythology works in a different way from science fiction. It starts in the cult of the profile or the document, from the virtual evidence culled in files, texts, photos, Photofits or forensic evidence which investigation must make real. Yet it proceeds quickly to the horror of gruesome killing. It gives us the horror documentary for the information age, and reproduces it as virtual spectacle. *The Silence of the Lambs* documents FBI procedures; *Se7en* documents the role of pathology in recording and diagnosing brutal murders; while *Henry: Portrait of a Serial Killer* is loosely based on the actual 'confessions', true or otherwise, of Henry Lee Lucas, its real-life villain. *Copycat* shows its professional cool by resourcing all the different kinds of murder practised by notorious serial killers and creating its own composite monster. The mini-holocaust of Stone's *Natural Born Killers* is a genocidal fantasy its maker tries to excuse with an equally amoral fantasy, the media circus as a global feeding frenzy, which Stone contrives to make one cause of the horror it clamours to investigate. Here seriality is no longer a matter of structure but the only alternative to chaos; or so it seems, until it becomes clear that even forty-seven killings cannot prevent Stone's picture from total stylistic collapse.

In general the documentary take on seriality is simply a spring-board, a narrative come-on for the spectacle taking many forms. In *Lambs*, Anthony Hopkins has steely deranged eyes recalling Lang's Peter Lorre in *M*, coupled with the crisp monosyllables of HAL, Kubrick's evil spaceship computer. In a rain-drenched LA straight out of *Blade Runner*, *Se7en*'s investigation room is an infernal chamber where Brad Pitt and Morgan Freeman pore over the body parts and recorded evidence of human depravity. In *Amerika* reflexivity is given a bad name by serial killing expert David Duchovny who unwittingly gives a ride across America in his car to serial killer Brad Pitt and is made to witness at first hand the substance of a topic he had previously consigned to scholarship. In *Copycat* the agoraphobic design of Sigourney Weaver's apartment, which seems to open itself at key points into an abyss of space, is equally a room of monstrous signs, a room embodying the evil which surrounds it outside, elsewhere perhaps but not far away. Evil, the audience feels, looms at its very door in the figure of the actual stalker who is so far only a virtual profile on her computer screen. Thus the horror of the serial killer works not only through documenting the enormity of crimes committed, but through repetition and its possibilities. The psychotic spree killer is by contrast a no-go area for Hollywood myth. The single bloody event is off limits because it defies seriality. It also defies Hollywood's pseudo-psychology. Plotting melodrama demands in effect a killer who plots, who will always have a next move, who will always strike and strike again when we are least expecting it. Instead, we might conjecture, teenage spree killing finds its filmic imaginary in that favourite of teen audiences, the horror genre, where, defying explanation, it is transposed into the supernatural.

Serial killing concentrates the mind of the viewer whose anxieties might be prompted by other more common forms of American, and increasingly global, mayhem, which involve the chance meeting of strangers. These include the terror Hollywood seldom features, mass random killing and child kidnapping ending in rape or murder. The serious crimes of strangers are those which have leapt in the statistics during the same period as the rise of the serial killer, and the collective fear, the terror of the strange rather than the familiar, has fuelled Hollywood's take on seriality. Seriality, after all, is a key ingredient of a melodrama where a series thought random is found to have an alarming pattern. Its suspenseful discovery by the shrewd investigator is the device which kick-starts the movie into life. *Se7en* places the bait for discovery ingeniously in the repertoire of the seven deadly sins, each of which one of the killer's seven victims is prone to committing. Each accordingly is punished ingeniously and gruesomely as 'revenge' for past 'sins'. Yet this is an uncommon subtlety. Most are, like Marion Crane, 'punished' for misdemeanours that bear no relationship to the psychotic atrocities of their killer, in other words not punished at all. As an extension of the horror genre, serial killing myth relies on this mismatch of cause and effect. The serial effect in other words creates the illusion of causality in the relation of killer and victim, a perverse vindication of their selection for gruesome fate.

In Denis Duclos's brilliant study of the American fascination with violence, he points out some of the things which serial killer fiction cannot do. Despite its cult of electronic profiling and its obsession with the hi-tech aspects of police investigation, the serial killer film is more concerned with the consequences of mayhem than with its source, with investigators and victims than with murderers.[31] Its prototype serial killer remains a non-being with little background and no childhood. Most serial killers by contrast have had too full a childhood, full usually of all the wrong things, which the two-hour narrative cannot hope to encompass, but also does not wish to. Instead the serial killer is a monstrous other who becomes a mythic artefact, a cast into which the liquid substance of a damaged psyche is poured and set as pure image. Duclos also points to the closeness of the actual killer and the virtual cyborg. Both are killing machines reared on repetition. While audiences can accept the killing machine as a futuristic cyborg, a malfunction of high-risk experiment, they cannot accept the mechanical nature of the contemporary killer who must be mythically represented instead as a cunning and sadistic monster. Here melodrama does what it always has. It provides audiences with conventions of evil they can recognise. The serial killer as liquidating machine is too cold and calculating to be romanticised like the cyborg whose 'monstrosity' can be written off as dystopian malfunction.

If there is a genre appropriate to the serial killer it is clearly the one foreshadowed by *Bonnie and Clyde* or *Badlands*, the road movie where the outlaw seeks to escape the constricting boundaries of place through a wide-open country which will hide him until he strikes again. The imitation of Malick has now become a dreary cliché, but the point remains. Confronting the cold but human killer, the homicidal loner, the systematic drifter, is to confront an existential void raising more questions than can be answered. The killer hates the world and takes revenge through killing, a metaphorical form of escape matched by the actual one which entails constant and countrywide movement, methodical evasion, stalking of victims. A further and powerful dysfunction is also lost in movie myth, that of communications breakdown. Movie-typical killers have to adhere to the laws of narrative suspense. Hence they are always portrayed as inveterate game-players intent on being one step ahead of the law and of their potential victims. That by itself is a source of their sadistic delight. Actual killers, Duclos claims, are more terrifying. They are fixated on overcoming the terror of solitude into which they have sunk by visceral communication with the body and flesh of their victims.[32] Long lapsed, communication stirs into life only with the dead and the dying, never with the living. Serial killers thus mimic the mechanical quality of the world in which they live, but are not, like cyborgs, the victims of its experiments. They are victims of its neglect. Yet in consumer culture the mildly paranoid mind-set seeking conspiracy as reassurance of totality cannot adjust to this randomness and indeterminacy of damaged lives, which later acquire their own deadly patterns. In filmic myth the pattern is everything.

American triumphalism does not involve here the forgetting of the social or the outcast. Indeed the mutant, the replicant, the cyborg are all malfunctioning outsiders operating in a world with a buried and stigmatic underclass; witness *Total Recall* or *Demolition Man*. This transposition of the urban dispossessed from present to future tense refers not just to a notional American city. It locks on to any metropolis worldwide where the movie product is big box-office, for its myth will contain an echo of that city's social disasters. In the filming of Los Angeles itself, a dystopian setting for the encounter of hero and under-class has often been Crown Heights, a decaying Hispanic area west of downtown now populated by drug dealers and illegal migrants and sporting the freeway tunnel now made famous by *Terminator*. After a day of movie shoots, the homeless nearby often scavenge the consumer remains left by the film crews, as the site of the futuristic slum of virtual spectacle becomes present, actual and banal again. The virtual film not only shunts the actual forwards into a dystopian future. It also shunts it sideways in the popular imagination, echoing general fear while naming no names or places, indeed taking controversy out of the public realm. Likewise, the imaginary transposition of the fear of nuclear war into a war of galactic worlds is a move forwards and sideways. The future world deflects us from the present one by mythic incorporation and the presence of the virtual danger makes us forget the presence of the actual danger. Its box-office success makes little sense, however, unless that underlying fear of catastrophe did not exist in some form, somewhere in our contemporary lives. Both kinds of displacement come together to vindicate Levi-Strauss's classic formula of myth. Filmic myth is indeed an imaginary resolution of real contradictions. The politics of virtual spectacle posits a fascinating variation, a paranoid interface of material dispossession (actual) for some, and potential catastrophe (virtual) for all. The networked society operating through an invisible cyberspace also offers up a visible conse-quence. Not to be networked is not to be connected, a sign of the exclusion that goes hand in glove with other forms of loss experienced by the 'new poor' of the networked society.[33] It is no wonder there-fore that the underclass and the excluded loom so large in its strange mythology.

Yet one vital question remains unanswered. Levi-Strauss cues us in to the form that myth will take, but we also need to explore its substance. What is central to the technological sublime, as Erik Davis has shown, is the Gnostic belief. Always cryptic and seldom open, it is the belief in a universal spirit beyond matter, to be revealed by new forms of communication.[34] The reaching out in cyberspace has its refracted image in the reaching out in outer space. The new material form has, in this particular cast of American optimism, a vast spiritual payoff that faces down the gloom of modern scepticism. It allows the spirit to transcend in new and unexpected ways. The term Davis employs for this mind-set, 'TechGnosis', is an apt description of the cultural frame within which Hollywood's spectacle-image has flourished. It is in part a Nietzschean Return, a template of inventions repeating itself throughout modernity, where at each stage its inventors were filled with the heady elation of spiritual discovery. Davis charts the Return throughout techno-history, in the imagined kinship of mesmerism and electricity, in the digital code of Samuel Morse's telegraph, the code to end all codes, in the spiritual transfusions which Alexander Bell imagined would charge his telephone lines, in McLuhan's vision of television as key to the electronic global village and in his prophecy that the computer would become the LSD of the business world.[35]

Cyberspace duly takes its place as a break with the past, which echoes it all too clearly. For Davis, the new prototypical Hermes of cyberspace is both ironist and visionary, 'dancing between logic and archaic perception, myth and modernity, reason and its own hallucinatory excess'.[36] This puts more clearly into focus than ever the impact of CLEANBLADE and its legacy. The spectacle-image easily absorbs irony and parody in his wider visionary ambit where TechGnosis reigns supreme. It is reassuring too. Despite its apocalyptic tone, it persuades us that glittering infomania, a veritable Gold Rush of the Microchip, is not only the source of great wealth in the Western world. Happily, it is the source of great spiritual richness as well, enhanced by invisible transmission. The spectacle-image reinforces this myth, triumphantly, resoundingly, without sleight of hand. This is the age of coeval connection. However dislocated your life may appear to be, however detached your telephone, TV or PC may seem from the centre of your brain or the source of your soul, you are connected to the great out-there and the great beyond. For the cinema audience of the spectacle-image, the viewing experience tells them much the same thing.

*Chapter 3*

# THE COLD WAR AND THE CINEMA
# OF WONDER

In the West, the Cold War produced two kinds of movie genre: James
Bond plus the spy thriller, and the irresistible rise of science fiction.
In Soviet cinema, too, were to be found equivalents for popular
consumption, with the nationalities of heroes and villains reversed.
Yet there is a richer legacy. As we have seen, comparisons between
*2001* and *Solaris*, or *Stalker* and *Blade Runner* continue to fascinate.
They are, indirectly, part of the geopolitics of the Cold War and if we
focus on the Eastern dimension we discover a different kind of cinema.
In so doing, we enter a contentious arena. Since 1990, the break-up
of the Soviet Union and the official end of the Cold War have provoked
deluded visions of world convergence in politics and culture.[1] In film
criticism they have also produced globalising tendencies that are
equally defective.[2] The link between film and geopolitics needs to be
rethought, to bring in other fault lines of modernity, cultural and religious, which militate against the tendency to assume common patterns
can be attributed to all things non-Western. Samuel Huntingdon has
discerned a new politics in a post-Cold War world destined to produce
key conflicts in the twenty-first century across civilisations. He has
analysed them from a conservative, Western point of view.[3] Yet these
fault lines remind us that film, as a vital form of world culture, is not
homogenous and never will be. While it aspires to be a universal
language, history shows us that differences remain. The film world
since 1960 has been not only that of Welles and Hitchcock, Godard

and Truffaut, Bergman and Fellini, Altman and Scorsese. It has also been that of Glauber Rocha and Tomás Gutiérrez Alea, Akira Kurosawa and Satyajit Ray, Angelopoulos and Kiarostami, Imamura and Oshima, Edward Yang and Wong Kar-Wai. Meanwhile, within the socialist world, film has brought forth among its many talents Miklós Jancsó and Andrzej Wajda, Sergei Paradjanov and Andrei Tarkovsky, Chen Kaige and Zhang Yimou.

There is a strong case for seeing a deep aesthetic in the cinema of the socialist world persisting, though diminished, into the post-communist present. From 1960 to 1990 a vital core of film-making failed to fulfil expectations either of the authoritarian state looking for ideological affirmation, or of Western critics looking for overt opposition and liberalism. How are we to understand this? The vexations of art, as ever, play off the vexations of politics in mysterious ways. The deep aesthetic of which we speak here is certainly prefigured by the cinemas of the West, by Italian neo-realism and the rise of the neo-modern. Yet within the tight frame of authoritarian politics and cultural censorship there is no second wave of modernism in the Western sense, and the Nouvelle Vague had only a marginal effect. The term 'modernist' seems largely inappropriate. Indeed neither official doctrines of socialist realism nor Western forms of modernism seem to apply at all. There *was* an aesthetic transformation in this period, but of a different order altogether.

Part of this lies in the Soviet background. The 1920s modernism in the silent cinema of Pudovkin, Vertov and Eisenstein was a specific form of the avant-garde in a revolutionary decade. Yet the second transformation of film aesthetics, which we can date from 1964, the year of Sergei Paradjanov's *Shadows of our Forgotten Ancestors*, was not overtly political. If there was an earlier Soviet model it was the pantheistic lyricism of Alexander Dovzhenko's silent film of 1930, *Earth*. *Earth* was the Ur-text of the new aesthetic, urging the centrality of landscape and nature in socialist film, turning it away from the industrial city and the technologies of the machine age. The new aesthetic, which inherited Dovzhenko's pantheistic vision, differed in one crucial aspect. Gone was the era of Soviet triumphalism, the triumph of the kolkhoz and the peasant over the kulak and the land, which underpinned Dovzhenko's film. Moreover, the new aesthetic was neither avant-garde in the style of Eisenstein nor a proto-Western form of dissonance, neither alienation nor Deleuzian bal(l)ade. For sure, there were key influences. Eisenstein and Dovzhenko were the Soviet models, while Bresson, Bergman, Buñuel and Antonioni were figures of inspiration from the West. Yet Japanese cinema was equally important. For Tarkovsky, Ozu and Mizoguchi were key figures in his formally composed sculpting of the cinematic frame, while Paradjanov's unique epic cinema surely has its closest precedent in the bold and daring paradigm of Kurosawa's Samurai Japan.

Produced under conditions of tough censorship, this new form is difficult to pin down. Juxtaposed, on a conceptual grid of prefixes, against both the Western neo-modern and its hyper-modern successors, we might call it *meta-modern* instead. It is an art exploration of modernity that tries to jump beyond the empirical boundaries of its explicit subject without resorting to the supernatural or the purely symbolic. It is materially grounded in a vivid life-world, in the realm of the material image, yet seeks transcendental meaning beyond official frameworks of materialism. Its narratives, we might say, create parallel worlds to the official discourse of politics. It preserves the quest for totality, which it inherits from socialist culture, but shifts it quite radically away from the world of ideology. If Lenin said that cinema was the most important art, the film-makers of the meta-modern have created their own perverse confirmation. They have explored the shifting boundaries of modernity and tradition in worlds apart from their own, worlds not easily incorporated into any political register.

In meta-modern film, this culture clash of the old and the new, of country and city, technology and nature, custom and freedom has been framed against the grain of a discourse using progress as its watchword and history as its end-goal. Here something very different happens. Progress evaporates, history becomes tragic, yet the marvel of life itself goes on. This generates a paradox. The meta-modern is part of the new, not its repudiation, but signs of 'progress' within the text are sparse. We have new worlds on film, new ways of seeing and new experiences, in short cinematic totalities, but no easy language in which to speak of it. As a way of glossing modernity, this is film-making on the outside looking in, extraordinary in its detachment. It strives to create the site of an artistic beyond, in which contemplation as a form of witnessing the immediate, the existential, the social, becomes something more, a form of meta-narrative to rival the meta-narrative of the state.

The range in form is enormous, shown by the flair of Andrei Tarkovsky in moving from medieval fable in his film of obscure icon-maker, Andrei Rublev, to futuristic fable in *Solaris*. Both differ in tone and voice, yet both are unmistakably Tarkovskian. This leads us to a vital speculation. Whether medieval, contemporary or futuristic, it may be possible to see meta-modern narrative as a *cinema of wonder*. What could this mean? Without mentioning film, Philip Fisher has defined the art of wonder as an artistic presentation of the intensely visual, the sudden and the unexpected occurring within the frame of the ordinary and the mundane. In modern art, he juxtaposes wonder against the aesthetic of the sublime but also against the devices of defamiliarisation and shock often held to be core signifiers of modernism. In nature, wonder is exemplified by the appearance of the rainbow, a sight at which we never cease to marvel.[4] As a model for art taken from nature, the rainbow is sudden and luminous, unpredictable in size and direction. Wonder is thus an aesthetic of the rare experience, but unlike the rainbow made by nature, the art wonder is recreated out of the crossover of the natural and cultural worlds. Meta-modern film is just such a recreation, which strives to capture the rare experience of wonder in the life-world through the art experience of the moving image. Yet the image of wonder is no sense idyllic. The rare and the unusual are not treated as exotic, but as part of the fabric of the ordinary and mundane, now seen and heard in a different light. In the realm of film theory, it seems an exoneration of Kracauer's view of the extraordinary and the marvellous as part of the filmic redemption of reality, a quest he endowed with a quasi-sacred mission,[5] but with a key difference. Above and beyond the rare and the extraordinary, the meta-modern project is the creation of new cinematic world.

In its desire to unfold the new and the startling within the familiar, the cinema of wonder differs from the manufactured sublime of genres like horror and science fiction. It is not so much a journey of fear and fascination as one of rare yet miraculous discovery. Of course the life-worlds that meta-modern film has glossed are not innocent of the depredations of culture or the catastrophes of politics. We might say just the opposite. In the cinema of wonder two rare happenings occur, metaphorically speaking, at the same time: the rainbow and the earth-quake. This, contra Fisher, is a deadly double metaphor that derives from events in the natural world beyond our power. It suggests a kind of film operating out of the very heart of catastrophe. To take the metaphor further, the experience of filmic wonder might be imagined as watching a rainbow during the sensation of aftershock. If the sublime is the metaphorical fear which clouds our optimism, wonder is the marvellous event that surfaces in the midst of a tragic sense of life. We can think in meta-modern film of many epiphanies of wonder, the fire-amidst-rain of the farm building in *Mirror* which the infant Alexei watches with his mother and sister, the search party in the river at twilight in *Shadows of our Forgotten Ancestors,* the German trooper in *Come and See* trapped by his parachute in the branches of dense forest, Kaidanovsky's dream in the Zone in *Stalker* where he hears voices uttering the prophesies of revelations. Familiar neo-modern idioms, such as the style adventure, the alienation effect, the lyrical diversion or defamiliarisation, scarcely touch upon this kind of effect. They are conspicuous by their absence in Tarkovsky's writings on film, where instead the theorising of time, memory and the image is paramount. Nor can we assimilate wonder to that range of shock effects now incorporating anything from surrealist outrage to the spectacle-image of virtual Hollywood feature. Even in future mode, the meta-modern is never 'TechGnostic' in the American sense of Erik Davis, but a fusion of the marvellous and the tragic.

The rise of the meta-modern was just one outcome of the constant obstacle race experienced within socialist states, of perennial resistance to a bureaucratic censorship that Tarkovsky patiently defied in all five of his Soviet features. The state, to its credit valuing film as a cultural medium, usually trained and funded the talented but often took away with one hand what it gave with the other. Stringently vetting projects before production, it could also ban them after they were made, or in that pernicious *via media* which so nearly grounded Tarkovsky's career, first demand changes and then delay or limit release in the hope that public interest had died away. Yet form itself cannot be explained purely through this institutional quandary, important though it may be. We must add to film form the cultural lacunae of socialism and their polyphonic stress on collective experience. This experience has been part of the turbulent clash between tradition and modernity where the contradictions people live out in their own lives has often had no voice outside of ideology. Covertly, perhaps, meta-modern cinema has provided one expression out of that array of muted polyphonic voices, and in some respects, the most important one.

The importance of tradition, of the past, of buried culture and buried worlds becomes vital. In socialism, tradition has been seen as a residue of the old, troublesome but eventually overcome by the long transition of history. In the Soviet Union, the end of the Second World War was viewed not only as socialist triumph but also as confirmation of the country's modern nature, of having arrived as a military-industrial powerhouse on the global stage. As a startling gloss on the nature of that war, Tarkovsky's early film *Ivan's Childhood* could well have seemed perverse in its experimental form and unamenable to the collective patriotic memory in its novel use of dream structures. Yet it did follow, admittedly at the very edge, a recognisable paradigm. The patriotic war against Hitler was, after all, a sacred subject which allowed cineastes to free up their filmic imagination, and still be seen and recognised by wide publics. It was only after Tarkovsky's path-beating work, here and in *Mirror*, that the true epic which alone could match the scope, and the barbarity and the suffering of war against Hitler surfaces at the start of *glasnost*: Elem Klimov's unforgettable chronicle of witnessing, *Come and See*. Here the dream-like wonder inherited from Tarkovsky eventually turns to expressionist nightmare in one of the most powerful war pictures in cinema history.

Earlier in 1964, however, a different kind of transformation has taken place. *Shadows of our Forgotten Ancestors* rewrote the rules of film-making and changed Soviet cinema decisively. Working out of the Ukrainian Dovzhenko Film Studio, Sergei Paradjanov went back to a remote nineteenth-century world of Carpathian peasants, a world untouched by the heavy hand of the Soviet dialectic. He proceeded, in all true senses of the word, with the epic recreation of a world apart. A few years later in *Andrei Rublev*, Tarkovsky told at great length the story of a little-known icon-maker of fourteenth-century Russia. The heroes of both films are not 'progressive' precursors of Soviet heroism but Christ-like figures who obey a different iconography, Christian, mystic and sacrificial. Within the Soviet orbit, this set a dangerous precedent. From the outset meta-modern film, always vulnerable and semi-official, defined its iconic value in an extraordinary way through the figure of Christ in a country whose official religion at the time was atheism. In Orthodox iconography, in particular, Jesus as a sacred figure can be erotic and mystic at the same time, a source of deeply expressive celebration as well as pietistic devotion. Yet Paradjanov and his followers link this erotic mystery to a pagan world of folk traditions as cussedly at odds with the rhetoric of Christianity as it is with the ideology of progress. This contradictory overlap of Christian and pagan is a vital iconic sign that reappears in the films of Larissa Shepitko, Tenghiz Abuladze, Alexander Sokurov and Konstantin Lopushansky. In its Byzantine dimensions, Orthodox iconography is also echoed in the films of Theo Angelopoulos in Greece, where it is underpinned by the legends of classical mythology with their different pagan traditions, and above all by the trope of the Homeric journey where the journey overland and the inland river replace the sea passage of myth.[6]

Firmly outside the Soviet sphere of influence, the films of Angelopoulos often seem connected through their Balkan setting and through Greece's tragic episodes of civil war and military dictatorship. To see his films as part of the forging of a national voice of cinema in trying times is to invite comparison with the work of Poland's Andrzej Wajda. Both deal with the historic tragedy of nations whose fate had been decided elsewhere, at Yalta in 1945 by the Allied Powers, but with opposite consequences. In post-war Poland, popular nationalism was sabotaged by a Soviet-directed coup to install communist rule. In post-war Greece popular socialism was truncated by a British-directed coup to install a pro-Western government and monarchy. As a result both countries suffered destructive civil wars. This mirror-image politics creates a cinematic paradox. Made within the socialist bloc, Wajda's films are profoundly affected by an emergent socialist culture and its many contradictions, yet resource both national romanticism and Western filmic influences. In Greece, Angelopoulos starts by exploring the defective pre- and post-war origins of Greek democracy in the light of its overthrow in the late 1960s by military dictatorship. While the rule of the Colonels was in force when he began work on *The Travelling Players*, the national dimension of politics was fused with the global dimension of art. His cinematic influences came from everywhere, from Europe, from America, from the Soviet Union, from Japan.

Wajda, within the Soviet sphere, is patriotic in his romanticism, socialist in his witnessing, but also deeply influenced by Italian neo-realism and Orson Welles. In 1957, Wellesian depth of field and back-lighting dominate the *mise-en-scène* of *Ashes and Diamonds*. In 1976, the Wellesian time-image and its contemplation of the false resonate throughout his reflexive meditation on post-war Polish history, *Man of Marble*.[7] Though Angelopoulos also takes his models of deep-focus and the sequence-shot, or *plan-séquence,* from Welles, he is more oblique and adventurous than Wajda in his use of time. He not only rejects linear time, but also the pattern of alternation between a recognisable past and present which is given by the conventional idiom of the flash-back. In this he is closer to Tarkovsky than to any Western director, as he also is in his exploration of the sequence-shot. Here he uses it as a means of transforming the spectator's experience of space and time, a filmic innovation in the cinema of wonder that parallels the work of Tarkovsky and the Hungarian director, Miklós Jancsó.

Let us start, however, with Paradjanov and his 1964 film that now seems at the very origin of the cinema of wonder. In *Ancestors* the epic frame runs much wider than its religious iconography. It reasserts the folk tradition as an authentic populism, sensuous, earthy, lyrical and at times barbaric. There is no sentimentality here but instead a sense of wonder evoked in the midst of an existence that is idyllic and ruthless, comic and tragic. *Andrei Rublev* was not the first film within the Soviet orbit to follow Paradjanov. In 1965 Jancsó made *The Round-Up,* a political fable of oppression set after the collapse of the 1848 revolution in Hungary. The nineteenth century is deeply politicised in this film but Jancsó follows through two aspects of Paradjanov's style and transforms them into his own. The long lyrical take and the exploration of landscape are fused into a film form of what Tarkovsky was soon to call 'sculpting in time', of establishing the duration of the shot as a rhythmic expression of human time. There is a geographic adjacency too in their different landscapes. Paradjanov's forgotten landscape in the Ukraine was, as the film's credits put it, 'a god-forsaken Carpathian region' inhabited by a forgotten mountain people. Jancsó, further west, had set his film on the eastern Hungarian plain and used its strong horse-riding traditions as a metonym to define the visual look of the film. The grim round-up of the Hungarian guerrilla bandits by their Austrian oppressors reads like an iconic reversal of the American Western which could well be called 'How the East was Lost'. The horsemen are the

Hungarian victims of the Austrian empire, rougher, coarser, cruder than their oppressors and also easily divided against themselves by interrogation and imprisonment. Paradjanov is sensuous, breathless and euphoric. Jancsó is abstract, meticulous and sombre.[8] Yet both take life to the point of death when it is unexpected, sudden and unpredictable, like an erupting earthquake.

Paradjanov's figures of folk tradition work differently from Jancsó's nameless subjects, who are framed by abstract patterns of composition. In *Ancestors* he starts from a tragic love-tale of the region, which he reassembles from song, lyric and dance into a narrative chronicle, a series of episodes prefaced by captions like the chapter headings of a fairy-tale. This dark fairy-tale reaffirms tradition, however, only by abandoning it. It is not an excuse for a traditional means of story-telling but rather the opposite. It is a starting-point for innovation in form where the greater freedom in portraying the pre-revolutionary past is one way out of the difficulties of representing the present under the watchful censor's eye. With similar ingenuity, Tarkovsky would turn to the future through science fiction. This is a complex and often tortuous route to the Calvary of art resurrection, yet in Paradjanov's case its effect was extraordinary. The immediacy of film as medium restores to presence the absent figures of folk history, the 'shadows' of forgotten ancestors turned into living bodies, earthy, garish, uncompromising, sensual. Yet Paradjanov is also deliberate and reflective, for this is a bold cinematic strategy. The aesthetic forges the narrative form of time past and brings it into life on the contemporary screen, as time present. The story itself, in springing to life by springing on to the screen, in turn regenerates film as art. It rescues it, in other words, from the monolithic images of modernity decreed by the state.

The film also creates a new language of location shooting in colour, moving seamlessly through the seasons but with equal ease through the landscape, fusing time and space in its elated palimpsest with an iconic force not seen in Soviet cinema since *Earth*. Paradjanov gives a deceptive simplicity to complex effects, fast-tracking through dense forest, using close-ups, low angles, swish-pans, hand-held witnessing and wheeling overhead shots in virtuoso combinations. In that respect his style is just as kinetic as Welles or Truffaut at their most ambitious, and his choice of shot almost flawless. The use of sound matches song and music to the sounds of the landscape with a lyric resonance elevating narrative form. What fascinates him is not just the over-coming of the forgetting of the past but the fertile mix of Christian and pagan motifs in folk tradition, defying through its very hybridity any pattern of intellectual abstraction. Through this discovery, meta-modern film distances itself from the pure individual predicament prevalent in the West and becomes a cinema of the collective: but this is a new kind of collective, very different from that demanded by political masters, an organic imaginary disconnected from abstract collectivism, and a vital platform for the art of wonder.

Paradjanov's key elements of style and theme were soon to be taken over by others. In the 1970s Tarkovsky used a mix of colour and mono-chrome in *Solaris* and *Mirror* and developed in *Stalker* his futuristic use of Christian iconography. In Hungary Jancsó fused Paradjanov's form with his own more abstract poetics in the remarkable *Red Psalm*. His story of a farmworkers' uprising at the turn of the century transformed the mix of Christian and pagan motifs into a triptych which adds social-ism as its third dimension, then culminates in an astonishing socialist rendering of the Lord's Prayer. In Georgia, Tenghiz Abuladze's *The Wishing Tree* recreated the lyric folk chronicle as living force on the eve of the 1917 revolution. Further north, the conjoined images of snow and crucifixion in the opening sequence of *Ancestors* recur throughout the *mise-en-scène* of Larissa Shepitko's partisan drama *The Ascent*. In the 1980s, the brief decade of *glasnost*, Paradjanov became more appo-site, not less. The raucous peasant rituals and songs in the Carpathians are echoed in the defiant peasant songs and customs of *Farewell*, the Klimov/Shepitko elegy to a vanishing Siberian community resisting in vain a confused Party plan to flood their island as part of a hydroelectric scheme. Paradjanov's idyllic boy-girl sequences in the forest recur in Klimov's *Come and See* with a more sombre hue. In tracking the couple's oneiric search for the boy's massacred family, Klimov too uses a following hand-held camera amidst images of birch and pine with the panning-upward tilts and whirring 360-degree turns at the heart of the forest which were pioneered in *Ancestors*. Here the lyric dream turns to jagged nightmare at the heart of a war of liquidation.

In the Balkans we can see, as the Soviet empire stutters to finality, his film permeating Emir Kusturica's startling Yugoslav 1989 fable, *Time of the Gypsies*. A central sequence in both films contains an almost identical image of wonder, yet is given opposite meanings in their respective narratives. This is the ritualistic image of burning beacons held head-high and moving over the current of the river at twilight, framed as a contrast between the primal elements of fire and water. In Paradjanov it is a tragic sign, marking the desperate and doomed search of the villagers wading through the torrent to find the body of Ivan's beloved Marichka who has slipped and crashed into the river from a cliff edge and been borne away. In Kusturica's film it is a brief redemptive sign, the beacons held aloft by boating parties enacting the fantasy wedding of young Perhan to his sweetheart, forged in the boy's vivid imagination to atone for his desolate life. Kusturica redeems Paradjanov's tragedy but only through the device of fantasy. Elsewhere, his tragic figures of Perhan and his younger sister repeat uncannily the figures on a landscape that are Paradjanov's childhood sweethearts, Ivan and Marichka. Later, the tragic death of Perhan's young wife repeats that of Marichka; his own at the film's end echoes the violent death of Ivan. The interface of the religious and the pagan repeats itself through Kusturica's film of Yugoslav gypsies, Balkan 'forgotten ancestors' of the present, mixing their tales and traditions with Muslim and Christian customs in a mixed community. Yet this is also a film of a different kind of present-ness, an interface with the modern where young gypsies are taken across the Yugoslav border and inducted by a village racketeer into crime and prostitution on the streets of Milan. The forms of betrayal among kin and among neighbours in Kusturica's film, which generate Perhan's tragic quest for revenge, now seem like a brooding premonition of the ethnic feuding and vicious blood-letting which marked the break-up of Yugoslavia only a few years later.

Finally, in a country where Christian iconography plays very little part at all, the sensibility of *Ancestors* finds a profoundly uncanny echo. In Chen Kaige's *Yellow Earth*, one of the first films of the Chinese fifth generation, made in 1984 and set in 1939 in the remote landscapes of the Yellow River in north-east China, we find traces of Paradjanov's *mise-en-scène* transposed to a different world. The geopolitical span is immense. The Chinese film style too is different, more formal and austere in its Asian framing and in its use of indigenous visual traditions.[9] Yet similarities abound: the poignant rendering of local peasant songs eerily weaving in and out of the soundtrack, the same meticulous filming of arcane village processions, the same shadows of forgotten ancestors made flesh. Yet again, this is brought forwards in time to the verge of revolution, and the modern is made manifest. Chen's young communist hero, avid collector of folksongs and resplendent in Fifth Army uniform, encounters the village peasants during the course of the Long March north, where contact with the unknown peasantry of the hinterland is seen as vital to the strategy of revolution. Yet during his stay in the village, collecting songs for the army, the hero is powerless to prevent an arranged child marriage that strikes him as a barbaric custom, and the life that so fascinates him still feels at the end like a distant mystery.

The beginnings of Chinese fifth-generation film in the 1980s, exemplified by *Yellow Earth*, *Red Sorghum* and *The Horse Thief*, show us a cinema which scrolls back to a pre-communist past, which recreates the remote, the primitive, the barbaric as a critique of the most oppressive forms of tradition, but is also a sharp reminder of other cultures which a monolithic ideology cannot contain, a resilient otherness which, as young urban members of the Red Guard sent out to remote lands, Chen Kaige, Zhang Yimou and Tian Zhuangzhuang all experienced at first hand. In terms of spectatorship, the dilemma is quite powerful. Contemporary audiences in Soviet and Chinese cities were not necessarily responsive to these films either as a veiled critique of the authorities or as cinematic registers of a common experience of which they felt a part. They, too, would be unsettled by such visions of the remote, the primitive and the unfamiliar. Thus in Zhang's films the star icon of Gong Li as an iconic figure from China's pre-communist past was placed in unequal competition with the new American icons of a China opening itself to cultural imports, the fantasy icons of Stallone and Schwarzenegger.

All cinemas of the meta-modern can lead critics badly into temptation. The easy option, about which Tarkovsky was so scathing, is to marvel at filmic wonder by calling it surreal, and then narrowing it down to a Buñuelian by-product of the exotic East. Magical realism, a term that is Latin American in concept and history, is often bandied around uncritically as a shorthand for anything Eastern, and tinged with abstract exoticism. Yet the term cannot accurately pin it down, and often translates instead into a bastardised form of Orientalism. The transcendental image of the meta-modern, which connects life, memory, dream and vision, is intended as something different, a composite image of wonder shared by the film-maker, by the imaginary subjects on screen and by the spectator, locked into a triangular circle of active contemplation. In the video age, this has its obvious ironies. In the West, the cinema of wonder is seen more often, if at all, on pan-and-scan tapes on a small monitor than in a fresh film print on a full-size cinema screen. The Hollywood-controlled market compromises spectatorship with the result that the only version of *Come and See* that mass audiences are likely to see is *Saving Private Ryan*.

Where film-makers within the socialist orbit moved on from Paradjanov, they moved on to a more recent history or into the present itself, the life-worlds of tradition, under threat, not sentimentalised but vibrant, and presenting the figure of the Other to modern audiences not as a species of the exotic so much as a form of the uncanny, that which in one's culture or country remains unfamiliar but familiar, unknown but also unsettling, recognised but repressed. The metamodern is thus different from the quest of Werner Herzog to adopt the posture of the global nomad, seeking out states of wonder in undiscovered cultures, a quest that latterly doomed him to be an eternal traveller cursing the ubiquity of the electronic image. It is rooted in time and place, sought out by Paradjanov's successors by confronting modernity as an ambivalent force, a force which necessarily disrupts the past for good and for ill. Paradjanov himself had no illusions, however, about being a popular artist for the younger generation. During his imprisonment in the 1970s he wrote to Tarkovsky suggesting laconically that his young tattooed cellmate with ten convictions, heavily into a life of crime, would have little interest in movies about 'the world of fairies, poets, story-tellers, Tsars of Kievan Russia'.[10] Yet much of what is enduring in the cinema of the socialist world and fascinating for worldwide audiences comes from his specific imprint upon the filmic imagination.

As if to spike the guns of the ideological monolith once more, Paradjanov's next film in 1969, *The Colour of Pomegranates*, moved from the lyric, the kinetic and the sensuous to the formal tableau of the still shot. A disconnected biography of Sayat Nova, an eighteenth-century Armenian poet, its central figure appears over an old map of his country drenched in the blood-red fruit of the title. Each tableau is framed as a dense fusion of Christian and pagan symbols, by the bewildering visitations of angels, and by the sex change of the poet himself submitting to his female persona, homoerotic but with controlled abandon. It is a film of the Caucasus, with Georgian and Armenian dimensions which contrast vividly with the spare, at times austere, imagery of the Russian Tarkovsky. Not released by the Soviet authorities until 1983, its hieratic and queer sensibilities seemed part of a double affront that may well have contributed to his imprisonment in 1975. The use of the still frame also went against the grain of the very aesthetic he had helped to inaugurate in his earlier film. It is the diametrical opposite of the sequence-shot, and a sign that Paradjanov himself in making the epic an entire world with a truly autonomous style, did not wish to be bound by any convention at all, even one he had helped to create himself.

## II

A key stylistic feature of the meta-modern, which Paradjanov abandoned, is the structured tracking take or sequence-shot, a style we often identify with Orson Welles or the Italian cinema. Here it is neither simply a form of operatic or lyrical expression nor, in the template of André Bazin, a fuller filmic representation of the lifeworld. The opening out on to the world differs from that predicated by Bazin in crucial respects. In Bazin, the moving camera, freed from the restrictions of montage and the static shot, unveils more of the world. Here it is much more again, a form of filming Tarkovsky has called 'sculpting in time', a means of enfolding the rhythms of human time as lived experience and memory within the duration of the shot. In doing so film ensures that 'time and memory merge into one another: they are like two sides of the same medal.'[11] One senses here, reading between the lines, that Tarkovsky's stress on time's inherent 'inner, moral qualities' is inseparable from the depredations of official discourse, the Soviet burying of complete areas of the collective Russian past, especially during the era of Stalin in which Tarkovsky grew up. In part, too, his writings on time can be considered a polemic against Eisenstein and the montage of attractions, which often excises time and memory as cinematic qualities at the expense of dialectics and the immediacy of the image, and active viewing at the expense of assimilation of the message. Yet just as Eisenstein's films are more than the sum of his writings on film, and *Ivan the Terrible* a powerful filmic transcription of Orthodox iconography long before *Andrei Rublev*, so Tarkovsky's cinema often outruns his own meditations.

We can sense in Tarkovsky's juxtaposition of time and memory a fruitful contradiction at the heart of the work. In his desire to dismiss the constrictions of montage, he rightly emphasised that the extensive shot should contain not only a sequence of action but also the weight of time passing, a feature he had seen in the films of Bresson or Antonioni. Yet his stress on the moral qualities of time takes his aesthetic into a new dimension that poses a vital question. If memory is reincarnated as part of the subject matter of the film, as it is in *Ivan's Childhood, Solaris* or *Mirror*, then it becomes a matter of theme as well as style, of plot as well as *mise-en-scène*. Memory directly poses, as Resnais had shown, the relationship of past to present as part of the texture of narrative itself. Thus the fusion of the two involves not simply duration within the shot but the edited composition of the relationship between shots. Although he claims that editing cannot determine rhythm, Tarkovsky admits as much in his discussion of *Mirror* where he confesses that until the very last moment, with twenty variations undergone in the editing room, he feared there would be no final cut of the film.[12] The film did not look as if its essential rhythm could ever be found, but Tarkovsky's essentialism convinces him the cut he eventually chose was the authentic film. It seems Eisenstein was not altogether wrong. The rhythms may be inherent in the shot but they can only emerge after the shot. The intrinsic problem posed by *Mirror* is not only the duration of time within the shot but also the crucial juxtaposition of different sequences of past and present, dream and memory. Questions of ordering, sequence and contrast still prevail. How else is the pattern of their relationship to be resolved? Here Tarkovsky's film still remains enigmatic, an open text to be read in different ways on different viewings. In that respect it is perhaps the most impersonal 'personal' film ever made in film history.

In the meta-modern the sequence-shot is a core aesthetic, an instrument for choreographing the precise double movement of camera and characters through physical space. It becomes crucial as a means of exploration stressing, unlike montage, the visual and acoustic importance of the out-of-frame, the constant unveiling of that which may be already heard, but which is yet to be seen. In exploring the life-world, or the world of dreams, the camera unveils and reveals. Tarkovsky has insisted that this is not simply a feature of watching films but of making them. Discovery for him lies in the elemental power of the extensive image. In Western cinema we normally associate Welles, Godard or Antonioni with specific long takes in *Touch of Evil*, *Week-End* or *The Passenger* that question the ontology of the image. More recently we might find it an excuse for pure virtuosity, as in the opening shots of *The Player* or *Snake Eyes*. Yet the films of Jancsó, Tarkovsky, Angelopoulos and Sokurov all set records for the low number of shots in the final cut. In *The Travelling Players* there are forty; in *Mirror* about 200; and in *The Sacrifice*, his last film, Tarkovsky relies on the sequence-shot more than ever.[13] Here *plan-séquence* defines the look and rhythm of the whole film. The cinema of wonder is an episodic chronicle of discovery which echoes and replicates the sense of wonder we experience in our daily lives by displaying things that are outside that experience, the new, the unexpected, the catastrophic, the marvellous. Here the sequence-shot has a double function. It is instrument and form, a means of revealing but also part of the nature of revelation. For this reason it must be dynamic. To contain and control everything within the static frame, – sound, image, figure – would be to undermine the aesthetic, which signifies a constant onward moving in space and time. What the spectator contemplates is always in motion, but in continuous motion unbroken by the cut.

Comparing Jancsó with Eisenstein can show the difference in political cinema, between montage and the meta-modern. Although Jancsó follows the Soviet director in his stress upon the collective subject and the unnamed protagonist, the close-up and the montage cut are eliminated from his work. In *The Red and the White*, made in 1969 and set in the Ukraine at the time of the Russian Civil War, Jancsó shows the tide of fortune changing often within the course of a single shot as Reds, then Whites, then Reds again contend for the riverbank territory surrounding a field hospital. Such sequence-shots seem to work on a higher metonymical plane, standing for the catastrophic sweep of contending ideological armies across the territories of Central and Eastern Europe throughout the twentieth century. Yet the delineation of their detail is local and precise. In one sequence the arrogant White officer, whose unit takes over the hospital and forces a nurse to identify wounded Reds for execution, orders them shot as they are forced to jump into the river. In the same shot, he finishes the act of elimination by watching, entranced, as a troop of White cavalry emerges at full speed along the far riverbank. Iconically it seems like a victorious movement, affirming his ruthlessness, but suddenly a single shot rings out, off screen, from the near side of the camera and he falls, fatally wounded. A Red officer emerges from *behind* the camera, revolver in hand, to take over with his own unit and it seems then that the White cavalry is retreating, not advancing after all. We are just as disoriented by the flux of war as the officer who watches the cavalry, vainly trying to measure the odds of advance and retreat. The tide has turned yet again and as it does, Jancsó choreographs within the sequence the transition of war from regimentation to chaos and back again. The film uses black-and-white Cinemascope to maximise width and depth. Horizontal and recessional perspectives are choreographed into a unified image that extends the plane of vision and enhances the possibilities of offscreen framing. In the famous final sequence we see a plainimetric composition of the Red platoon, spaced and marching in line down to a White position by the river. At the start of the shot they stretch the width of the frame but their advance makes them recede to mere black and distant figures; they remain sharply etched in deep focus until the point at which they are massacred.

In the uninterrupted take, the camera is on a journey of discovery, not in Bazinian mode as a replica of the human gaze but as its metamodern enhancement. The time-image for Tarkovsky is seldom the medium of the hand-held or out-of-focus shot, or of the close-up. Just as the camera's depth of field, its even panning and sharpness of vision are things just beyond the power of the gaze, so its steady glide is more like sleepwalker's procession then any normal human stride. It treads the path of human trajectory yet is unerringly superhuman in its power of imaging – that is to say, *inconspicuously* or invisibly superhuman. For the move is not a reflexive one in which the camera advertises its presence or its virtuosity. Rather it takes the mundane gaze into the trajectory of dream, oneiric in echoing the power of the dreaming brain to free up bodily perception and float through space. Its disembodied mimicry of the body thus has a power beyond the body's material being. This is reinforced by the doubling effect of the dream-work. In Tarkovsky the camera, as it appears to be dream-like in its journey through space and time, also films dreams. In Angelopoulos the sequence-shot, which often uses the crane, sometimes floats through mid-air as if defying gravity. It can also travel back in time as it floats forwards through space, as if the superhuman movement of the latter paves the way for the hallucinatory or metaphysical time-travel of the former, which then is no longer overtly metaphysical, since different time-frames operate within the same visual field with no signifying cut.

In societies with tragic and turbulent histories, often censored histories, the Tarkovskian idiom so vital to the uncovering of the past is the memory-film, and *Mirror* is its most complete expression. In an age of official whitewash, where dark aspects of the past are excised from collective memory, the highly personal film of the cineaste is more than refreshing antidote. It is an artwork which fuses the levels of the public and the personal, so that Tarkovsky's autobiographical 'persona' who never appears on camera as an adult, only as a boy, is himself placed within history by a fragmented chronicle of public events, elliptical sequences pulled from the documentary archive. While the life jumps generations, back and forwards, through dream and memory, the newsreel images move forwards in linear fashion through the respective generations of mother and son, from the Spanish Civil War, the Soviet war against Hitler, to the border clashes in the East with Chinese Red Guards signifying present time. None of these is arbitrary but is chosen for the specific weight and wonder of the documentary image. Indeed the footage of Soviet troops wading across Lake Sivash in the Ukraine to mount a surprise offensive against the retreating Nazis suggests a talented cameraman, soon to be killed in battle, whose style of filming was Tarkovskian *avant la lettre*.

Both public and personal narratives are fragmented, disconnected, asking to be recomposed by an active viewer faced with an acerbic irony. Is the absent father of the opening sequence a poet who has deserted his wife and children, or is he, like Osip Mandelstam, a poet whose absence signifies political disappearance to the Gulag? If the life is lyric enigma, a mosaic of dream and recollection, how do we connect it to the collective memory that is often anything but? Here the composite document of actual events is equally baffling, composed of shards and fragments devoid of the reassuring voice-over that normally narrates a continuous history for us on film. Moreover the pre-credits sequence features an actual event which is not part of that official history at all – a speech therapy session, roughly in time present, where a woman specialist cures on camera the severe stammer of a teenage boy. This too is taken from the archive, but how can so specific, so 'personal' an event be read as part of the historical narrative to come? The viewer must make the active connection and maybe it lies in the discovered fluency of the impaired voice, a metonym perhaps for the adult Tarkovsky's wish to exorcise the ghosts of childhood through the image.

Tarkovsky's film was even more personal than Fellini's 8½. The poems of his father Arseniy voice-over key sections of the early narrative. The 1930s family house at Tuchkovo was reconstructed from family photographs on the very spot in the countryside where it had turned to ruin, while adjacent land was rented from the local kolkhoz to turn its clover and rye back into the buckwheat he had known in childhood.[14] This is filmic recreation at its most precise and daring. Yet this is no ego trip. Unlike Fellini's film where the director played by Marcello Mastroianni appears in Fellini's fedora hat, larger than life, Tarkovsky's strategy is the opposite, an aesthetic of self-effacement. No image of the adult director appears in his film. We have instead the linked images of childhood, the 1930s infant and the wartime boy, and in the early 1970s the offscreen voice speaking to wife, mother and son. This decentring of authorial persona is stressed even more by the doubling of roles, Margarita Terekhova as both mother and wife, and by the same boy actor cast as Alexei, and in the present as Alexei's son, Ignat. 'Mirror', taken from a line in one his father's featured poems, was a title Tarkovsky arrived at late after 'A Bright Day' and 'Martyrology'. It seems a clear pragmatic recognition of the doubling process that unfolds in the film. This is a complex and mirrored doubling, as complex as any in modern film, the doubling of personae not only as a doubling of images but as a doubling of generations, centred on Tarkovsky's transfer of Terekhova into the role of Natalia, Alexei's estranged wife, after her brilliant performance in the role of Masha. This Oedipal transfer quickly enters the realm of the uncanny, but does so because the active witnessing of postmarital malaise by us and by Ignat, the son of Alexei and Natalia, fills in the earlier absence of marital encounter between Alexei's parents. The elusive void of the first generation is filled out in the plenitude of the next, but with a difference. Alexei is heard but never seen so that absence remains a haunting legacy.

The mindscreen images of the film are similarly dispersed and at times open, where dream is nearly always in black and white and memory in colour. Through retrospective understanding, the active spectator adduces the early dreams and memories to be those of the absent author of the film, a fragmentary portrait of an artist as a young boy; but there is always ambiguity. The monochrome sequence of Masha rushing in anxious terror to the printing house is surely her mindscreen. Other sequences raise the question of shared mindscreen. The visit to the wartime neighbour after evacuation to the country from Moscow, where Masha sells her earrings for food and beheads a chicken for her depleted table, suggest a shared memory of something which could be equally vivid for mother and son alike from the stand-point of the present, when they are now grandmother and father. The boy is struck by the retreat behind closed doors to bargain over the ear-rings, a humiliating comedown for his malnourished mother. It thus appears to be his memory. In the final shot of the sequence, the look of trepidation on Masha's face as she prepares to axe the chicken is so strongly felt, conveying an emotion which seems to be too intense for Alexei's childhood response, that it seems to be her memory. The ambi-guity lies in the absence of the POV shot in Tarkovsky's *mise-en-scène* at vital moments. From which point of view is the action seen? From which point of view is it felt? The movement of the camera continually objectifies the memory and gives no obvious answer. In the mirror, metaphorically speaking, there is no obvious reflection.

The opening post-credits sequence is even stronger in its ambiguity. Voice-overed by the adult Alexei, a brief commentary frames the appearance of a figure approaching the remote house through the wheat field. It turns out not to be the absent father the woman wants to see, but a doctor, so he claims, who has lost his way from the station. It is Masha sitting on the fence that dominates the sequence. Only a cutaway shot from her backward look reveals the two infants resting or sleeping on a hammock nearer the house. Yet we are never sure. Is it the resting Alexei who sees the encounter of mother and stranger from beneath half-closed eyelids and his adult persona who brings it forth as a first memory of childhood, or is this solely Masha's mindscreen, her remembrance of an ambiguous meeting with sexual implications?

An objective profile shot establishes Masha's face over Alexei's voice-over, and then cuts to a rear shot which tracks forwards past her head out towards the approaching stranger. We may start in the sequence-shot with the POV of the sleeping infant but without a cut the shot clearly incorporates the POV of the watching mother, and then embodies her experience of the encounter. The shot may start as Alexei's infant memory but the circling camera establishes a tight relationship of detail and an erotic tension between the two adults no child of that age could detect. It has a clear sexual edge, the stranger looking to persuade the husbandless woman of his interest in her, she facing him down with uncertain resistance. Her backward look to the hammock may well be that of a caring mother worried about an intrusive stranger or it may be a calculating look to measure the chances of distraction. The collapsing fence, on which the couple sit side by side, breaks the spell. The chance has gone. There is no editing suture here to suggest conflicting POVs, the child's naive vision and the mother's knowing vision. Just as we cannot know for sure who sees, we cannot know for sure what Masha feels. The look is enigmatic in its concealment of thought and feeling, so that we are both inside and outside her sensibility at the same time.

A generation later, in Alexei's Moscow apartment, we see drawings by Leonardo whose work will reappear in Tarkovsky's films. This again might be a clue to the look of Masha, often seen in a half-profile with gaze turning towards the camera but always at an angle, never making contact. It may well be an iconic sign of a blonde Mona Lisa of the moving image, ironised certainly, but whose plasticity differs crucially from the still portrait. While Leonardo's enigmatic Mona looks at the spectator from every angle with a firm and knowing fixity, with a trace of a smile, Terekhova does the opposite. She preserves the trace of the smile but her eyes flicker and avert the gaze, moving her look constantly as if aware of imminent contact and avoiding it, the evasion a studied posture midway between indifference and transcendence. This is the one actress in Tarkovsky's cinema who fascinates in this regard, a tribute not only to the subtlety of Terekhova's performance but also to the director's play upon the filmic convention of not-looking, of pretending the camera is not there. Mona Lisa's mystery of the look is replaced by Terekhova's mystery of the non-look, an enticement that is nearly but never quite asexual. There is a lure but the lure is not really erotic at all. It lies in that oscillation between an image of pure spirit and an image of pure caprice. The perplexed spectator might attribute this to conventions of distance. After all, the stranger is seeing her for the first time, and the son is too young to know what he sees. Yet at the end, when the absent husband, known to us by his poetry, is brought into an intimate memory shot with her for the first time, lying together on the grass outside the house, we have the same impression. As he asks her whether she wishes to give birth to a boy or girl, she fails to reply and her gaze wanders in response as if it has its own rhythm and its world.

For Tarkovsky the enigma of Terekhova's look is also the enigma of looking which permeates the camera. The mirror is both metonym and metaphor for this looking, and for the poet-husband's quest to reach its other side. Here Tarkovsky is indebted to Bergman but also moves away from him into another dimension. The female double is the central icon of both *Solaris* and *Mirror* and both spring out in different directions from Bergman's *Persona*. Indeed Bibi Andersson, who played such a central part in the latter, was keen to take the part of Hari in *Solaris*, and Tarkovsky keen to cast her before he decided in favour of the younger Russian, Natalya Bondarchuk.[15] From Lem's novel, Tarkovsky took the central theme. This is the strange relation of the deserted, damaged space station with its prophetic shades of Mir whose lifespan in space survived that of the Soviet Union, to Solaris, the planet it monitors, possessed of a mysterious life-giving ocean. In the screenplay he expanded on the family background of Kris Kelvin (Donatas Banionis), indisputably Russian, and on the theme of the female double, the galactic haunting. Here the 'Hari' whom Solaris objectifies and turns into flesh out of the signals of his brain, is sent to the space station as a fruition of his wishes. Yet she resists the role imposed upon her as replica and reincarnation of the woman he had married on earth and who had earlier killed herself.

Tarkovsky thus provides variations on those great neo-modern films exploring double identity, *Vertigo* and *Persona*, yet he does so in a Soviet context. As in *Stalker* he uses science fiction to analyse the plight of the Russian intelligentsia in the Soviet world, *Stalker's* world of the Zone, or here in orbit around a distant planet. Both are contingent worlds and worlds of wonder, yet also metonyms of detachment, intellectuals becalmed not in the country home as they had been in Turgenev or

Chekhov but in the experimental zones of science or space. Officially functional, they still feel despairing and redundant. One the one hand they are stoic about their condition, but on the other they philosophise about it endlessly and sense no way out. Instead of resolving the strange plight of astronauts being fed the emanations of their inner life by the Solaris Ocean, a plot that would be the stuff of melodrama, Kelvin succumbs to the disease he seeks to cure. This is an example of the destructiveness of science, not because it malfunctions, as in American science fiction, but because it is fundamentally flawed and helpless before the forces of the cosmos, a true source of wonder beyond human comprehension. The films are as far removed from the ideological optimism of the space-race as it is possible to imagine, and lead us back to a basic predicament of his cinema pinpointed by *Solaris*. One the one hand, there is a schizophrenic split between emotion and science, tradition and modernity. On the other hand the passion in space between Kris and Hari transcends the failure of marriage on earth. The point cannot be understated. Amidst the stray detritus and cool desolation of circular corridors and rooms with circular walls and tables, we see enacted the one truly passionate love affair in the whole of Tarkovsky's work.

Why is this? Perhaps because Tarkovsky creates a *mise-en-scène* where the metaphysical, as a searching beyond the *physis*, is immersed in a sense of wonder. 'I am not Hari!' Bondarchuk cries at one point, recalling Bibi Anderssons' anguished cry in *Persona*: 'No, I am not Elizabet Vogler!' Kelvin falls in love with the reincarnation of the woman he had failed to love on earth, but the cosmic ghost stubbornly struggles to be human, and to be unique, not a projection of his own desires. The power of the doomed passion lies in the contingent images Tarkovsky creates, but also in the juxtaposition of spacecraft and metropolis – here the business district of Akasaka-Mitsuke in Tokyo[16] – with natural landscape and country home. Schizophrenic culture, we might say, equals schizophrenic passion.

*Solaris* is flawed by the one enduring motif in Tarkovsky's work, which undermines the complexity of his images of wonder. This is the installing of the patriarchal icon who, in reactionary mode, is meant to atone for modernity's void. In his two non-Soviet films, we have further variations pointing up Tarkovsky's insecurity. In *The Sacrifice* the nuclear threat to the world at large is equated, regressively, with the threat to

Erland Josephson's patriarchal authority and his special relationship with God. In *Nostalghia* the Botticellian interpreter Domiziana Giordano is portrayed as a woman whose beauty and independence are a threat to male authority, to be remedied, it seems, by a good dose of religious piety. In *Mirror* there is no trace of these reactionary elements, for a good reason. It lies in the double image of the absent father, which is both haunting and enduring and whose power resonates throughout meta-modern cinema over the next twenty-five years.

Here are some key examples of the absent father in that same generation. The first is the orphaned Flyor in *Come and See* thrust into the harsh world of the Partisans and its rough and ready fighters who take an authority role when his family is massacred. The linear newsreels of *Mirror* are run backwards in Klimov's final sequence where Flyor repeatedly shoots in a puddle's reflection the newsreel images of Hitler scrolling back in time to his childhood. The infant who should never have been born becomes the ultimate father-figure tyrant, whose policies of liquidation are metaphorically matched by Flyor's Oedipal liquidation of the tyrant's image. In post-Soviet film, the key surrogate father of the period is surely to be found in Pavel Chukrai's *The Thief*, where an army officer usurps the role of the absent father in post-war Russia, trading on the power of his military uniform to dazzle widow and son alike, but acting all the while as a usurper and a thief. Chukrai's film can be read as an allegory of Stalin as the false surrogate father but equally as a fable of emotional ambivalence, where a love and an authority that are false become real in their consequences. In the same post-war period, the tangled Yugoslav politics of the absent Stalinist father is highlighted in Kusturica's *When Father was Away on Business*, yet Chukrai's film is the more powerful, not least in its final flash-forward to the present, where in reprising Tarkovsky's leap between generations, the fatherless son has now become an army officer with no authority, or rather, there may de jure authority in his wearing of combat fatigues but all de facto authority has been removed as he retreats with his wretched platoon and nameless civilians from a war-torn zone reminiscent of Chechnya.

In the 1990s work of Alexander Sokurov there is a very different response to the Tarkovsky paradigm. Set in Siberia *The Second Circle*, which adopts Tarkovsky's depth of field and slow-motion tracking, concerns the return of a young man to mourn and bury the corpse of his dead father. In *Mother and Son* Sokurov creates the iconography of a reverse *pietà* as a son nurses and cradles his dying mother on a windswept landscape infused with the austere and doomed romanticism of Arnold Böcklin or Caspar David Friedrich. The films constitute a diptych, a sequential *Liebestod,* as the pastoral mode of Dovzhenko and Paradjanov is updated to a form of living death. By mourning his father in *The Second Circle* the hero finds life in death. By cradling his dying mother in the later film, the hero finds death in life. *The Second Circle* is a lament and an exorcism, an elegy to a world that has expired but also a sharp reminder of Russian mortality and the presence of early death.[17] In contrast, *Mother and Son* suggests a healing process, allegorically a nursing of the shattered 'motherland', in the Edenic landscape of a new Russian romanticism made credible by the power of the image. In that sense, Sokurov is a clear successor to Tarkovsky but also a rare and fragile point of departure.

## III

Theo Angelopoulos has often been compared to Tarkovsky not only in style but also in substance, because of a common religious heritage. Yet he himself has been quick to point out the main difference. As he sees it: 'I am Greek and Greek Orthodoxy passes through paganism. Slav Orthodoxy is mysticist. Greek Orthodoxy swims in the light.'[18] Yet his films also challenge the tourist view of Greece with a vengeance. His cinema is not so much that of the South in summer as the North in winter, where Athens and the islands are conspicuous by their absence. Invariably, his films are bathed in northern winter light and one of his great epiphanies of wonder, in *Landscape in the Mist,* illustrates this perfectly. Brought to a local police station, the film's two lost children are left alone in the corridor with a madwoman as all the officials rush out to greet the unexpected arrival of snow. This is a deep-focus long shot that holds on the woman and children long after the police have disappeared. The door from the corridor into the interrogation room is open so that we see right through to the window on the far wall and beyond to where the snow is falling, a shot reminiscent in its own way of Welles's first childhood shot of Charles Foster Kane in the Colorado winter.

A few years later, in the 1990s, two films by Angelopoulos stand out as exemplars of this extraordinary fusion between the sequence-shot and the forms of feeling it generates: *Ulysses' Gaze* and *Eternity and a Day*. They are both films that touch on frontiers and a wider geopolitics. While Greece has come closer to Western Europe through the European Union, the break-up of federal Yugoslavia has entailed a rethinking of relations with Balkan neighbours. Both films confront this. In *Eternity and a Day* a poet plagued by illness (Bruno Ganz) tries to rescue a Greek-Albanian boy from an immigrant mafia who trade orphans to Westerners. Like *Time of the Gypsies*, the film glosses the relationship of the richer to the poorer nation and the cruel exploitation of the young sucked into the trap of begging and street crime. *Ulysses' Gaze* is much broader and deeper in scope, and can be seen not just as a Greek film but a Balkan film. It traces the Homeric journey of a Greek-American film-maker (Harvey Keitel) across the borders of Greece, Albania, Macedonia, Bulgaria, Romania, Serbia and Bosnia in search of three elusive reels of film by the Manakis brothers, which are at the very origins of Balkan cinema and of the cultural heritage Keitel feels he has inherited. Just as their film had been forged against the background of the Balkan conflict which preceded the Great War, so Keitel's journey of discovery and retrieval takes place during a similar decade of strife, a double convulsion in which communism is overthrown and federal Yugoslavia dismembered by militant nationalism and civil war.

Not since *The Travelling Players* had Angelopoulos created such a complete parallel universe in film, a meta-narrative of culture and politics spanning frontiers and generations. It is a kind of cinema fusing story and history, terms tracing their etymology to the Greek *istoria*, and thus vies with and reflects upon the route of history itself. Whereas the 1974 film had contemplated a recent history from 1939 to 1952, the later film is set in the present, 1995, from which it unpeels the layers of the past. Keitel's route across dangerous frontiers follows the route the film had taken in an earlier generation, and ends in Sarajevo with tragic consequences. His journey through space is also a journey through time, forwards and backwards. Without a cut, Keitel travels back at the Bulgarian frontier to the time of the Manakis brothers and doubles in his imagination as Yannis, the political intriguer who is interrogated and about to be shot. Later, without a cut, Keitel is greeted at Bucharest station by his mother welcoming him to the new post-war Romania of 1945, the literal portrait of an artist as a young boy, imagining himself back into childhood. The sequence shows Keitel leaving his lover and alighting from a 1995 train carriage, then returning with his mother through the same door to an adjacent 1945 carriage to take them to Constanza on the Black Sea. When they arrive at the family home, the next sequence-shot frames successive New Year's Eve celebrations after the war, again without a cut, during which relatives and furniture are spirited away by the secret police as a signal for their impending departure to Greece. In the same sequence the film turns Keitel's homecoming into his family's forced departure, which is itself a kind of homecoming as they prepare to return to Greece.

Angelopoulos not only cuts within the frame spatially through the device of exit and entrance, where the movement of the camera abandons one subject only to usher in another. He also cuts through the time-image where exit and entrance signify temporal transition. The New Year party forms and reforms through the ritual of the dance which affirms life and the knock at the door which negates it, both punctuated by the sound of the piano changing tune and mood, dramatic devices successfully transposed from the rhythms of Vincente Minnelli and the American musical. When earlier Keitel is pulled over to the customs office at the Bulgarian border control, the camera tracks his progress blind on the outside of the building until its finds an entry point, by which time we are back to the world of Yannis Manakis and his arrest on charges of terrorism. As the uniforms and personnel change in that brief instant of invisibility, so Keitel changes identity, but remains in the same clothes. Hallucinatory time-travel dispenses with the flashback and edits within the frame. In the film's prelude we have the perfect expression, through compression, of the method. We see the ageing Yannis Manakis filming a blue sailing ship as it moves out to sea, and then dying of heart seizure in the arms of a contemporary film buff relaying his story to Keitel. As the camera pans right away from Manakis and brings Keitel into shot, it also brings into shot the contemporary shore and skyline of Salonika. As Keitel takes up the story by walking back left to where Manakis has fallen, the camera follows but Manakis has vanished, even though the ship sails on until it is out of shot. Within the sequence shot

Angelopoulos has shifted time around in unexpected ways. The film buff appears to be an anachronism, intruding into the time-space of an earlier history, but as the camera moves back, it retrospectively turns Manakis into a figure of history, who has intruded into the time-space of the present, that of Keitel, his distant successor. Thereafter we follow Keitel's world.

This startling innovation in the time-image brings us on to the general question of style. In his debatable view of Angelopoulos as a late synchronic force of European modernisms, Bordwell has, none the less, perceptively demonstrated the stylistic and expressive influence of Antonioni. He focuses in particular on the long tracking take, the three-quarter rear-view shot he calls '¾ dorsality', reversing the convention of the frontal shot: the devices of de-dramatisation, the alternation of recessional and plainimetric composition, and the pervasive tone of melancholia.[19] We could add others, notably the visual reconstruction of the found object. While Antonioni effectively redesigned parts of the industrial landscape in *The Red Desert*, Angelopoulos used bombed buildings and ruined streets in Vukovar and Mostar to evoke a Sarajevo then under siege. In *Eternity and a Day*, he reconstructed the poet's family home out of the villa of the Italian consulate in Thessaloniki and a half-formed facsimile built by the sea, so that in the final memory-sequence there could be a moving shot which passes through an opening window over the veranda and the courtyard right down to the water's edge.[20] The close detail of Bordwell's argument is very impressive, yet key differences between the two directors remain. While Angelopoulos, Jancsó and Tarkovsky have consistently used the sequence-shot, Antonioni moved away from it in his later work. While the Italian is minimalist in his use of soundtrack music, the plaintive scoring of Eleni Karaindrou sets the expressive tones of the Greek director's films and matches, in its lyrical use of sound, the interior rhythm of the director's sequence-shots. Where Antonioni questions quite fundamentally the ontology of the dramatic, Angelopoulos reworks the dramatic, framing it in new and startling ways.

This can be seen at the end of the first episode where Keitel appears in Florina in northern Greece for a showing of his latest film, only to find the town divided between willing spectators and religious fanatics evicting them from the cinema. It climaxes in the street confrontation between the two crowds divided by a line of riot police, and is filmed in long shot to contrast the umbrellas of the spectators and the torches of the fanatics, an abstract arabesque signifying opposing elements of fire and water. Yet moments earlier, in the next street and the same shot, we witness Maia Morgenstern's first entry into the film, in many respects the key to Keitel's journey. As he walks with a friend from Athens to take his taxi and leave, she enters right from out of the frame, walking in the street in front of him. From the spectator's standpoint, this is a ¾ frontal shot transformed into a ¾ dorsality shot as she turns the corner and walks away down the street. From Keitel's POV, as the camera pans and tracks after her, it is a *continuous* dorsality shot. He never sees her face. It is as if we see her face for him, and are forced to fill in that recognition which is never explained. We see her face without recognising her. He recognises her without seeing her face. As he follows her and Karaindrou's theme swells on the soundtrack, his unseen voice declares his return to her as the start of another journey. She does not respond, disappearing between the procession of fanatics and the line of riot police into another street. As the police overtake the following Keitel, the umbrellaed spectators follow behind. The climax of confrontation begins, then ends in the sequence in a sharp cut. The figures of the walking couple, which had just defined an empty street, are swallowed up in a triple-layered crowd. This is the dorsality shot as a way *not* of draining drama from encounter but of intensifying it in unexpected ways. It also provides the audience with a tough challenge. We see the beautiful face that will launch Keitel's journey briefly in real time as she passes in the street. We are then asked to hold the image on that glimpse and match it to its later reincarnations. We are also asked to do so at the very climax of the sequence, where the fleeting contact of lovers is overwhelmed by the clash of crowds.

Not only in the realm of the dramatic are there disparities between the Italian and Greek cineastes. Antonioni's trilogy, which inspired Angelopoulos in his student days in Paris, deals with the disaffected bourgeoisie, with boredom and disconnection, financial and sexual corruption. Angelopoulos, in contrast, focuses on the vulnerable, the liminal and the rebellious. Conversely, two key pictures show that where the cineastes *are* comparable in theme, they diverge in terms of *style*. The key match is *The Passenger* and *Ulysses' Gaze*, reinforced by the casting of American stars, whose characters have a double nationality. While Keitel plays the Greek–American 'A', Jack Nicholson had been cast as the Anglo-American reporter, Locke. In both performances, style and delivery differ sharply from their American work. Deliberation, in speech and movement, makes them integral elements in their director's vision, while their characters are intense witnesses of the visual whose border-crossing journeys are framed by their profession. Both enact a form of tragic repetition. Set against the journey of the Manakis brothers from the Greek Diaspora along the Black Sea to the homeland, and later the journey of his own family, Keitel goes in the opposite direction, creating his bleak passage into Balkan worlds of cruelty and chaos. In the earlier film, Nicholson had shed his identity as a reporter for one as a gunrunner, only to end up moving back to the point of his persona's origin in North Africa, acting out a circle of return instead of an existential flight.

Both films are also romance narratives that play upon the return of the same. Nicholson takes up with Maria Schneider, an architecture student he meets in Barcelona, but whom the camera has already caught with him in the same shot in Bloomsbury outside the British Museum. In *Ulysses' Gaze* the repetition of the image is more complex and less contingent. The Romanian Morgenstern plays all four different women who cross Keitel's path, modern versions of figures in the *Odyssey*: Penelope, Calypso, Circe and Nausicaa. Yet Angeloupolos intends something more. The three women Keitel meets on his journey all seem in variation of dress, manner and nationality to be versions of the woman who leaves him on the streets of Florina. Aided by Morgenstern's versatility and lack of star stature, Angelopoulos is able to play on the variations of the same actress as forms of the erotic uncanny. Her spaced reincarnation in different guises is not only a sensuous eruption into narrative, which gives it both structure and drive. It is also inflected by Keitel's prior perception of the woman who walks past his waiting taxi without a backward glance, an imprint that seems on a second showing of the film to predetermine each encounter to come.

The stylistic framing of narrative in the two films is as different as the themes are similar. Antonioni's framing is *intensive*. Locke's existential flight is played out as three parallel and intersecting narratives, jigsaws on different perceptual planes that finally dovetail together. By contrast, *Ulysses' Gaze* is made *extensive* by the sequence-shot. The

Italian cineaste cuts elliptically between time frames; the Greek cineaste explores the sequence as a form of contiguity, made poetic by
the internal cut, the fluid exit or entrance, the time-lapse with no
truncation. This is the exploration of a unified space within the range
of the moving camera, which is also here equivalent to the pace of
human movement or the vehicle of that movement, the truck, the
bus, the ship, the train, all of which Angelopoulos uses so well. For
him a cut through space is usually a cut through time, the opposite
of parallel montage, as a different episode begins. The aesthetic of
wonder which is implicit in Antonioni in specific sequences only, such
as the desert sequence which begins his film, is crystallised here as
the very essence of the narrative.

That sense of wonder inflects narrative with a questioning of its
own ontology. Is Keitel's journey really happening? In what sense are
the places that act as way stations on his journey real? The perilous
river trip from Belgrade to Sarajevo is never shown in naturalistic
mode. Instead it is punctuated by Keitel's encounter with a Bosnian
widow in a deserted and ruined landscape, where Morgenstern is a
Circean figure both past and present, helping Keitel to dress in her
husband's uniform to escape along the river. Here she seems an erotic
motif in Keitel's dream, an archetypal Balkan woman of the century,
Bulgarian then and Bosnian now, helping him to journey to Sarajevo
in the present but also to escape from the Greek Diaspora of the Black
Sea – she traces the route in the moisture of a windowpane – to the
homeland in the time of Yannis Manakis. Her double persona reflects
that of Keitel himself, who is now living as two different film-makers
at opposite ends of the century. This synchronic time-travel, in which
two epochs appear simultaneously in a single shot, is repeated in
*Eternity and a Day*, where writer Bruno Ganz steps back a century
within the same shot to confront a poet-ancestor who is both his
double and his progenitor. By this time Keitel's journey seems very
real, but also hallucinatory, like the journey in *Voyage to Cythera* or
the imaginary border between Greece and Germany, which exists in
the minds of the two wandering children of *Landscape in the Mist*. 'Is
this Sarajevo?' he demands in vain of people fleeing distant gunfire
and unseen shells amidst ruined apartment blocks. In production
reality it is not, since the sequence was shot elsewhere. Is this then
the Sarajevo of his imagination, shot on location in other war-scarred

cities? The question remains open. The power of the image lies not in forcing us to choose, but in forcing us not to choose. For we cannot choose. The Sarajevo of *Ulysses' Gaze* is both place and non-place, real and imaginary at the same time. In that conundrum lie both the power and the provocation of the film.

*Chapter 4*

# CONSPIRACY THEORY: *JFK* AND THE NIGHTMARE ON ELM STREET REVISITED

The flipside of TechGnosis, both cult and mythology, is the paranoia of the disconnected. The mythic package which contemporary culture offers, buys in the two as the day and night of the information age. It is a double-sign of the domination of a peculiar rhetoric. Instead of the soul being wired to the fount of Gnostic wisdom, the soul is severed from its electronic source. The source of disconnection is then read as conspiracy, what *they* do to *us*, or at its most desperate, *me*. In Freud's classic formula, delusions of grandeur accompany delusions of persecution. My importance is confirmed by widespread conspiracy so that I am at the centre of a secret orchestrated campaign to mislead, to deceive, to persecute, or to do all three. One of the fascinating features of 1990s cinema is the persistence of conspiracy theory beyond its value as a guide to action. In the United States of the 1970s, speculations about the Kennedy and King assassinations and the true nature of Watergate were linked to radical opposition to the American political system. Such oppositions no longer exist on the same scale or act with the same intensity, yet conspiracy theories do. They survive, as it were, in the absence of a clear politics but they also survive because power politics is always secret and conspiratorial. At the extreme end of the scale conspiracy theories about the Branch Davidian deaths at Waco, the murky details of which are still not clear, indirectly provoked the terror-catastrophe of the Oklahoma bombing.[1] Yet conspiracy remains for the most part apolitical, a sign of detachment from the system which produces isolated terror, often apocalyptic and deeply troubling, on the one hand, and mass inertia, equally troubling, on the other. The circulation of conspiracy theories on the Net about such events is a sign of a subterranean militancy, which usually has no cause to surface in order to prove itself. When it does, however, it can be murderous.

In this context conspiracy movies are ideal fodder for paranoid networks and electronic lonely hearts. The villains can be set in stone as Agency people of whatever intelligence branch of government comes to mind. The mythic strength of the Hollywood narrative here lies in the transition from total incredulity about the hero's claims, to one of mythic conviction where the audience is prepared to suspend disbelief because conspiracy and cover-up have been revealed. In *Conspiracy Theory* taxi driver Mel Gibson gives out a different name to his customers from the one on his cab ID, and lives in a fortress apartment where even the doors on his fridge are padlocked. His idea of cab conversation is to spew out at motormouth speed a whole series of incoherent riffs on famous conspiracy theories. We are meant to read him as hyperactively deranged but for very good reasons. With the love and rational brain of a good woman, attorney Julia Roberts, he finds out that the subliminal flashes in his mind are memory fragments of a CIA experiment officially suppressed. Afraid his memory is becoming lethal and will expose the scandal, the rogues of the Agency try, and fail, to eliminate him. With better special effects, *Enemy of the State* does much the same as the hapless Will Smith, good family man, is fortuitously left with the incriminating film that shows a political killing. As the rogue NSA (National Security Agency) operatives get on his trail, things happen to himself and his family that should never happen to any democratic law-abiding citizen. The things that happen are the stuff of paranoia, but here they are also the stuff of devious plotting and round-the-clock surveillance. This is the enemy of the state as the enemy of the lawless branch of some agency of the state blessed with an omniscient electronic eye, which turns out not to be all-seeing after all.

A different version of the fight against the electronic eye is *The Truman Show*. That it should be such a commercial hit in the age of the television soap shows with no small irony the power of the TV medium on the film audience. Their desire to back Jim Carrey's fightback, as he finds out his whole life has been the subject of the country's longest-running TV soap combines two things: complete dependency on the medium with a deep desire to resist it. It also marks the crossover between TechGnosis and paranoia. Being networked means being the virtual and vicarious neighbour of the fictive characters who appear on the screen week in, week out and are taken so much to be real that virtual neighbours discuss their 'lives' in their own lives, at home, in café, pub or office. Yet what if the democratic medium connecting us all, because we watch and 'live out' the same soaps, should be the prime movers of *our* lives? What if we are no more actual than our fictive counterparts on screen? Weir's talent here is to touch this raw nerve in the virtual body. When Carrey looks out fondly at the moon rising over his island suburb, little does he know that there actually is a man-in-the-moon, Ed Harris as Christof, media orchestrator of his life's daily drama, or that the moon is a satellite monitoring his movements and those of the real-life actors around him. The information age is thus source of both delirium and fear, the buzz and hype of being connected set against the phobic suspicion of the unseen instrument that sees all, the orchestrating panopticon.

Like Weir's salutary fable, *Enemy of the State* updates *The Conversation* to the digital age. The eponymous Gene Hackman plays over the role he earlier played in Coppola's film, and though Harry Caul now 'becomes' Edward Lyle, he remains an extension of the same surveillance persona, witness the NSA photofile shot Scott inserts of Hackman as Caul twenty years earlier. The film, which starts out a solemn warning of the new surveillance politics in an age of space satellites and Bill Gates, ends in hacker's paradise as Hackman – what's in a name? – teaches Smith the rudimentary counter-power of the electronic eye. Fittingly, Jason Robards, Ben Bradlee in *All the President's Men,* plays the congressman murdered because he wishes to limit the NSA's increased powers. The film in effect replays the 1970s for the 1990s, but does so without the politics or without the real time of investigation, things which the films of Coppola and Pakula had mastered so well. Investigation as a labyrinthine search for truth is subordinate to paranoia as the imagination of endless pursuit. The spectacle-image of the chase replaces the time-image of the search. Melodrama resurfaces triumphantly, as the bad guys lose and the good guys win out. Though the cultic severing of conspiracy from politics seems new, we can see in turn its connection to the recent past. The greatest challenge for the American time-image, we might say, was the moment of Kennedy's assassination, constantly rehashed in remembrance of conspiracies past. Oliver Stone's film *JFK* is perhaps the most dazzling, the most hyperactive and densely impacted chronicle of recent history ever made. It is also, through its many weaknesses, testament to a dilemma that will not go away. On the one hand the living past cannot be written out of history. On the other hand it can all too easily be turned into living myth. Here film is inseparable from culture as a whole, from fiction, drama, journalism and political investigation, which all pass over the same terrain and recompose it in different ways. At the century's end Stone's film appears as the lopsided culmination of an immense culture of inquiry, which has verged on obsession. Let us now look back to where it all begins.

I

The story so far: the Warren Commission concludes that Lee Harvey Oswald acted alone in killing John F. Kennedy by firing three shots from a sixth-floor window of the Texas Book Depository. Soon after, Mark Lane challenges the official findings in *Rush to Judgment*. New Orleans DA Jim Garrison brings charges of conspiracy to assassinate against a local entrepreneur, Clay Shaw. The charge is fuelled by speculation surrounding Oswald's own murder in custody at the hands of Jack Ruby, a Dallas club owner. In two recent American surveys 77 per cent and 89 per cent of all respondents thought Kennedy's murder was a part of a widespread conspiracy that has never come to light. Now read on.

Despite Garrison's failure to produce evidence of conspiracy and Shaw's acquittal, doubts about Dallas resurfaced during the Watergate hearings of 1974 as the extent of President Nixon's role in the cover-up surrounding the burglary of Democratic Party HQ there become apparent. Suspicions were increased by other forms of Nixonian duplicity in matters of foreign policy, the covert bombings of Laos and the opportunistic invasion of Cambodia during the Vietnam War while proclaiming a policy of disengagement. Nixon's chequered career had been a connecting link between the Cold War paranoia of an American Right persecuting real and imaginary Communists through the HUAC (House Committee on Un-American Activities) hearings and the

Vietnam paranoia of a Republican administration besieged by war protesters in the streets and troubled by mutinies in its conscripted army at the front. In this climate of mistrust Seymour Hersh added fuel to the fire by uncovering an abortive CIA plot, Operation Mongoose, hatched after the Bay of Pigs to assassinate Fidel Castro through the use of Mafia connections. The role of the Kennedys in that plot remains ambiguous.[2] Yet if fact proved stranger than fiction in 1974 many assumed the same had applied a decade earlier. The Watergate burglary and cover-up showed due contempt for democratic process. Critics encouraged by the Watergate hearings, the investigative journalism of the *Washington Post* and the new Freedom of Information Act found case after case of illegal action by federal agencies – surveillance, illegal entry, violence and intimidation by *agents provocateurs*, all made systematic by the FBI COINTEL programme in its hounding of the peace movement, student radicals, Martin Luther King, Black Power revolutionaries and the American Indian movement.[3] Conversely the paranoid fix of the American Right no longer worked. The protest movements of the 1970s were too widespread and fragmented to be written off as machinations of a Marxist cabal and the FBI was reluctantly forced to abandon J. Edgar Hoover's myth of world Communist conspiracy. The time thus seemed right, for many Americans, to re-open the case of Kennedy's assassination.

Surprisingly it has become fashionable among sociologists like Jean Baudrillard and Jeffrey Alexander to discount the importance of Watergate for the issue of democratic legitimacy. Baudrillard claims that Watergate was a trap set by the political system to catch its adversaries, a 'simulation of scandal to regenerative ends'.[4] This claim of simulation, which discounts the actual crisis of presidential legitimacy during the Vietnam War, is the springboard for Baudrillard's sneer about Watergate's 'vertigo of interpretations' and his nostalgic claim in 1981 that Kennedy was the last serious American president. What Baudrillard seems to forget is that Kennedy's murder prompted 'the vertigo of interpretations' in the first place and that Watergate, by comparison, became a goldmine of revelations. Indeed the excellent BBC *Panorama* documentary of 1994, whose interviews with the politicians involved have brought much new evidence to light, showed the cover-up ran deep and defied all democratic accountability. Watergate cannot be dismissed as a mere form of game-playing while Dallas is accorded the status of a major event. Indeed it was Watergate-as-revelation which revived the obsession with Dallas-as-unsolved-mystery. Some mysteries about Watergate clearly remain. Nixon has denied any involvement in the burglary, only in its cover-up, and his tapes do not clear up the matter for us. Did he or did he not know? Perhaps we shall never know. In any case triumphant investigation had a knock-on effect. After his ignominious resignation under the threat of impeachment, a House Select Committee (HSC) on Assassinations was formed to re-examine the evidence of the end of Kennedy.

Closely watching Abraham Zapruder's home movie, which captures the gruesome moment of murder and calling new witnesses to testify, the Committee came to very different conclusions from Warren. It found out more about the chaotic transfer of the corpse to Washington, the sloppiness of the Dallas police during the interrogation of Oswald and the failure of the FBI to keep close tabs on Oswald when he was officially under surveillance. It found out more about Oswald's strange life first as a marine in a US surveillance base in Japan, then as a defector to the Soviet Union, and finally as a returning Marxist with a Russian wife who mixed freely in the Texan circles of right-wing *émigrés*; but the crucial evidence lay elsewhere. Faced with conflicting ballistic evidence and the enduring puzzle of the simultaneous shooting of Kennedy and Governor Connolly by the so-called 'magic bullet', the HSC concluded there must have been more than the three shots claimed by Warren, and for that reason there was probably a second assassin firing from the grassy knoll to the front right of the presidential car on Elm Street. In 1978, after a marathon investigation costing nearly six million dollars, experts still disagreed on the meaning of their visual and acoustic data. Moreover, the HSC produced no evidence of who had planned the murder. In effect it gave the public a conspiracy without conspirators.

The report opened the floodgates to a new wave of alternative conspiracy theories as critics also re-examined the murders of Robert Kennedy and Martin Luther King. The published views of Lane and Garrison, Edward Jay Epstein, Anthony Summers, Robert Groden and Jim Marrs were just the tip of the iceberg as conspiracy went into overdrive. Up to thirty different people were named as plausible assassins, including one Ramón Benítez (a real person?) as the gunman on the grassy knoll by Don DeLillo in his powerful docufiction *Libra*

(1988). In 1991 the new rhetoric was consummated, for want of a better word, in *JFK* at the cost of at least fourteen million dollars more than the report of the HSC. Here nebulous multiple conspiracies blend with Stone's mythologising of the Kennedy era as the American Garden of Eden. Kennedy's exploding skull, immortalised to universal horror by Zapruder's film, stands in as dubious metaphor for the bitten apple from the Tree of Knowledge. In the nostalgic aura of the Kennedy cult, it is the emblem of the Fall, a mythic knowledge of dreams unfulfilled. Yet in Stone's movie, knowledge is not at a premium and very little is revealed about Kennedy's death. Instead we have an optical mythology where Clay Shaw and the New Orleans gay underground merge with the CIA, the FBI, the Chiefs of Staff, the Dallas police, Lyndon Johnson, Cuban exiles and unnamed half-seen assassins to kill the President in a turkey shoot while Oswald, in his own words 'the patsy', is the fall-guy with a dud rifle who couldn't shoot straight. In the Elm Street scenario, Stone sets new standards for expensive obsession. Freezing frames on the Zapruder home movie became the paranoid's favourite sport. As a result Kennedy left the arena of history and entered that of folklore, murdered by almost everybody except his most obvious assassin.

In Dallas the conspiracy industry became part of the heritage industry, where even Stone's difficulties with the local authority in gaining access to Dealey Plaza can be presented by Groden as evidence of deliberate obstruction of the truth. Coffee-table conspiracy books, TV documentaries, talk shows with witnesses and survivors all abound. As time goes by, false memory syndrome takes over. Marina Oswald, probably the only person to know of her husband's attempt to kill General Edwin Walker, now bends her ear to conspiracy, having repudiated it for years. Testimonies from ex-Soviet officials, free to talk since 1990 and presenting their view of Oswald as an unstable loner, became grist to the conspiracy mill. In Dealey Plaza assassination tours are a regular tourist attraction while diverse memorabilia now on sale have attained the status of Chaucerian relics. In 1993 new archive material, which contained 800 000 pages of information, was declassified and opened to public inspection in Washington. So far it has shed little light on the dark matter of conspiracy.[5]

As Kennedy's death traumatised a nation and much of the Western world, intertextual vertigo has become the vortex of the collective memory. Many remembered exactly where they were when the bad news broke. The bad news is still with us but in different ways. The cult of information has been replaced by the cult of tenuous connection. Convicted Texan contract killer Charles Harrelson falsely claimed to be one of the assassins disguised as a tramp in Dealey Plaza. His son, Woody, now plays a serial killer in the road movie, *Natural Born Killers*, directed of course by Oliver Stone. Stone's rival for the essential Oswald movie was John Malkovich's projected adaptation of *Libra*, allegedly scuppered by Stone using his superior studio connections. Malkovich then took a play version to his old stalking ground, Steppenwolf Theatre in Chicago, but has also appeared in Hollywood's alter ego version, its right-wing riposte to Stone's retro-paranoia. *In the Line of Fire* has Clint Eastwood as a veteran Secret Serviceman who failed in his youth to turn and draw in the back-up car on Elm Street. Making amends thirty years later, he comes back to protect a Bush-clone President from a would-be assassin – Malkovich playing a renegade CIA killer. The ending, where Clint gets his man in the nick of time, is mythic atonement for Kennedy but also, one suspects, for the serious wounding of Reagan by John Hinckley in 1982, now unremarked because it was clearly a conspiracy of one. Looking like a dead ringer for Oswald in middle age, Malkovich becomes a master of disguise whose different names and faces flip over on FBI computer screens in a reprise of the many alleged sightings and known aliases of Oswald in an earlier age. He thus passes as a version of Oswald the undead, now deemed CIA in the mythic realm of conspiracy and reminding us that Oswald's connection with the CIA has never been proved or disproved after all these years. Yet the film has its popular impact. If, as Levi-Strauss claims, myth is a resolution of social contradictions, this is an effective stitch-up. Malkovich is both lone psycho and ex-Agency, the rogue killer's mythic ground of being upon which the Warren Commission and Oliver Stone might embrace in reconciliation.

The plot, however, thickens. Hinckley was obsessed by *Taxi Driver*'s Travis Bickle (Robert De Niro), the Vietnam vet on speed who gets a Mohican haircut and plans to kill a populist politician – a clear reference to the Kennedys. Bickle is infatuated with the twelve-year-old hooker, played by Jodie Foster, whom he tries to rescue from pimp Harvey Keitel. When Foster later went to Harvard she received unsolicited mail from the obsessed Hinckley. Meanwhile the CIA also turned to fiction. While agent Howard Hunt, the Watergate plumber accused of being a tramp in Dealey Plaza on the fatal day, wrote spy novels, David Phillips, a CIA disinformation specialist in Mexico City in 1963, died in 1988 leaving behind an unpublished story in which a CIA man in Mexico City claims he is one of the two case officers giving Oswald the task of assassinating Castro. He has to share the guilt when Oswald kills Kennedy instead.[6] On a lighter note Stone makes a guest appearance as himself in *Dave*, a comedy in which a local dimwit (Kevin Kline) is a dead ringer for a dying president and is forced by ruthless aides to take his place so that a dumb public will fail to notice the difference. In a sound-bite interview Stone vouches for President 'Dave', then in the fashion of the stars that send themselves up in Altman's *The Player*, claims he is not paranoid. Stone's most recent film *Nixon*, however, is a film about his favourite *paranoid* politician whose intense perception of rejection has an uncanny resemblance to Stone's own. Connections recycle in the culture as mythic variations on a single, obsessive theme. They prove nothing but what is in the mind's eye, but then, they still are in the mind's eye and don't go away.

Facile profiles of conspiracy critics lure us into the temptation of an amateur sociology of knowledge. Stone's uncritical praise of Kennedy and his bitterness at the Dallas murder derive without doubt from his own disillusion with American politics after his stint as a platoon officer in Vietnam. With Kennedy's death, so legend had it, the rot set in. 'They' must have got him. Meanwhile Stone's main movie property, Garrison's *On the Trail of the Assassins* (1988), has been attacked as a crude catalogue of Garrison's settling of scores with old rivals. Such a rival was successful right-wing businessman Clay Shaw, whose open homosexuality had enraged Garrison. Garrison hounded neo-fascists Shaw and David Ferrie as much for their sexuality as their politics, so critics claim, and then hounded witnesses to testify against them. At the same time rumours abounded about Garrison's failure to prosecute organised crime and his predilection for teenage boys, leading to charges against him of homophobia and more recently to gay protests at Stone's reprise of the Garrison 'homophobic' tendency in *JFK*. Inconclusive, the debate rages on. Meanwhile Stone has admitted that while his belief in a conspiracy is undying, he has no conclusive evidence to offer.[7] In the film version of Shaw's trial, Garrison (Kevin

Costner) reveals little credible evidence and so preaches sanctimoniously to the courtroom before playing to them the horrifying evidence of the Zapruder home movie. As the fatal shot detonates on Kennedy's head, Stone cuts to a reaction shot of Shaw (Tommy Lee Jones) wincing in his seat. Guilt is established not by rational representation of evidence but by the Hollywood lexicon of signs. The usual guilt by association with the Party, with Cuban exiles or with the CIA gives way to a even cheaper guilt – guilt by association with the image. Stone's sharp reminder of the seedy underbelly of right-wing extremism fails to end up as conspiracy, except in the annals of myth which in his own country is often more potent than history. Hence his mythic simulation of the real is the imperfect copy of history many, including college students, take for history itself. This after all is the age in which the moving image has triumphed over the written text, and where what is seen on screens is what is most remembered.

Yet the written text is still a vital element. The Texan journalist Jim Marrs also fed Stone the sweet honey of paranoia in *Crossfire: The Plot that Killed Kennedy* (1990), where many are potential suspects but no new assassin is named. As with Stone, true paranoia entails the deferring of naming as if the final naming of names is a form of brain-death for the authentic conspiracy critic, an act of crudity which rules out the bliss of unending possibility. The Free State itself, with its luxuriant gun culture, has also become a source of paranoia in its own right, especially where celebrity and murder are concerned. Oswald himself was a *locus classicus*, as his brief encounter with the FBI, his desire to be a spy and his avid consumption of Ian Fleming novels all show. His assassin Jack Ruby was another, coming to believe in jail that, on the floor of the prison below him, millions of Jews were being murdered. Another was Russian *émigré* George de Mohrenschildt, Lee's Dallas mentor who told conspiracy critic Jay Epstein in 1977 the CIA had asked him to monitor Oswald's behaviour. A few hours later, de Mohrenschildt shot himself, but only after trying to kill himself three times in the previous year while claiming that an FBI and Jewish mafia were out to get him.[8] All this shows how paranoia feeds off itself, the mindset of victims and perpetrators alike, a contagion which never stops, both cause and consequence of the nightmare on Elm Street. Meanwhile the truth quotient of the confession by de Mohrenschildt, said by some to be on a CIA mission and not a business trip in Haiti when Kennedy was shot, has yet to be established.

Two low-budget movies to come out of Texas, David Byrne's *True Stories* (1986) and Richard Linklater's *Slacker* (1991), treat us to rare confessions of paranoid belief, a comic device which sends up paranoia as dozy natural attitude. In *True Stories* an evangelical preacher in the imaginary town of Virgil weaves together the murder of JFK, the death of Elvis, the media, credit cards, and the shortage of Kleenex and toilet paper as evidence of a giant secular conspiracy. A huge TV screen behind him flashes over images of robots, skyscrapers, politicians and gold bullion. 'What's the link?' he demands, while in the background his evangelical choir repeatedly chants 'Puzzling evidence. Puzzling evidence'.[9] Less grandly, one of Linklater's slackers, an assistant in a seedy Austin bookshop, tries to score with a woman customer by displaying his conspiracy shelf and selling her a copy of Mark Lane's *Rush to Judgment*. *Slacker* also features a darker scene near the clock tower on the college campus where a year after Dallas another ex-marine became a killer from a great height as he shot students at random with a high-powered rifle, evidence of a one-man turkey shoot overlooked by conspiracy buffs. Ruby's moment of notoriety in a Dallas jailhouse found its grim echo thirty years later in the quest of another paranoid seeker of publicity, David Koresh, ex-rock singer and founder of the Branch Davidian of Jehovah's Witnesses. Turning his cult's compound into an armed fortress in Waco, he provoked a battle with federal agents who tried to storm the building. During the second assault the building caught fire and was razed to the ground, killing most of its inmates and providing material Armageddon for those amongst them who thought the end of the world was nigh.

Many conspiracy narratives abound in authorial bias. Here are two of the more interesting. The first is the Mossad training school where the art of dissimulation was top of the curriculum. According to Victor Ostrovsky, a Mossad graduate, instructors computing their own angles of fire from the Dealey Plaza shooting claimed the Mafia had planned to kill Connolly but hit Kennedy by mistake, while Oswald was the proverbial patsy. Not only did this imply an error of great ballistic sophistication, it also echoed the standard Mossad sting operation Ostrovsky relates in which nothing is obvious and agents regularly do one thing while pretending to their victims to be doing exactly the opposite.[10] A second more crucial instance is that of Howard Donahue, whose cover-up mania was nourished by his own induction into the Dealey Plaza replay culture of media investigation. As a firearms expert Donahue had done a simulated test for the CBS TV re-enactment in 1967 where he had proved it was possible to fire three bullets accurately from a Mannlicher-Carcano rifle in even faster time than Oswald had done. Instead of being quietly satisfied, Donahue became an investigator himself, the ingenious author of the magic bullet theory – the second shot passing through Kennedy's neck to wound Connolly's arm and thigh – whose plausibility has been increased by recent computer enhancement technology.[11]

Donahue, a godsend for the single-gunman critics at this point, then changed around and became a conspiracy buff with a cover-up but no conspiracy. Working as a gunsmith in the frontline of Baltimore's gun culture, an ambience of gruesome accidents and scary near-misses clearly influenced his esoteric version of events. He computed the origin of the third bullet to come not from Oswald but from the back seat of the Secret Service back-up car, fired from a Colt AR-15 rifle with a more powerful copper bullet lacking a full metal jacket. For Donahue this would explain the powerful explosion of the bullet disintegrating in Kennedy's head. From this he surmised that Secret Service agent George Hickey had accidentally fired forwards, hitting Kennedy, after picking up his AR-15 in order to shoot back at Oswald in the rear.[12] The imagined scene of the accidental shot comes not from the movie-book of Oliver Stone but from that of Robert Altman. Unfortunately, among the hundreds of witnesses in Dealey Plaza, many of whom had contradictory testimonies, none claimed to have witnessed a blue flame spurting out of the barrel of the AR-15 or heard the very loud retort which would have accompanied it. Donahue and his journalist collaborator Bonar Meinunger are left instead with the faint chance of an FBI cover-up, and are thus fated to pursue the Secret Service, including Hickey himself, in vain for confirmation or denial. In his book *Mortal Error* (1992) Meinunger adds Donahue's twist to standard forms of third-shot pathos. First there is the shot from the grassy knoll which beats Oswald to the draw – in DeLillo's novel: 'Lee was about to squeeze off the third round, he was in the act, he was actually pressing the trigger.'[13] Second comes the pathos of the simultaneous double-hit, of third and fourth shots simultaneously fired from opposing angles and rocking the head backwards, a coincidence thought possible by a minority of experts.[14] Finally we have Donahue's pathos of the bodyguard who fired accidentally in the wrong direction.

The most sophisticated works of the conspiracy and anti-conspiracy schools, *The Kennedy Conspiracy* (1989) by Anthony Summers and *Case Closed* (1993) by Gerald Posner, have produced identical forms of praise from literary rivals, Norman Mailer and William Styron. Both hailed their favoured reconstructions as *literary* narratives. Mailer wrote of Summer's conspiracy epic: 'Races along like a novel by John le Carré . . . I began it again as soon as I had finished.' Styron said of Posner's powerful attack on conspiracy theories: 'With the skill of a good novelist . . . Posner fully convinces me that Oswald acted alone when he killed Kennedy.' Mailer is not only a paranoid reader in Brian McHale's sense, already looking forward to his next fix with the next paranoid text.[15] He has also been, like DeLillo and James Ellroy, a key player in the paranoid school of fiction itself, and one who, until recently, was a firm supporter of Stone's *JFK*. His major donation to conspiracy genre has been *Harlot's Ghost*, a tortuous, baroque meta-faction of CIA skulduggery from its origin until Kennedy's death. One notable feature of this opus (1300 pages plus) is the author's postscript meditation on the skill of interweaving historical and fictional characters, and then providing a huge bibliography of names, places and 'foreign phrases'. Just so that his reader is clear about who in the text is real and who not, Mailer allocates an asterisk to 'all real historical personages and all actual cryptonyms'. His book is an end-of-history narrative comparable to the more staccato fiction of James Ellroy's *American Tabloid* (1995). For both novelists, history stops on 22 November 1963. Mailer's secret CIA wars build up to their nemesis. Ellroy's villainous triumvirate of Howard Hughes, Jimmy Hoffa and J. Edgar Hoover prod viciously into motion the events that end in the Dallas Fall. It is interesting to note that in *JFK* Mailer look-alike Ed Asner played drunken ex-FBI racist Guy Banister who features in both novels and whose office in New Orleans Oswald was alleged to have frequented: and this, conveniently, is the point of re-entry for our own narrative. For, given the cultural freight of conspiracy, it is predictable that Summers and Posner should have versions of Banister's link to Oswald so different they do justice to Kurosawa's *Rashomon*.

The *Rashomon* variations are all the more bizarre because they spring largely from the same source, the testimony of the dead Banister's secretary and ex-lover, Delphine Roberts, testimony proving once again what sociologists hold most dear – the power of positive interviewing. Seen as an unreliable witness by the HSC, Roberts gave interviews to both Summers and Posner, both of whom noted her extreme right-wing politics. The similarity ends there. For Summers she held the key to Oswald's connection to the neo-fascist networks of New Orleans, confiding to him, though not to Warren or the HSC, that Oswald came into Banister's office to enrol as an undercover agent and seemed to be on familiar terms with her boss.[16] To Posner she told a different story. Claiming to be the last person to see the sacred scrolls which God had put into the Ark of the Covenant, she also claimed she had told Summers her story largely because of the fee his programme was offering her and the free dinner which went with it.[17] Her daughter, who had told Summers that Oswald had a room in the building for storing equipment, now told Posner that Oswald did not have an office in the building but lived in an apartment there for two to three months during a period that Marina Oswald claims her husband never left Dallas. An interview is an interview is an interview.

Another instance in Summers' book, powerfully told, illustrates the different worlds of conspiracy and anti-conspiracy. This is the incident soon after Kennedy's murder where Oswald is walking rapidly through Oak Cliffs and is finally arrested after the murder of Patrolman J. D. Tippit. Summers' narrative technique here illustrates the general tenor of his book and is repeated elsewhere by lesser critics. Summers and Posner chart Oswald's progress along 10th Street but with different versions of intent, versions that remain, as they would admit, speculative. For Summers he is most likely to be seeking a pre-arranged meeting in the Texas theatre where he was actually arrested, there to be spirited away by accomplices and possibly assassinated. For Posner, as for Warren counsel David Belin, he was possibly heading towards a bus stop where he could board a transfer for the Greyhound connection to Mexico, the fare of which would have fitted the amount of money in his pocket when arrested.[18] For Summers he needs seven-league boots to walk the nine-tenths of a mile into Oak Cliffs in ten minutes. For Posner he has fifteen in which to hurry at a brisk pace.

Posner recounts the sightings of five witnesses to the shooting and seven other witnesses to Oswald's immediate flight.[19] Summers lists the contrary accounts of two detractors, which contradict each other, and mentions only one positive sighting, which he discredits. He adds in his second edition that Tippit, a married man, was having a steamy affair with a married waitress.[20] His technique is common. It is to use Warren as the official version, omit the detail of eyewitness testimony that does not fit the case, then offer statements, one never made public, which do not corroborate each other. Serial objection becomes a *trompe l'œil*. His narrative appears to be rushing towards an alternative revelation but never actually reaches it. Like the delirious montage of attractions in Stone's brilliantly edited movie, it is cumulative and compelling. It aims for accretion of effect and the breathless bypass technique – not stopping long enough for reader or viewer to figure out if the critical questioning implies a ready answer to the view questioned.[21] It was not even necessary to deny Oswald's murder of Tippit, or to prove conspiracy or cover-up in Dallas. For once conspiracy is on a roll it becomes hard to stop.

The most extreme form of the paranoid fix affirms Oswald's total innocence, the patsy as holy fool who not only did not kill Kennedy, but also did not kill Tippit and did not even try to kill General Edwin Walker. The vertigo shifts into ceaseless spiral. Someone else in Dallas impersonates Oswald. Oswald is not the guy in the picture holding the Mannlicher-Carcano even though it isn't a gun that could kill anyone at that distance anyway, and anyway the photo was a fake, and anyway he was a lousy shot. Oswald was not in the Russian Embassy in Mexico City even though Soviet officials say that he was, because it was someone else impersonating him and expertly faking his signature. Jack Ruby was seen in a truck at the same time as he was in the offices of a Dallas newspaper, so there must be two Jack Rubys. And yet Oswald *was* in and out of Guy Banister's office in New Orleans, even though no hard evidence exists that he used a room in the building as Stone's movie suggests. Though avoiding these extremes, Summers' questing narrative becomes a series of blind alleys down which he takes his reader, objecting en route to the official version but offering no way out of its relative certainties. He refuses, that is to say, to turn from defence to prosecution because of insufficient evidence. Yet his narrative starts out in style as a classic detective quest and the book's hype, more restrained than the going rate for most conspiracy junkets, still suggests the final fix for the reader of something nearing complete discovery. After 550 pages, however, and Summers is the best on show, the payoff never comes. *The Kennedy Conspiracy* fails to prove conspiracy.

Yet in *Case Closed* Posner fails to close the case. Questions go unanswered. The CIA appears to be sitting on information it will not declassify over events in Moscow, Dallas and Mexico City. There were multiple sightings of Oswald with David Ferrie, the rabid Democrat hater and gay New Orleans paramilitary in Clinton, Louisiana, a sequence filmed by Stone for *JFK* but left out of the final cut for reasons of length. Cuban *émigrée* Silvia Odio was visited in Dallas shortly before Kennedy's death by a man identified as Oswald, a 'third man' in the company of two anti-Castro Cubans. This has been explained as the hysteria of a double trauma, a young mother troubled by recent marital breakdown and then further disturbed by Kennedy's death, but an FBI contact, who at first claimed to be the 'third man', later retracted his statement. De Mohrenschildt, Oswald's mentor, remains a mystery, a chameleon with CIA connections baiting liberals with Hitler salutes and singing the praises of communism to Texan fascists, a model perhaps for Oswald's imaginary double-life. There is also the small matter of a campfire photograph of the teenage Oswald in the company of Ferrie. So it continues. Psychiatrists profile the typical paranoid as utterly humourless in the pursuit of conspiratorial truth, a point proved by Kevin Costner's sombre acting in *JFK*; but Oswald, alias O. H. Lee, alias A. J. Hidell, must be laughing in his grave.

For Sherlock Holmes it was so much easier. The sensible search for clues was predicated on getting a result. It has had little place in the conspiracy theories of the late twentieth century. Here there are professional abuses of reason the amateur detective cannot hope to emulate but equally vast bureaucratic labyrinths the amateur cannot hope to navigate. Besides, the ambience of Baker Street was a key to Victorian optimism. Franco Moretti suggests that 'a good rule in detective fiction is to have only one criminal. This is not because guilt isolates, but on the contrary, because isolation breeds guilt.'[22] What matters to Holmes and early modern detectives is the uniqueness and mystery of the killing, the killing of lone victims by lone criminals in secluded rooms.

'Detective fiction is rooted in a sacrificial rite,' Moretti claims. 'For the stereotypes to live, the individual must die, then die a second time in the guise of the criminal.'[23] The narrative of discovery and arrest restores things to the *status quo ante*. Life is untouched after all by the violation which threatens its social ordering. In the act of reading, the reader undergoes a parallel journey. He or she is restored to innocence and learns nothing by the compulsory process of discovery. Rather, as the reader continues to read detective stories, discovery becomes an addiction, an empty compulsion to repeat. Between the beginning and the end of narrative there is only 'a long wait', a mystery to be overcome by a pre-ordained solution.

In the Kennedy magical mystery tour, the long wait has turned into endless vertigo. The single villain is replaced by a chain or series of connections in which the original villain (Oswald) is the central figure who becomes displaced by the chain itself. Who Oswald 'knows' determines, on this reasoning, not his relative guilt but his relative innocence. The links in the chain, however, become secondary in conspiracy theory to the chain itself. Thus the pure paranoia of Stone's movie which indicts without evidence a person deemed secondary (Shaw as fall-guy), only to offer pseudo-evidence of transindividual complicity, where human agency is replaced by collective agencies employing faceless gunmen, agencies immune to the act of naming because they are corporate, impersonal entities. Thus the *reductio ad absurdum* of all conspiracy theory – the CIA did it – is transcended by implying all agencies conspired to do it, and whatever their degree of complicity, it was anyway in their objective interests to see that it was done. In this scenario, Kennedy, who actually enjoyed good relations with his CIA chief at the time, the fervently anti-communist John McCone, becomes the equivalent of his main adversary in the hemisphere, Fidel Castro. The anti-Soviet and charismatic President is repackaged as the politically correct 'enemy within' who defies the American power élites. The grassy knoll gunman who figures in the scenarios of Marrs and Groden is the invisible enforcer of the universal conspiracy in which one particular group, the CIA, the Mafia or the anti-Castroites may well be *the* agency but all serve to gain.

This single event, conclusive but inconclusive, explicit but mysterious, has helped transform the landscape of narrative fictions both written and visual, landscapes equally of book and film. The key 1960s texts in this transformation of Western narrative occur less than three years after Kennedy's death and chart the course of paranoid fiction up to our present decade. These are Antonioni's feature film *Blow-Up* and Pynchon's novella *The Crying of Lot 49*. In both the quest narrative is reborn as the endless waiting of Beckett's Godot in which nothing is known and nothing finally resolved. The 'long wait' extends to infinity. In both different formations of the thin grey line between paranoia and critical reason emerge. In *Blow-Up* the evidence is visual. The central document is the roll of film on which a fashion photographer (David Hemmings) thinks he may have shot evidence of a murder in a south London park. In Pynchon the evidence is verbal, the central document in all its different textual versions, a Jacobean revenge play, 'The Courier's Tragedy', with its elusive traces of the Tristero, an underground communications network spanning centuries, a conspiracy of preterits who flaunt their posthorn symbols in the face of Calvinist damnation.

In her nocturnal journey through San Francisco, perhaps a hallucinated journey of mind, Oedipa Maas, Pynchon's questing heroine, sees such posthorns, the Tristero symbol, everywhere. Her options mirror inversely those of the Kennedy investigator. Either the Tristero network is real, a richness of true connecting beneath the official tissue of Establishment lies and the ballast of an overloaded postal system; or else it is the overwrought dream of an overworked investigator[24]; or else it is a ploy by Pierce Inverarity, Oedipa's former lover now deceased, to lure her into false connections, an elaborate sting with a cast of thousands, the familiar scenario for most of the Dallas cover-ups whose logistical feasibility depends on hundreds of people faking evidence in the right place at the right time with the utmost precision. Here Inverarity, whose legacy contains the possibility of a secret plot to ensnare Oedipa, becomes a combination of Oswald the undead and the reflexive author of Pierce's fiction, the elusive Thomas Pynchon currently doing unto his readers what Pierce has done unto Oedipa. The fiction becomes a sting about a sting about a sting and paranoia is dispersed into an infinity of mirrors.

The compulsive seeing of the posthorns echoes the hearing of the make-believe tennis ball striking the imaginary racket in the student's mime at the end of *Blow-Up*, but the connections in the film are firmly visual. In his studio Hemmings plots the sight-lines of Vanessa

Redgrave's anxious gaze over her lover's shoulder towards the dense bush behind, yes, a picket fence on a grassy knoll. A blow-up of his photo of the bush reveals to his mind's eye the contour of a man in profile pointing what appears to be a gun. At the same time Hemmings has almost simultaneously 'shot' a picture of the embracing couple, giving a metaphorical echo of the double-hit scenario of the final rifle shot on Elm Street. Twenty-two years later a British reconstruction for Central Television, 'Who Killed Kennedy?', did the same with a bystander's photograph of the picket fence on the grassy knoll at Dealey Plaza where the producers hoped for visual confirmation of 'badgeman', an armed gunman dressed in the uniform of the Dallas police. The blow-up appeared to this viewer at least to be all in vain. He could see nothing. Yet there was still a certain sense of *déjà vu*, of documentary laboriously imitating art in the pointing of the gun over the picket fence. This was *Blow-Up* revisited, but then in *Blow-Up* we cannot tell whether or not Hemmings is hallucinating the contours of a figure in the blow-up or if, when he returns that night to the park, the corpse he sees at the foot of the tree is actually there – which explains its absence the next morning at daylight when he returns for the last time. Coates has suggested that the photographer's 'shooting' of the couple echoes the Oedipal motif of exclusion from the primal scene which then becomes paranoid,[25] but the film is as much about the suppression of the paranoid temptation as about capitulation to it. Hemmings finally becomes stoical about its infinite uncertainty, his failure to grasp totality. In the real world the producers at Central Television were more positivistic. Relying on the unreliable testimony of Christian David, a drug-trafficker in Leavenworth jail resisting extradition to France on a murder charge, they named three Corsican hitmen, one long dead, who had operated out of Marseilles and were alleged to be a Mafia assassination squad airlifted in from Mexico.[26] All of a sudden *Blow-Up* has turned into *The French Connection*. The two living accused then produced evidence claiming to show they were in France at the time of the assassination.

If the CIA and Charles Colson of Watergate fame can turn to fiction, so too can those in the legal eye of the conspiratorial storm, the lawyers themselves. The publicised murder trials of the rich and famous have brought to prominence in America a new breed of super-lawyers like Leslie Abramson, Lee Bailey, Johnnie Cochrane, Alan

Dershowitz and Robert Shapiro, whose profiles come to rival, as their fees grow fatter, the celebrity of their clients. Conspiracy fiction has also created a new breed of super-lawyer novelists dispensing best-selling fiction. In general they have taken paranoia out of the high-aesthetic mode of DeLillo or Pynchon, eschewed the stylistic experiments of Mailer and Ellroy, and put it in every airport book-shop in the world. Scott Turow, John Grisham and Richard North Patterson have commodified – better cannibalised – the liberal para-noias of the 1970s by turning them into thrillers with heroic lawyers and then selling the movie rights. Here Holmes would clearly have been out of his depth. For the new fictional investigators have to deal with political, Mafia or corporate conspiracies grown to great size. Such is the power of the new liberal paranoia – of which Mailer and Ellroy also are a part – that the political Right has had to produce its own brand mark under the name of Tom Clancy. Richard Patterson's novel *Degree of Guilt* (1993) has a famous lawyer, once responsible for a Watergate-type exposure in the 1970s, investigating a murder in the 1980s connected to a cover-up in the 1960s of the death of a film star, suspiciously like Marilyn Monroe, involving a famous politician, suspiciously like Robert Kennedy. The archaic fantasy of lone killers and lone victims in secluded rooms is a thing of the past. In Grisham the lawyer-heroes are not truly paranoid, only wisely mistrustful, because their suspicions, which appear at first to be absurd, then conveniently turn out to be true. On the one hand they inherit the Woodward/Bernstein dream ticket and their lawyer-author is an omni-scient version of 'Deep Throat' throwing his embattled heroes super-clues. On the other hand, the triumph of the law appears to have been replaced by the triumph of lawyers. They venture where no JFK conspiracy can go, compensating in the mythic imagination for the lack of discovery in the mystery that still matters most, and matters most because it is still a mystery, the mystery on Elm Street.

In John Grisham's *The Firm* or *The Pelican Brief* there is no dozy Watson to play foil to the primly clever Holmes, who in his own eccentric way is part of the Establishment. We have instead the lone investigator with a sidekick of the opposite sex, thrown back on their own resources and trusting nobody. In theme, his novels echo the format of Watergate dramatised by *All the President's Men* for readers in waiting rooms and departure lounges, long-distance trains and planes. In the age of mass travel, they give us good speed. Grisham's heroes are finally triumphant and while their victory echoes that of Robert Redford and Dustin Hoffman in Alan Pakula's movie, there is more – and less. For the films of both books verge on the level of mediocrity. In *The Firm* Mitch McDeere (Tom Cruise) is investigating his Mafia-run law firm while pretending not to because he himself is under the firm's constant surveillance. His every move is being watched, the cross that the flustered Garrison claimed he had to bear, in his questing for the 'assassins' of Kennedy.[27] In *The Pelican Brief* Darby Shaw (Julia Roberts) is intended as the dream of every female researcher come true, solving the mystery of political murder in the archive. Yet as an ambitious law novice being watched and threatened, she has to cling on to truth with the help of a cynical knight in shining armour, a *Washington Post* (sic) photographer (Denzel Washington). The lawyer-investigator is the stuff of which Lane and Garrison's dreams were made. Sadly their subject matter proved intractable, and still is. Fiction knows no such limits. McDeere and Shaw are the model investigators who *solve* their mysteries in face of the paranoia which threatens to engulf their initial uncertainty. Like Eastwood 'in the line of fire' they are making amends for a double failure of American history, failure to prevent Kennedy's murder and failure to track down the deeper connections thereafter. The atonement is mythic, acting through fiction as a way of reconciling historical past and lived present. The nightmare of history – the nightmare on Elm Street – is exonerated by the promise that history will not repeat itself. At the level of the unconscious, myth reconciles.

DeLillo, like Stone, appears to be offering his own version of counter-myth, the myth that does not heal the wound, but with greater documented accuracy. Posner's book puts in doubt key passages of the speculative faction. Yet read as narrative, his faction has that hard-nosed edge with the clinching biodetail which stirs the adrenaline. His Oswald is compelling from cradle to grave. There is something unsettling which makes his book very different from Stone's film. The narrative *caveat*, which annuls the charge of naive belief in conspiracy, lies in the framing of the quest. In the archive preparing his report on Kennedy's death for the Agency, retired agent Nicholas Branch (which branch?) is clearly in trouble. The juice of detection flows but the detective's psyche has dried up. At one level his resolution of the assassin's plot is hard and certain. At another it is hallucinatory, pure delirium in the archive. It is a dream version in the same way some critics have seen the ending of *Gravity's Rainbow,* where the last Nazi rocket to be fired falls on Los Angeles and destroys the world, the drug hallucination of a Vietnam officer, annulling the war he is fighting by fictionally destroying its (and his) possibility of ever having existed.

Branch has been in the archive for fifteen years, an image out of Kafka or Borges, but not one associated with a streetwise New York writer. Yet Mark Lane published *Rush to Judgment* in 1967 and *Plausible Denial* in 1991, a time-lapse of twenty-four years. Between times he had exercised his creative paranoia on behalf of the American Indian movement.[28] Branch, by contrast, could still be in the springtime of his labours, except that he is a retired Agency analyst, a prophecy seven years ago of retired analysts now mainlining on the Oswald case and other conspiracies. Bred to promote conspiracy while forever denying it, they are now free to look for it.[29] For many, the never-ending mystery has turned into the trauma of not knowing in one's own lifetime. It is the dark side of the farce which has overcome Watergate, where convicted cover-up artists are now celebrities uncovering secrets of the conspiracy for avid audiences and even, like Charles Colson, writing born-again Christian conspiracy novels.[30] If John Dean and Gordon Liddy can never agree on the detail, who cares? The main thrust is there for all to know. While the new breed of retired experts are free to work for themselves – free at last! – Branch is, however, still working for the Agency, which moreover is refusing to give him all the data he requests, having loaded him with more than he can cope with.

DeLillo thus reverses the thrust of certainty and sends us into free-fall. The anxieties of Branch punctuate the fictional move towards showdown with sad disclaimers of 'a wayward tale'. Here the image of Oswald is impossible to pin down. He changes from one photograph to another, from one eyewitness testimony to another. In Service photographs his fellow marines look more like him than he does. Oswald is both 'a grim killer and baby-face hero'. Faced with this heady oscillation Branch takes refuge in his research notes but feels the time will never be ripe to turn them into 'coherent history'. The data are endless and 'the past is changing as he writes.'[31] Thus *Libra* is a form of schizo-writing which oscillates between doubting all and discovering all. Dreams of discovery are set against nightmares of hallucination. Its 'true fiction' straddles two adjacent artefacts. On the one side we have the commodified paranoias of Grisham, Turow and Clancy and for sci-fi freaks the cyberpunk surrogates of *Blade Runner* and William Gibson's *Neuromancer* which changes the noun Watergate to the verb Watergating. On the other side we have *Blow-Up*, *Lot 49* and their offshoots, among them DeLillo's earlier novel *The Names* (1982) and the filmic conspiracies of the 1970s, the ontology questing of *Klute*, *The Conversation*, *Chinatown* and *Blow-Out*.

Like Pynchon, DeLillo plays knowingly with the paranoia of his hero but Nicholas Branch is also clearly an authorial persona. While *Blow-Up*'s ending is deeply melancholy, echoing Adorno's pessimism about the arbitrary power of the dead commodity, the unsignifying sign, the Americans by contrast harbour a secret optimism. Paranoia is, like Maxwell's Demon, a medium for the conversion of energy into information which will in turn, the hope is, recycle itself as pure energy, thus breaking the iron hold of entropy upon the rationalised world. The choice is no longer between life and the lie. The paranoid wager on truth elides the boundary lines and transforms the will-to-power into the will-to-truth. Information is no longer petrified into cultic rite, but inhabits a force field where the play of forces is always uncertain. Moving on from Nietzsche, Foucault has tried to freeze the frame within the force field and discovers discourse as the key to power. In our own time this becomes a moot point. If the power discourses of conspiracy ward off entropy, then Oliver Stone is a necessary evil. If, however, they spiral out of control into fantasies which bring persecution in their wake, that is another matter. In *Nixon*, Stone seems to have found a powerful alter ego, his demonic other, feeling persecuted in the act of persecuting, where the President's rejection by his people is a cracked mirror of Stone's perceived rejection by his critics. There has to be a check and a balance. If critique degenerates into paranoia, some form of communicative reason must bring it back once more to critique. It is the same with the transparency of the gaze for which critique strives. The transparent gaze cannot be omnipotent, as Rousseau desired, because then it is no longer the enlightened gaze of human knowledge but the disguised gaze of a Divine Being, who sees everything. In order to see, we have to confess opacity.

## II

In the aftermath of Stone's film, there have been two significant developments in the conspiracy stakes. On the one hand, greater weight has been attached to the connections of Oswald with the American Mafia, but on the other Mailer and DeLillo, the top guns of American writing who believed in some version of conspiracy, have now changed their minds. In *Oswald's Tale*, Mailer, now sceptical of conspiracy, patiently sifts and confirms the looseness of the loose ends in Posner's unclosed case, the Clinton sightings of Oswald, Silvia Odio's unnerving story of the 'visit', and Ruby's Mafia connections.[32] He also gives the best account yet of Oswald's ties with George de Mohrenschildt, ties the CIA would like suppressed, and probably has. To those who continue to argue without evidence for CIA conspiracy to assassinate, we have the strong possibility of a different kind of trauma here, the Agency's failure to prevent assassination by someone under its surveillance. Moreover, while no clear evidence exists that someone was keeping Oswald in mind, somewhere in the Agency, for Operation Mongoose in Cuba, no clear evidence exists to contradict it. In a subject which film now seems to have exhausted, this is the only credible pitch that is left. It duly changes the focus once more. Mailer now follows DeLillo in recognising that the focus of the tragedy should be on Oswald himself, on that unique and extraordinary 'tale' in which fact is stranger than fiction. In comparison, Stone's weakness deepens. His movie dominated by the Capraesque figure of Garrison–Costner,[33] he now seems at a fatal disadvantage, cued by Mailer's subtitle for his new opus, 'An American Mystery'. So, for Mailer, it is. For Stone it is the opposite. In his desperation to eradicate mystique, to reconstruct the past with the technical fervour of Yankee knowhow, Stone is in denial. There is no mystery in *JFK*. In fact Stone wants to deny it, just as Hickey, O'Neill's evangelical salesman in *The Iceman Cometh*, had wanted to annihilate all pipedreams, including his own. For all his iconoclastic rhetoric, Stone imparts a deep hatred of that curse of modernity, ambiguity.[34]

Conspiracy here becomes a clear case of Gnostic conviction, of a belief in deeper connections than can ever meet the eye. In the making of this film, in which Stone mixes colour and monochrome, news footage and fictive re-enactment, real characters and professional actors, he is truly TechGnostic. This is pure hyper-modern montage,

in which Costner's voice-over orchestrates a dazzling play of intertextual signs, where history, memory and fantasy all merge into one
pseudo-cosmic image. The look of the montage is still impressive,
both an immense technical feat and a poetic orchestration of history's
random events. Yet the imprint of Costner's voice throughout leads
only in one direction, in the paranoid conviction that, to borrow the
title of Welles's film, *it's all true*. Thus Stone annihilates the time-
image in the process of transforming it. Subscribing to the rhetoric
that time past is knowable, unconditionally and in its entirety, he side-
lines the problematic that has sent him into overdrive in the first place.
For the mysteries of time-image in the 1990s we will have to look
elsewhere, particularly to the challenge of *The Usual Suspects* and *Lost
Highway*, where the past is never what it seems, and what it seems
is itself filmic enigma. It is not that Stone is un-American. It is more
that he is too American. He has absorbed both Welles and Capra but
cannot unify them. His film thus stands on the aesthetic fault line,
covert, subterranean and deadly, which separates the maverick truth-
teller from the powers of the false.

1. 'The Father's Poems, the Mother's Look: Margarita Terekhova. *Mirror*.'

2. 'Searching in *Winter* for the Absent Father. *Landscape in the Mist*.'

3. 'Portrait of the Artist as a Dying Man: Nigel Terry. *Caravaggio.*'

4. 'Ambiguous Figures in the Viewfinder. *The Draughtsman's Contract.*'

*Chapter 5*

# THE ART OF IDENTITY:
## GREENAWAY, JARMAN, JORDAN

———⊸⊂———

Film is at its most effective when it challenges national identity, when, far from confirming it, it points out contradictions or the frailties of perception, when it unveils discord or division. As a culture industry it is not so much a medium of true nationhood, more a *jeu sans frontières*, happily taking money and personnel from wherever it can if that means all the difference between mere intention and final execution. The higher the budget, the more the American market looms for any other nation, the more this applies. Often it raises the question, to what country does this film belong? For the cause of the true nation there is no comforting rhyme or reason. Yet the cineastes forming the subject of this chapter have identities that are national and reputations that are international. Peter Greenaway, Derek Jarman and Neil Jordan were key figures in the British and Irish renaissance of the 1980s. With very different and distinctive styles they probe a similar point of connection – that of the personal and the national. In varying degrees they explore the identity of the person in harness with the identity of the nation, only to pinpoint the different forms of breakdown that occur between the public and the personal. Their work then can be seen in the neo-modern continuum of dis-association, here the dislocation between selfhood and nationhood, but also at the threshold of the hyper-modern, the filmic response to the dense accretions of the information age. Their art of identity is thus discomfiting for it challenges both conventions of self and of nationhood, Jarman and Greenaway in England, Jordan in Ireland. Yet it is also visionary. Its refusal of bad faith has been a constant

107

warning against the complacencies of the contemporary film industry, and the key to the challenges which cinema faced in the changing worlds of culture and politics as it moved towards the end of the twentieth century.

I

Let us first take the English legacies of Greenaway and Jarman in a wider context. One great source of commercial strength in British cinema has been the literary adaptation and the heritage film. Yet this has produced some strange combinations. Many of England's most successful heritage movies have been made by a polyglot trio: a writer from a Jewish–Polish family living much of her life in India, Ruth Prawer Jhabvala, a producer from that same country, Ismail Merchant, who now lives in New York, along with James Ivory, the American director completing the triangle.[1] What is essentially English about any them? Very little. Yet they are gifted in the art of screening English fiction and Ivory is especially effective in bringing out the best in his English actors. To stress the point of otherness we might note that two 1990s heritage hits *not* by Merchant-Ivory, *Elizabeth* and *Sense and Sensibility*, have Asian directors, Indian Shekar Kapur and Taiwanese Ang Lee. If film-makers are from somewhere else, might not the location shoot be a truer guide to nationhood? It is not always so. Michael Winterbottom's *Jude* has given Thomas Hardy's vision of Christminster, a coded disguise of Oxford, an even thinner disguise by crossing the border to Edinburgh's Old Town. The visuals of replication depend on what architecture is left standing from any century and any country. Yet even the authentic location can land us back in the arms of the foreign director. London had its first taste of 1960s modernism from Polanski's *Repulsion*, Losey's *The Servant*, Antonioni's *Blow-Up*. The paradox thus remains. It is often film's cosmopolitan voices that give a universal edge to the particular, to the landmarks of time, place and essence.

In analysing the composite nature of British cinema, other nuances come into play. The weakness of auteurism here would tend to affirm Adorno's stress upon the impersonal nature of the artwork over the persona of the artist.[2] This is confirmed by the recent triumph of two genres in British film history. The first is the biopic, which from 1970 onwards has resurrected the notorious 'celebrity' of post-war England. We can think of *Dance with a Stranger*, *10 Rillington Place*, *Prick up your Ears*, *Scandal*, *Sid and Nancy* and *Love is the Devil*, all with dubious heroes or heroines – Ruth Ellis, John Christie, Joe Orton, Christine Keeler, Sid Vicious, Francis Bacon. The second genre is the filmic translation of F. R. Leavis's 'Great Tradition', the literary film which has seen Austen, Eliot, Dickens, the Brontës, Conrad, James, Hardy, Forster and Lawrence all successfully brought to the screen. While the first genre of reincarnation is vaguely satanic through its notoriety, the second genre is vaguely angelic through its literary pedigree. In the 1990s a director to succeed in both genres was Iain Softley, first with his Beatles biopic from the early 1960s, *Backbeat*, and then with a bold version of *The Wings of the Dove*, which brings the Jamesian text a decade forwards out of the late Victorian age. Points of contact between Stu Sutcliffe and the lads and the complex rituals of courtship in late James would seem slim, but in Softley's versions they are subtly connected, first through a bold reworking of English history in different decades of the century, second through the fine-tuning of a love-triangle doomed in a foreign country and third in a tale of two cities, one English, the other European. *The Wings of the Dove* dovetails historical London with historical Venice. *Backbeat* matches industrial Liverpool to industrial Hamburg. Both stage cultural encounters of a transnational kind.

Yet this achievement seems impossible without the landmark films of Jarman and Greenaway, who remain two of the most inventive English cineastes in the late twentieth century. In 1986, Jarman's *Caravaggio* and Greenaway's *The Belly of an Architect* exposed key confrontations between Englishness and Otherness, which not only charge the powerful intimacy of a doomed love-triangle, but also invoke the broader canvas of Europe's cultural heritage. This breadth of vision can be measured not only against the English biopic, with which both films play in subtle ways, but also against that great strength of Anglo-Scottish film-making in particular, the autobiographical picture. Three of the National Film School's critically acclaimed directors have defined themselves in this way: Bill Douglas in his 1970s Edinburgh trilogy, Terence Davies in his 1980s Liverpool trilogy and Glaswegian Gillies MacKinnon in his recent film-memoir, *Small Faces*. The latest Film

School graduate to add to this prestigious list is Glaswegian Lynne Ramsay with her debut feature film, *Ratcatcher*. In contrast to this, Jarman and Greenaway opted to move outside the realm of autobiography, projecting their own experience on to a wider canvas. What they might lose at times in the remembrance of time past, they gain from imaginative extension of both past and present as objective histories. It is true that Jarman sometimes appears in his own films in order to frame his singular vision. Yet in the work of both there is a movement away from the known experience, which acts as a powerful spur to filmic innovation. As a result both have often been seen as overreachers, keen to explore the very margins of cinematic possibility, and never afraid of idiosyncrasy as a mark of original vision.

Here they have many things in common: a background in London art school (Jarman at the Slade, Greenaway at Walthamstow College), a concern with the vexed identities of England past and present, a cryptic rivalry for the role of art auteur in the British cinema of the 1980s and a conscious vision of film as outrageous narrative designed to provoke and shock. These provide a necessary template for measuring their differences. Jarman's *mise-en-scène* is often spare and minimalist; Greenaway's is usually ornate and baroque. Jarman's roving camera seeks out English city wastelands. In Greenaway, they are conspicuous by their absence. Greenaway has shot standard feature-length films in colour and 35 mm or 70 mm with European funding and co-production, moving to video only in its recent digital phase. Despite faithful support from the British Film Institute, Jarman had a rough time with any kind of collateral funding, insisting with great impatience on mixing different low-budget formats, monochrome and colour, Super 8 mm his preferred format for exteriors, and pre-digital video, using 35 mm blow-up for theatrical distribution. Moreover, Jarman's films raise more clearly the imperatives of standard length that distribution imposes upon contemporary film-makers. In cinema time and space have their own ironies. Length matters in a way that it does not in either stage drama or fiction. Duration matters in a way that size does not in the painter's canvas. Jarman's predilection for the shorter film, say in *Blue* or *The Garden*, meant not only a sacrifice of large cinema audiences. Channel Four producers were more attracted to the standard feature lengths of Greenaway and other talents which they funded in the 1980s renaissance of British cinema.[3] Here Jarman clearly came off second best.

Pairings of key films can enable us to continue this assessment of sameness within difference, of key variations in adjacent visions of English society. In *Jubilee* and *Drowning by Numbers*, for example, there is a subversive proto-feminist echo of the English music hall tradition which pervades the Ealing and later the Carry On comedies. In their very different versions of the same Shakespeare text, *The Tempest* (1979) and *Prospero's Books* (1991), narrative is dominated less by plot and more by meticulous *mise-en-scène*. Mutual concern with the politics of 1980s Britain also provides a fascinating contrast. Jarman's low-budget expressionist assault on the legacy of Thatcher's decade in *The Last of England* can be set against Greenaway's allegorical deconstruction of the same in his baroque *The Cook, The Thief, His Wife and her Lover*. While the former is a location movie, largely improvised, the latter is a studio movie, pre-planned in great detail. Outside of England, the existence of Italy in *Caravaggio* and *The Belly of an Architect* is a source of primal vision and cultural Otherness, of a strange transcendental release for both in their quest for artistic origins. Yet here the roles are reversed. Greenaway shoots ambitiously and flamboyantly on location in Rome while Jarman shoots within the confines of a London studio set tautly designed by Christopher Hobbs. For Greenaway's American architect the present of the eternal city is chained to its past. He cannot escape from the imitation of a history whose evidence surrounds him. For Jarman the historical enigma of Caravaggio is chained to present predicament, the fatal intersection of art and sexuality. Finally both provide their own variations on the filmic double, a central theme of *A Zed and Two Noughts* and a passing motif in *The Tempest* and *The Garden*, and both capture different kinds of English country garden in *The Draughtsman's Contract* and *The Garden*. If we wish to celebrate their original vision, we can only do so by stressing that the visual look each has forged in his work is also a shared look, as any film is. On the one hand Greenaway developed that look with Sacha Vierny, the photographer of *Last Year at Marienbad,* a superb technician equipped to handle his labyrinthine adventures into cool baroque. Jarman, using different cinematographers through his career has the look of nearly all his films indelibly stamped with the visual design of Christopher Hobbs, an expert in functional staging and in minimalist form.[4]

Their respective work also illustrates the intertextuality of cultural form. Both respond to the trends and movements in modernist painting that preceded their work in cinema. Jarman, as Michael O'Pray points out, responds critically to the Pop Art sixties idiom of Hockney and Peter Blake and their cultural network of which he was briefly a part.[5] Indeed, he was brave enough to attack Hockney, a fellow gay and by then a cult figure, for his embrace of all things American. During the cultural flowering of the New Left in the 1970s, he took a strongly libertarian as opposed to a rigidly Marxist position. Greenaway, as David Pascoe notes, integrated his interest in modernist art directly into his films. Right from the start of his film career he resourced the high modernism of R. B. Kitaj with its conceptual usage of grids and frames that had strongly influenced his pre-filmic painting.[6] Greenaway's flair for abstract and deliberate composition of the filmic frame is above all painterly, and in that respect Kitaj was a more seminal influence than Alain Resnais. In addition, both directors have emerged from the visual force field of Francis Bacon, which had so clearly defined *Performance*, the one British film of the late 1960s keying into their own work.

Their debt to English theatre should not be ignored either. First, we can point to its dynamic representation of historic legacy in new productions of Renaissance tragedy or Restoration comedy; second to the political renaissance of such forms in the 1970s drama of Edward Bond and Howard Brenton.[7] Such radical dramaturgy, in which Bond argued polemically for specific aggro-effects to augment the use of the Brechtian gestus and its alienation-effects, has its parallel in the disruptive power of audiovisual shock that Jarman and Greenaway use, not to heighten narrative in the idiom of Hollywood melodrama, but to disturb it and to interrogate the very nature of its fabric. Jarman's connection with the 1970s English stage is also firmed up by politicising anachronism, rendering it integral to his film aesthetic in *Jubilee*, *Caravaggio* or *Edward II* just as Bond had make it central to stage aesthetics in *Lear* and Brenton even more so in *The Romans in Britain*. Both plays move gesturally and aggressively in their use of shock tactics from a distant past in which the audience feels safe into an immediate present that is clearly discomfiting. Moreover, past and present are brought in tandem by anti-historicist and anti-psychologistic means. Both playwrights thus undermine the methods of naturalist theatre while retaining their themes. Likewise, Jarman undermines the realist cinema while sharing many of its themes. For Greenaway, filmic theatricality draws on the acting idioms of the London stage, and on talented actors like Michael Gambon, Helen Mirren, Joan Plowright, John Gielgud, Janet Suzman and Alan Howard, whose experience in English tragedy became a crucial resource.

While both absorb theatre into film, they also extend film form by other means. We need here to look more closely at their different usages of time and space. While both are concerned with history and its present meanings, Jarman's systematic use of anachronism and palimpsest provides a key contrast with Greenaway, who uses them more sparingly and sticks, by and large, to the rigours of narrative continuum. While Jarman is largely fascinated by the temporal frame-within-the-frame of film narrative, the leap of epochs as disruptive shock not only to the viewers' sensibilities but to their sense of linear history, Greenaway in contrast is more obsessed by the spatial frame-within-the-frame, the viewfinder, the painting, the photograph, even the photocopy. The 1960s challenge noted by Noel Burch and Pascal Bonitzer to the enterprise of film itself, how to signify within the frame the absence of the offscreen presence,[8] that field of the perpetual out-of-frame defining the rectangular limits of film stock and screen projection, is turned by Greenaway into an even more self-conscious and cerebral meditation. Recently this concern for the frame has found its most extreme expression in *The Pillow Book*, with its complex multiple screens forcing us to read simultaneous text and images. While for Jarman time cannot be absorbed by film's duration, for Greenaway space cannot be absorbed by its technical projection. In both cases film is a problematic of multiple worlds which remain unresolved but lead to different emphases. Following Eisenstein, Jarman gives us montage juxtapositions as forms of temporal shock, but then dissolves the boundaries of time itself. In *Jubilee* Jenny Runacre is Elizabeth I and all of a sudden the leader of a gang of female punks in 1970s London, the casual assassin of Elizabeth II. In *Edward II* the historic murder of the homosexual king jumps centuries directly into strident footage of a Gay OutRage demonstration of the 1980s. Likewise *Caravaggio* is both a Renaissance Italy reinvented in a London studio and a random summation of everyday artefacts from the intervening epochs of European history. *The Garden* improvises ad hoc the crucifixion of a modern Christ against a mystic, Blakean but familiar South Coast backdrop. Yet at the same time it is a hallucinated vision of Jarman, the film-maker who constantly sleeps and wakes through its errant passage.

In Greenaway the rectangular screen is a frail aesthetic that sets off contrary movements since its frame is equally a source of fascination and a form of impaired vision. Either self-conscious framing like the draughtsman's viewfinder that draws attention to that deficiency signals its limit, or that limit is obliterated by the richness of content within the frame, a radical compression of layered artefacts into a finite field. Often, in hyper-modern override of Simmel's tragedy of culture, which laments the dilemmas of accretion,[9] Greenaway crams as much as he can of history's collectable objects into a single deep-focus shot. The artefacts themselves are collected largely from cultures of extravagance and adornment. Ornate or baroque in their original setting, these qualities are amplified by the time they have travelled through culture and technology into Greenaway's final cut. Here his European heritage nurtures a strident dualism. His mimicking of Fellini's Rabelaisian appetite and Pasolini's sacrificial excesses of the flesh offsets the cool spatial framing of his 1960s mentors, Resnais and Antonioni, but while Fellini collects the gross, the kitsch, the sensuous and the grotesque with effortless gusto, Greenaway usually oscillates between excess and refinement, between good taste and its complete negation. Collecting cinematic influences as voraciously as art-objects, he often falls between two stools.

At its best, Greenaway's framing has a deceptive simplicity. One thinks in *The Draughtsman's Contract* of the hero's viewfinder centred within the frame of a still camera. Here the landscape and the house that are seen, and meant to be seen, by the viewfinder are filled with the intrigues of intruding figures who are clearly not meant to be there. In terms of the contract they are not meant to be present in the final illustrations yet their significance is vital to the fate of the draughtsman himself. The selective conceits of the pastoral, which Greenaway stresses through the saturated greens of landscape, are followed through in the depopulating images which move humans out of the frame to capture a 'nature' more congenial to posterity. In the dining-room of *The Cook* Frans Hals's portrait of the Haarlem officers who stare down from the back wall mocks the latterday chevaliers of Albert Spica who sit parodically framed under their portrait doubles in similar sashes, similar saturations of red and black. At its best, self-conscious framing leads to the creation of multi-layered images whose richness is enhanced by widescreen, by saturated colours and by depth of field. At its worst, the technique degenerates into well-meaning kitsch.

The opening track in *Prospero's Books* along the Renaissance library of the exiled hero is a visual conceit which tries to turn Prospero's first book, his self-conscious book of Genesis, into Greenaway's first image: 'In the beginning was the Word and the Word was Greenaway. And Greenaway said let there be light, and there was light.' The image springs out of the book, in this case the book of water, which leads on to images of water and tempest but never gets out of the library. The dilemma is acute but typical. In making the bookish literal and Prospero his own double, Greenaway is forced back on to contrivance. The composite facsimile of the Renaissance library is a crowded museum overpopulated by figures from Renaissance painting and kitsch models from twentieth-century fashion. This anthropomorphic conceit – the figures of paintings coming to life, as in the lovers' chess game – is generically kitsch in Adorno's sense of the word,[10] the cue for the educated audience which values its own powers of discrimination to applaud the lifeless facsimile of the Renaissance or Baroque without realising its deathly mistake. Greenaway's kitsch, we might say, is the unconscious dumbing-down of cultural capital. By contrast, the allegorical bite of *The Cook* derives its *mise-en-scène* of conspicuous consumption from clusters of objects which resonate with a corrupt and recognisable present. More than that, consumption in the modern sense of celebrating plenty is restored to its more primitive sense of consuming-as-devouring. The items on the daily menu at Le Hollandais exist, it seems, only to be devoured in perpetual travesty of an ancient sacrificial feast. This reaches its nemesis in the beaten and tortured lover's forced devouring of the bookish text on which he chokes to death and then in Spica's unwitting consumption of the sacrificial flesh of his victim. Such clinching images are precisely what *Prospero's Books* lacks. It mistakenly tries to collect the classical and the revered into a single frame yet the clutter of the past becomes devoid of life. The 1990s turn in Greenaway has indeed shown the layering of excess at its worst, frames within frames within frames, object upon object upon object, and for the spectator the nightmare of a mad Mabuse museum without exit, a labyrinth forcing upon the viewer cultural death through asphyxiation of the senses.

We might say then that Greenaway and Jarman appropriate contrary signs of cultural capital. Greenaway is the manic collector acquiring the refined loot of the European art world before extending his reach to the Orient. Jarman wants to ritualise excess in a different way by obsessively repeating sacred ceremony as a camp gesture. Here ritual becomes an excuse for extravagant fun. Thus one can speculate that Jarman is high camp because he was also in upbringing High Anglican, because he needed the visual surety of sacred spectacle if only to make it profane. His sacrificial unconscious, where thankfully the sacrificial images of his surrogate Christ-figures run deeper than his self-conscious posturing, are flavoured by fetishistic ceremonies of consecration which are often too formless to be taken seriously. Where they are serious and visceral, as in *Caravaggio*, they can be devastating. When they are jokily camped up in a parody of subversive gesture, they degenerate into a peculiar form of kitsch. His English eccentricity pleads to be accepted by being hysterical. He aims at times for the eccentric feel of earlier English film comedy but lacks its formal control. His intellectual concern is really to inflate his subject matter rather than deflate it and for most audiences he draws the sting of tragedy without compensating through humour. Campness can mean that, unlike Pasolini, his images lack genuine sacrilegious power; though when he does forgo it, as in *Caravaggio*, he can match Pasolini frame for frame.

His low-budget operation can thus seem like a feverish impatience with form coupled with a naive delight in instant effect. At their worst, his improvised Super 8 images become tedious and repetitive, like a child playing with film stock for the first time. At his best what disturbs in this format is an inspired fusion of montage and expressionist gesture where human anguish inhabits a void, where any rational explanation for such anguish is impossible. The more uninhibited or outrageous Jarman becomes, the more one senses something remains unuttered or utterable, as if freedom merely reveals the depth of repression. The loudest of images can thus have a mute resonance. One thinks of Tilda Swinton's dress tearing at the end of *The Last of England*, a touch overwrought but still impacted with a visual power landscaped by vast unyielding spaces of urban desolation. Here lack of definition in the Super 8 image, matched by the presence of twilight, conjure a genuine alchemy which elsewhere Jarman sought obsessively but often failed to find. Often sexual display follows the same pattern. His naked male couples are so obviously kitsch and camp that one senses a hidden denial of Eros rather than homoerotic celebration. The sharp epiphany of lovemaking between victim and masked SAS terrorist is arguably the most erotic gay sequence Jarman has ever filmed outside of *Caravaggio*. Word has it that in the filmed sequence the masked SAS 'man' was played by a female stand-in, in which case the love that dare finally speak its name finds Eros in a reverse transvestism, the erotic woman masquerading as male aggressor. In the artwork true Eros lies in concealment not display, while the auteur, one feels, desperately wishes it were the other way around.

*Jubilee* and *The Last of England* have left a mixed legacy in the filming of London. Many of the features which were to follow in Jarman's wake draw greater power from their neo-naturalist framing and linear narrative. Clarke's *The Firm*, Loach's *Riff-Raff*, Leigh's *Naked* and Oldman's *Nil by Mouth* all negate Jarman's aesthetic but often do greater justice to his didactic intent than his own films. Gay director Ron Peck's neglected *Empire State*, set in the changing vista around Canary Wharf, equally asked questions of Jarman's extreme anti-naturalism. The greater 'freedom' which Jarman claimed to find in Super 8 was often his undoing. Greenaway's 35 mm landscapes, both garden and shoreline, are more consistently powerful in *Draughtsman* and *Drowning by Numbers*. Even allowing for his clear debt to Fellini's *Roma*, no current film-maker has ever systematically reinvented a modern city as Greenaway does with Rome in *The Belly of an Architect*. On the other hand, only *The Cook* rivals the uses of interior space that Jarman had developed in *Caravaggio* and *Edward II*. Despite his own wishes, it is precisely the match of structured setting to semi-structured narrative that has worked best for him. As MacCabe astutely notes, the labyrinthine spaces of Prospero's country house, which disorient the eye in *The Tempest*, are a perfect visual match for Jarman's serious concern with the surveillance politics of the Elizabethan state.[11] All the history films show the power of stylistic and loose narrative framing to liberate Jarman's filmic imagination. Here their political and sexual politics are a fluid and labile interior space, a space of conspiratorial epochs that creates its frisson of Machiavellian intrigue. It contrasts favourably with the library or museum interiors, which can sometimes be oppressive in the later Greenaway. They are mausoleum interiors reminding us just as much of death's presence as Greenaway's exhibited corpses.

The danger facing Greenaway is often the greater presence of the corpse over the living actor, who is sometimes reduced to an item in a curator's collection. Indeed his compulsion to collect is sometimes so obsessive it goes beyond any credible claim to be a new aesthetic. While Jarman's high camp extravagances often give the viewer the sense of a liberated boy scout troop attempting a nativity play, Greenaway's obsession displays a mania for refinement which has its pedigree in good English breeding and taste. Once the camera starts to whir, however, it goes awry. The anxieties of collecting and exhibiting dominate the narrative until it becomes a constipated clutter, an unconscious parody perhaps of the still life in Dutch painting. Only when they are reflexive, as in Stourley Kracklite's stage exhibitions, or destructively wasteful, as in Spica's predatory feasting, do they have the right kind of impact. When Greenaway pointedly deconstructs his own devices in creating them, he shows a powerful and controlled intelligence. Otherwise the compulsion to collect merely arouses suspicions of the director's own monomania, which leads at times, it must be said, to an intellectual dead-end. More recently the desire to be a new Darwin, to adopt the Victorian genius of natural selection as his own double and as a metaphor of omnipotent film-making, seems like muddled self-indulgence. For in the various library tableaux of Greenaway's television documentary, Darwin seems to elide the roles of curator and creator, framed like a Victorian patriarch at the centre of his facsimiles of natural selection. In the same way the 'natural selection' in Greenaway's narrative, which charts decay, decomposition and death, is patently not that of nature but that of Greenaway, the contrivance of his imaginary narratives. At its best, Greenaway's work does not need Darwinian framing in any way at all. It is most compelling when his male paranoiacs are tragic victims, when Neville, Kracklite and Spica appear as victims of the complex interface between culture, politics and their flawed egos, victims of the world and of themselves.

The mythic 'necessity' of Darwin is an oblique version of Englishness that shows the tenuousness of the very term, a vain search for roots which founders on excess. Another oblique version of this excess is Jarman's love–hate relationship toward the British Army uniforms of the twentieth century, a fetish source of fear and attraction he may well have inherited from his childhood in the domestic quarters of an army barracks he thought of more as prison than as home.[12] The more he rails against the uniform, the more he demonstrates his unspoken love for it. The stilted awkwardness of characterisation, which comes from this cultural enclave, brings to mind that other middle-class Englishman whom Jarman so admired, Michael Powell. The irony is that Powell's conservative vision of the end of colonial Britain is followed by the radical Jarman's apocalyptical vision of the end of England *per se*. Yet England has not ended. The Greenwich waste-lands which featured in Jarman's films as images of decay are now host to the Millennium Dome, a project more suited to Greenaway who, one suspects, would have clear ideas on how to fill every available inch. It is a suitable moment at which to pause and take stock. At the turn of the century we are now in a position to assess the legacy of both directors. They show us that film as art is not only about national identities but also about their transcendence. Only among a host of other compulsions do they meditate on a sense of Englishness as an acquired heritage to love and hate, to construct and deconstruct, to worship and to lampoon as myth. We should end too with a brief meditation on the very fragility of nationhood and identity in the transnational world of the information age. It should be remembered that Jarman's army officer of a father was actually a New Zealander while Greenaway was born not in England but in Wales. England is more than ever a country full of people from somewhere else. At a time when essentialism is coming back into fashion, hybridity appears to have the last laugh.

II

To speak of Neil Jordan as Irish exemplar of the art of identity after viewing Jarman and Greenaway as English examples is to place the smaller nation against the larger, the homogenous Republic against the United, or disunited, Kingdom. Culturally, there is no complete separation, as geopolitics proves time and again. In film, relations remain close; yet equally close has been the American connection of which Ardmore Studios in County Wicklow have been a key beneficiary. Sandwiched between the British–American axes, we have opinion polls deeming Ford's *The Quiet Man* Ireland's most popular film about Ireland, while critical opinion has tended towards Carol Reed's classic *Odd Man Out*. That wartime hymn to English patriotism, *Henry V* was also shot on the green fields of the neutral Isle, as was Boorman's *Excalibur* and the current hymn to Scottish patriotism, Gibson's *Braveheart*, while a cluster of films by English directors have spanned the post-war period, from Lean's insipid *Ryan's Daughter* to 1990s versions of Roddy Doyle's fiction by Frears and Parker. As if to set the seal on cultural invasion Boorman returned to make *The General*, a black-and-white biopic about a North Dublin gangster. Yet Parker and Boorman's 'invasion' of Dublin can easily be countered by Jordan's 'invasion' of London in *Mona Lisa* and *The Crying Game*, showing that film-making will always break down boundaries that critics try to establish.

The national dilemma remains, however. In a small island population only a few have made their mark as cineastes, able to use the frail resources of elusive funding to reach international audiences. These include Jim Sheridan, Pat O'Connor, Joe Cornerford, Thaddeus O'Sullivan, Terry George and Jordan himself, the most controversial and productive of all. This paucity contrasts with the profusion of published talent in Irish writing, but one thing Irish cineastes have in common with their literary counterparts is the catalyst of the Troubles, a key source over thirty years for the urgency of art. In that respect, Jordan is like many Irish film-makers. Yet his vision is much wider. For this the Irish themselves have not always appreciated him. Some demurred at the global success of *The Crying Game*, and it was not until the huge hit of *Michael Collins* in Ireland that Jordan in effect came home. All this was achieved despite an advance blitzing of his project from revisionist historians and vitriol from the right-wing British press. While the film's reception may not have been enough to arrest previous ambivalence in Irish circles, it was a national triumph for an epic of great ambition nourished for over a decade from conception to completion.

As a fiction writer moving into film, Jordan's career was beset by controversy. His first feature *Angel*, produced by Boorman for whom he had worked on *Excalibur*, was the sole beneficiary of state funding in the Republic in 1981 and jointly financed by Channel Four, which provided 80 per cent of the backing. Some, ignored by the Irish Film

Board, denounced Jordan's project as apolitical and colonialist. Others saw it as influenced by the Americanised values of Boorman's *Point Blank*, while other voices thought it self-consciously arty in trying to imitate European cinema. In a pincer movement Jordan was attacked from different directions. In this myopia lay a kernel of truth. Most of Jordan's work lies at a critical juncture between European and American film-making, between the neo-modern innovations of European cinema in the 1960s and the transformation of popular genre in the American New Wave. Like Jarman and Greenaway, he is a key figure in the belated modernism of 1980s British cinema, giving it a distinct Irish spin. The nature of that spin lies in Jordan's heritage. The low-budget *Angel* now seems a fusion of the surreal-expressionist artworks of the Europeans with the legacy of what Eagleton has called 'the archaic avant-garde' in Irish writing, a form which matches the modernist fracturing of the text to indigenous myth.[13] Though a fiction writer, the legacy of Irish theatre has also made a mark. Following Beckett, his dialogue is supremely minimalist; his *mise-en-scène* has faint echoes of the gestural, hyperbolic staging of Yeats, Synge and O'Casey, whose poetic dialogue, however, he repudiates. His Irish films show us a precise, detailed world with a hallucinatory edge. The minimal voice, with its ludic play on common cliché, is framed by the fantastic and the unexpected. Jordan's oblique take on Irish theatre thus follows in the footsteps of Bergman's intricate take on Ibsen and Strindberg, and Cassavetes' affinity with the performative psycho-dramas of O'Neill.

The hostile reception given to *Angel* in Ireland pushed Jordan towards exile in London, a familiar Irish plight where cunning became more the order of the day than silence.[14] His career was soon linked to producer Steve Woolley and Palace Pictures, an independent company whose rise and fall coincided precisely with the 1980s British renaissance. *Angel*, given the kitsch title of *Danny Boy* in the USA, pinpointed a dilemma for Irish films about the Troubles. While American audiences could provide an interest based on fascination and ignorance, British audiences, all too close, could react with hatred or indifference. For Jordan and Jim Sheridan the transatlantic connection has been crucial. Yet *Angel* remains troubling for mass audiences. Its dark vision offers no entry point for the viewer's sympathy or easy outrage at deep injustice, features simplified by more accessible narratives like *Cal*, *Hidden*

*Agenda, In the Name of the Father* and *Some Mother's Son*. Its politics was veiled and inexplicit, refusing to spell out chapter and verse. One of its few obvious clues was the Jewish police inspector Bloom whose name is both homage to *Ulysses* and a marker, in Irish terms, of a neutral tribe. Thereafter its narrative seems to move very quickly from the real to the surreal and leaves the viewer with expectations of a political thriller well and truly stranded.

Here Jordan's refusal to name obvious names is matched by the creation of visual motifs that disorient the eye. Far from giving us clear markers of Irishness, such motifs connote damaged identities seeming at times beyond repair. Indeed we might say that Jordan uses cultural landscape to fracture the relationship between personal and national identity, to pinpoint rupture and breakdown. The national level of identity remains partly formed, since the northeast is politically excluded. One result is that personal identities suffer a double curse, on the one hand a geopolitical divide, and on the other social and religious constraints, north and south, which damage the fragile psyche. Here the pitfalls of Catholic religiosity feature with bittersweet irony, at times with dark humour. Yet Jordan also goes beyond this to echo the wider predicament of Western modernity. Politics and religion are catalysts to something deeper. The despairing unvoiced 'Who am I?' echoes through his work, as Jordan's male heroes threaten to disintegrate. *Angel, Mona Lisa, The Miracle, The Crying Game* and *The Butcher Boy* all quicken their narrative pace as psychic crisis looms. In contrast, *Michael Collins* externalises the crisis. The stoicism of Collins, the sense of his imminent death, is due to a situation that is beyond him, in the political divisions of Ireland itself. His personal tragedy is also a political tragedy. Jordan's epic is memorable for containing that which the other films omit. It is that brief historic moment of Irish revolution when the personal and the national fuse on a transcendental plane in the face of coming tragedy. Elsewhere in the work, identities conspire to fall apart. The personal and the national cannot hold, as Jordan films for very high stakes indeed.

This collapse is anything but one-dimensional. It is different in each picture, rich and diverse in terms of history, of myth, of pathology, of sexuality. In *Angel*, for instance, subtleties of neo-modern stylisation blend with subtleties of close observing. In his framing of the touring showband Jordan uses bright, saturated interiors we might associate with Hollywood musicals of the 1950s while the exteriors, by contrast, are drab and seedy. The emotive power of the musical numbers is offset by the strange dissonance of the *mise-en-scène*. Sax player Danny (Stephen Rea) and singer Dee (Honor Heffernan) perform not only obvious standards but 'Thicker than Water', 'Danny Boy' and 'Strange Fruit', and Dee's very name could well be homage to Synge's *Deirdre of the Sorrows*, her bluesy phrasing transposing the keening effects of lament into lyric for the Irish dancehall; but the numbers are performed in settings that serve up a host of alienation-effects. At 'Dreamland', where Danny meets the deaf-mute girl, Annie, soon to be gunned down by paramilitaries, intense and garish colours predominate. Blue lighting against a blood-red backdrop, colours of the Unionist flag, dog the opening number. Later Dee sings Billie Holiday's 'Strange Fruit' for a gig in a mental asylum in front of its silent inmates, a montage sequence cut elliptically against a scarlet backdrop, while 'Danny Boy', unofficial Irish anthem, is played in a neon-pink seaside bar, the band performing in Day-Glo purple suits while Dee is dolled up in stilettos and cutaway leopard-skin dress. In a comic echo of Adorno's sombre warning about the devious ways of modernity, the show band commodifies itself as a cheap facsimile of American culture for the locals. After Annie's brutal murder, however, Danny is transformed from the 'Stan Getz of South Armagh' into a vengeful gunman, turfing the sax out of its case and replacing it with a sub-machine-gun. As he hunts down his quarries with manic stride, we can see clear echoes of gangster Lee Marvin in *Point Blank* and, of course, De Niro in *Taxi Driver*.

Yet Jordan is doing something very different. *Angel* is not a genre picture and Danny is not a formulaic avenger. Drawing on Velázquez, he frames an ironic angelic encounter, the nocturnal love-scene between the deaf-mute and Danny on wasteland outside a ballroom strewn with circular pipes and wires, makeshift images of unlikely haloes. It cues us in, we later realise, to the ambiguity of the film's title. Is Danny an avenging angel, avenging a deaf-mute angel who is brutally shot? The politics of tragic intimacy crystallise as Jordan contrasts the abortive lovers, mute angelic innocence against the future angel of death. Here a further gap appears between Jordan and his genre mentors. Danny's descent into killing derives from the traumatic imprint in his witnessing, the terrified gaze cast on the slaughter of the innocent. Instead of the psychotic rage of the macho avenger, we have the perpetual trauma of the mute hysteric which time cannot heal and passion – the affair with Dee – cannot exorcise. Generally hysteria which can neither articulate grief nor replace it by rage is considered unmasculine in our culture and, as Showalter has pointed out, is seen as a public embarrassment, something to be suppressed.[15] The cuing of post-traumatic stress, never specific but visually ever-present, explains the robotic nature of Danny's revenge. Like Noah Render, the insurance man handling the trauma of fire in Egoyan's *The Adjuster*, he seems trapped in a state of mechanical shock.

This points forwards to the key trauma of *The Crying Game*, where IRA volunteer Fergus, again played by Rea, witnesses the gruesome death of Jody (Forest Whitaker), the black squaddie he has been ordered to execute. The same guilt is felt and shown on Rea's anguished face but in the later film there is also a glimpse of hope, the chance of expiation through love. In the crucial sequence which leads to Jody's freak killing the tone is dark yet romantic, moving away from the bleak despair of *Angel*. The running sequence with the desperate Jody fleeing the pursuing Fergus, his would-be executioner, has much of the pathos and power of the chicken-run sequence in *Rebel Without a Cause*. The echo of Ray's romantic defiance of death comes not only in the editing, its controlled breathlessness and suspense, but also in terms that go deeper into the politics of tragedy.

In both of Jordan's films trauma results in perceptual disintegration. They employ forms of the 'free indirect discourse' which in 1965 Pasolini had seen prophetically as the future of film narrative,[16] where a clear homology exists, a double register, between the collapse of the neurotic subject and the cineaste's delirium of film form. The film appeared soon after the charged circumstances of the Long Kesh Hunger Strike, but Danny's dementia offered little to either concerned liberals or militant republicans. Outside of politics, the use of the new subjectivity gained Jordan more plaudits, especially his recreation of the disturbed mind of the vulnerable young teenager, the dreaming Rosalee in Angela Carter's *The Company of Wolves*, or the troubled figure of Francie in Patrick MacCabe's *The Butcher Boy*.

These fables of teenage daydream and nightmare have had a softer critical landing. In adapting *The Company of Wolves* with Carter, Jordan retained the strong element of the Freudian fairy-tale and made the film an expanded reverie of a teenage girl who dreams herself into a timeless world of Merrie England with its age-old village in a forest full of wolves. The wolves act as a source of both fear and attraction and the film spirals into a set of tales within tales as Grannie (Angela Lansbury) spins yarn after yarn about the dangerous creatures of the wild. The figure of Lansbury helps to objectify the girl's dream world and provide a key narrative filter. When the wolves spring the trap of the dream and invade the family's country house, moving with her from the past back into the present there is again the fear and attraction of Gothic revenge. Yet overlaying the sexual reading of the tale there may well be a political fable in this animal invasion. Rosalee's prosperous English family seem to a live in a safe world but she dreams herself back into a world of ancient danger, the Anglo-Saxon settlement threatened perhaps by a Celtic or barbarian menace, personified in the figure of the wolf-man with his eyebrows joined in the middle. One finds here the Gothic element of the vampire which may have been inspired by an earlier Dublin writer, Bram Stoker. The ending has an ominous sense of the thin veneer of the civilising influence and suggests the film can be read ambiguously as a fable of history's eruption into the present with barbarian vitality.

*The Butcher Boy* offered a different challenge, a tale told in the first person of a twelve-year-old (Eamonn Owens) living a recent past in a small Irish town. The style has been deemed 'magical realism' by many critics and certainly bears comparison with Kusturica's *Time of the Gypsies*. As Martin McLoone has pointed out, it contains 'the voice of Ireland caught in the cusp between tradition and modernity'.[17] Yet in the framing of narrative around a central teenage figure there is a crucial difference. Jordan's camera is much closer to Francie than Kusturica's is to Perhan, the tragic boy-hero of his Yugoslav fable. For it adapts the novel's tunnel-vision narrative, governed by the demotic idiom of Francie's voice, directly into film. If Perhan's magic vision has its singular being within the world, Francie's vision *is* the world. We see the world exclusively through Francie's eyes and hear it through his voice-over. Jordan thus abandons the free indirect for a free direct mode of filming and raises at once a critical question of form. How is it possible to judge beyond the fantasy of a twelve-year-old's disturbed imagination, since we are completely locked into that vision? Disturbed it surely is, too, by the destructive marriage of his drunken violent father (Stephen Rea) and clinically depressed mother (Aisling O'Sullivan), and by the resulting stigma in the town which Francie noses out in the airs and graces of snobbish Mrs Nugent (Fiona Shaw) just returned from England. The main distancing effect is the voice of the adult Francie – in fact Rea's voice-over – which recounts the grisly teenage tale of its young persona, but Jordan brings in other devices too, notably the icon of television, a new medium for Irish culture in 1962, and establishes an objective yardstick of a world outside the town. Yet that world in turn is dark and feeds into Francie's fantasies, since Jordan foregrounds events not in MacCabe's novel, the Cuban Missile Crisis and the threat of nuclear war. There is then an objective correlative between global and psychic disturbance, almost as if the pathology of the boy and the pathology of the Bomb perversely mirrored one another in their destructive potency.

Though Jordan shoots on location with an effortless ease, post-production effects are vital for Francie's visions, among them atomic ruin, the Bomb exploding in the picture postcard of a lake he visits with his friend Joe, and the dream visitations of the blessed Virgin. Francie's world of fancy relies desperately on euphemism and make-believe, as if we had a updated portrait, inspired by Synge, of the Playboy's younger brother on the threshold of a new age. When Francie claims things are at their best, the townsfolk want to believe him because he reminds them so much of things at their worst. If he has tunnel vision, so in a sense do they. Jordan thus veers danger-ously close to a version of small-town idiocy, even insinuations of contempt, at those points when his narrative fails to forge distance by its use of the free direct form. Yet in most instances he can pull back through the interplay of comedy and irony. The visions of the Virgin, here assuming the form of that public critic of the Pope, Sinead O'Connor, are not only topical but also convincing as ethereal images in a rural world. Milo O'Shea's cameo of the abusing priest at reform school, equally topical, is a *coup de grâce*. It is only in the ending perhaps, with the murder, that Jordan's powers of invention seem to desert him. The pace becomes too frantic, the townspeople too moronic, the irony of the visitation that leads to the sighting of Mrs Nugent's corpse too obvious. As an ironic epiphany it lacks the power of Danny's encounter with the boy selling charms at the end of *Angel*, or Jimmy in *The Miracle* demanding of the Saviour's statue in the church that He live up to the title of the film and redeem a sinner's carnal error.

In making any film about the Troubles, Pasolini's free indirect form seemed a puzzling aesthetic for those demanding easy truths. Yet this is an effective method by which Jordan creates his distinctive film form, and the figure of Stephen Rea, laconic, vulnerable, quietly desperate, is a clear alter ego for the cineaste, positioned by this use of the double register in fraught and dangerous situations. This speculative interrogation of circumstance, pushing to see how figures act under particular kinds of extreme pressure, is what makes Jordan so controversial. A cineaste, however, is neither journalist nor historian. Jordan's political project is precisely one of derealisation, of dissolving the stable conventions of the life-world so that justice, evil and suffering are all elusive forms. That project has its origins in the Irish film that pioneered the method, *Odd Man Out*. As shot in expressionist monochrome by Robert Krasker, Reed's 1947 picture follows the flight of wounded IRA gunman James Mason on the streets of Belfast after a botched robbery, a flight punctuated by hallucination and surreal encounter, a *mise-en-scène* of damaged subjectivity daring for its time. Yet Mason remains the romantic and humanised hero still wishing to be redeemed for his mistakes both by God and by the love of his loyal sweetheart. The framing of empathy is so powerful here it carries the film. While echoing the tragic flight of Mason, the itinerant Rea has a more fearful subjectivity where the trauma of violence begets the violence of vengeance and where neither God nor sexual passion has any power of redemption.

It is this bleakness in *Angel* that separates Jordan from Reed. In part *The Crying Game* is much closer and Rea's vulnerability is humanised with a delicate touch. Yet Jordan's use of irony and his knowing take on the perverse separate his film from Reed's convention of invisible narrative and his flair for lyrical melodrama. Through Krasker's cinematography and in the snow-filled streets of the final sequences, Reed uses urban landscape as an uncanny harbinger of hope, but Jordan's rural landscape in the later stages of *Angel* is unremittingly bleak. Green fields are seldom to be seen, desaturated or else covered up, as in the seashore killing, by heaps of sand.[18] The clothes worn are much the same. The garish and artificial colours of later sequences replace mute or natural colours worn in early sequences. Rea is Jordan's

political other, the embattled soul who crosses over to the politics of
the gun, a journey the director has never made, but each journey is
distinct and unsettling, not amenable to ideological endorsement.
While Danny conducts an insane one-man crusade, Fergus draws back
from the Republican movement after the trauma of Jody's death.
Neither odyssey is comforting to militant Republicanism but neither
does it slot into the progressive melodramas of Goldcrest, Robert
Redford or Costa-Gavras, which claim to have history on the side of
their heroes. Jordan's heroes are hesitant anti-heroes, tormented souls
who make the wrong moves rather than ordinary guys who turn into
resolute men of action.

Jordan has mentioned kidnapping as a key link between *The Crying
Game* and Brendan Behan's IRA drama *The Hostage*, where there is
even a subplot cuing the transvestism central to Jordan's film.[19] Equally
*Angel* seems to invert O'Casey's dramatic strategy in *Shadow of a
Gunman*; the saxman with the gun in his music case replaces O'Casey's
'poltroon and poet' just as robotic action replaces rhetorical fantasy.
In *The Crying Game* Jordan shifts back again in the shock and disillusion which Fergus feels after Jody's death. At first sight the two
films appear to take Jordan out of the Irish romantic tradition. In his
quest for Annie's killers, Danny abandons Dee in the middle of their
affair or rather she rejects him as 'unclean' when she sees him killing
in cold blood. In *The Crying Game* Fergus transfers his cryptic affec-
tion for the dead Jody on to his perverse but plausible passion for
Dil, Jody's lover. Yet the use of modernist tropes fails to exorcise the
dark romantic sensibility. The famous last sequence played out in
prison between Dil and Fergus and tailed off by Lyle Lovett's version
of 'Stand by your Man' is a brilliant stroke of irony but fails to undermine the covert strain of romance. Homosexual love, at first hidden
through Rea's failure to read the signs, momentarily transcends differences of nation and pigmentation. Yet in so doing it rejoins and
re-echoes the troubled sexuality of *Angel*. The perverse object-choice
has tragic consequences radiating out into the troubled world of politics
of which it is a splintered mirror. In both films, Jordan's take on the
perverse is a powerful continuation of the European legacy of Buñuel
and Fassbinder, hitting the raw nerve of transgression not only here,
but also in *The Miracle* where Oedipal fate comes home, somewhat
casually, to the Wicklow coast.

The skein of this perverse sexuality contains its own enigmas. This refusal of romance as heterosexual convention is itself romantic. Specifically the denial of romance is a romantic denial of the conventions of Irish romance. Jordan's male Irish hero acts out a perverse attraction to the cultural other as object of desire, a desire for the deaf-mute, the dark-skinned, the sado-masochistic, the lesbian, the transvestite, the Oedipal. One might even include necrophilia, as in Francie's doting love in *The Butcher Boy* for his father's sitting-room corpse. What remains engraved on the eye, however, comes from the sense of conviction in Jordan's narrative strategy. Often his pairing of flawed 'lovers' has been inspired, like that of Bob Hoskins and black prostitute Cathy Tyson in *Mona Lisa*, or Rea and hairdresser Jaye Davidson. Indeed before Davidson was cast, Jordan was made to suffer for his boldness since Channel Four were reluctant to bankroll a picture with such a daring sex-change scenario.[20] Yet the casting confirms his uncanny powers of transmitting the perverse, of filming the sensual signs of misrecognition. Though Jimmy's misrecognising in *The Miracle* is more casual, it is also more extreme. For what cryptically romantic Irish teenager could ever imagine that a glamorous American actress old enough to be his mother, actually *was* his mother?

In Jordan, the erotic other is the forbidden, but this simply takes to its furthest point the convention of romance as a continuous form of transgression, a violation of social mores. Jordan's talent here is not only to make the transgression credible to the viewer, but also to make its timing and consequence sources of suspense. Interestingly, while this is the sign of narrative power, it is also a sign of incipient weakness. After the revelation of the forbidden other, there is often a void he tries to fill by the quickening of pace, the intensification of events. In this enervated rush, montage suffers and the last twenty minutes are always a critical period in the Jordan narrative. Often too much happens as the pace quickens and editing rhythms accelerate beyond control. Many of the films vitiate and weaken in their attempt to do too much, too quickly. Yet Jordan always provides great final scenes to compensate, the return to the ruined ballroom in *Angel*, the prison visit in *The Crying Game*, the ambush in *Michael Collins*, the flash-forward to the adult Francie in *The Butcher Boy*. It is always a renewal of strength that seems to follow premature exhaustion and reconnect with the power of vision. The sign of greatness, perhaps, lies in the director's second wind.

Events in the Troubles provide the springboard for the political films. The honey-trap which snares Jody at the start of *The Crying Game* had been a well-known Provo tactic, while the brutal killing of the band's manager in *Angel* echoes the sectarian massacre of the Miami Showband, ambushed on its way home to Dublin from a gig in a Protestant border town. The Irish setting in both pictures is border territory, the bandit country of South Armagh, while the border is never far away either in *The Butcher Boy*, shot just over the other side in the town of Clones in 1960s Monaghan, the home town of its author. In all three films, border territory is a disorienting territory of terror. Jordan makes the border, as a division within Ireland, work upon the spectator's subconscious, a lurking presence never explicitly shown but felt in the weight and the pressure of narrative. Border territory is both actual and metaphorical. It is implied in the repre- sented image but also in the weight and pressure of the boundary as an unwanted imprint on the soul, a cross the sacrificial hero unwit- tingly must bear.

There is a clear contrast here with the city films of Jim Sheridan. Yet what links Jordan and Sheridan in practical terms is the use of the Southern location in the Northern picture. The seaside, arcade and fairground sequences Jordan brings back repeatedly are born out of his upbringing at Bray on the Wicklow coast south of Dublin. The bridge sequence that opens *The Crying Game,* with its slow lateral track echoing the start of Tarkovsky's *The Sacrifice,* uses the bridge over the Nanny River from Jordan's childhood also appearing in *Angel* and in *Michael Collins*. While Jordan's South-for-North shots come from the coastal suburb, Sheridan's South-for-North shots, which open *In the Name of the Father,* spring from the working-class areas of North Dublin where he grew up, and where he triumphantly simu- lates a Falls Road riot. Again, in his Oscar-winning biopic about Christy Brown, *My Left Foot,* the sequences are largely contiguous with their North Dublin setting and this gives Sheridan his surety of touch. Equally his flair for depicting father–son relationships helps to fix in the filmic image the patriarchal working-class family of his own time and place. Yet Sheridan has little of the feel for London that Jordan does. When he goes beyond North Dublin what lingers in the mind is the enclosed interior, the powerful suspense of the prison melo- drama. Jordan, by comparison, is as surefooted in his London locations as he is in his Wicklow settings. Significantly the scene of Collins's assassination is displaced from West Cork to the Wicklow Hills where Jordan persuaded his producers to build a road through a glacial valley to act as the setting for the fatal ambush.[21]

There is another contrast between the two directors in the iconography of stardom. Each uses a central figure in their work for opposite effects. In Sheridan's films, Daniel Day-Lewis is a heroic prototype of working-class sacrifice, an unwitting victim of circumstance in varied guises, and delivers his roles with a Stanislavskian power of utter absorption that is deeply cinematic. He is best at his most extreme, with his rendering of the disabled Christy Brown where he conveys his hero's wish to break the stigma of the family idiot not only by forcing his neglected intelligence on them and on his neighbours, but on us the audience. Just as Day-Lewis is charismatic, assertive and agonistic, always challenging us to empathise with his quest for exoneration, so Stephen Rea is precisely the opposite. His performances are downbeat, laconic, as quiet as Day-Lewis is loud, marked by stoicism and a quiet desperation that verges on the tragic yet indicates a basic will to survive. When Jordan broaches charisma in the Irish context, it is of course in *Michael Collins*. Yet the charismatic presence of Liam Neeson as Collins and Alan Rickman as De Valera is of a different order. Whereas Sheridan resources the underdog's heroic struggle against victimhood, Jordan is interested in the dialectic tension between two forms of active will in two contrasting figures. The death of one, needless to say, is a tragedy for both. Yet just as Collins and De Valera had written themselves into history, so the performances by Neeson and Rickman should do the same for film history. Neeson's rhetorical yet earthy exchanges with the market town crowd at Granard provide a fitting contrast to Rickman's 'rivers of blood' oration on the eve of civil war. Neeson as Collins senses the mood of the crowd because he is like them but also one step ahead of them, able to persuade them to move on. In Rickman's eloquence before a vast heaving crowd on the O'Connell Street set, there is an icy quality of ethereal detachment, suggesting a greatness not given to ordinary mortals but also a disastrous distance from their material concerns, of a sense of fate beyond human scale. The struggle of Irish history which intersects the two figures becomes on screen a struggle of voice, of posture, of expression, of presence.

At its most intense, Jordan's sense of political tragedy here merits comparisons with Wajda's Polish trilogy, with *The Travelling Players* of Angelopoulos and with Bertolucci's *The Conformist*, all of them cinematic milestones which deal in retrospect with Europe's fascist curse and its pitiless aftermath. As a chronicle of the breathless surge of terror and counter-terror at the heart of the city, it echoes Pontecorvo's lyrical *Battle of Algiers*. Yet Jordan's chronicle heralds a greater sense of history's complexity and perfidy, breaking with the simple linear optimism in Pontecorvo's Marxist melodrama. More recent predecessors also spring to mind: Warren Beatty's self-styled 'revolutionary romance' about John Reed, *Reds*, Bertolucci's Hollywood epic about the politics of modern Italy, *1900*, and Goldcrest's money-spinner about the forging of Indian independence, *Gandhi*. Let us take them one by one. *Michael Collins* is of a period with Beatty's film, retaining the same freshness of the historical instance but without the latter's looseness and the preening narcissism in Beatty's own performance. It has the tight focus of the Indian independence struggle in *Gandhi* but is filmed here firmly from the inside, its focus on the colonised, not the colonisers. Lastly it avoids the temptation of the never-ending epic, which finally vitiates Bertolucci's narrative. It gains through compression what *1900* loses through the over-stretching of time. It shares the same practical fate, namely a meeting of the European imagination and Hollywood money, but shrewdly avoids the damaging consequence faced by Bertolucci of a picture considered too long for general release.

Unlike his pictures actually set in the USA, *Michael Collins* does not turn the American connection into an albatross around Jordan's neck. For sure, there are key influences. The taut montage of political killing is closer to the ending of *The Godfather* than it is to Eisenstein. Yet in framing, it still retains a European sensibility. It is an artistic reprise of history, not a glamorous forging of myth. When the dawn blitz around Dublin takes out the 'Cairo Gang', the cream of British intelligence, Collins is canoodling with Kitty in a hotel room, twirling a red rose in his fingers and placing it on her breast. At the end of the film when Collins in turn is being taken out by the Diehards of West Cork, Kitty is busy shopping in Dublin for her white bridal gown – parallel montage in repetition to prove a political point, and engage a mass audience with a maestro's touch. On the one hand, Jordan stamps a lyrical rhythm upon the film that is clearly his own. On the other, he carves out a tragic sense which is different from that of Yeats's '1916' but equally valid for the Uprising's consequences. At times the divide between tragedy and melodrama can be thinner than a whisker. Yet it remains intact. Instead of exorcising the romantic as he had done in *Angel*, Jordan endorses it in its Irish form through the montage of American melodrama at its most inspired. It shares Coppola's tight narrative hold on the conspiracies and betrayals of power but, crucially, uses a different register. While the romance of *Reds* hovers insanely between continents, Jordan is ruthlessly pursuing the path of romanticism in one country in order to achieve something beyond it, a structure of feeling both tragic and epic at the same time.

At times the spectacle-image is no substitute for the complexities of the political event. Anachronisms like the Dublin car bomb and the armoured car massacre in Croke Park are too neat and too spectacular, shorting major circuits of history. The dockside killing of Harry Boland (Aidan Quinn), much changed in detail and too melodramatic in *mise-en-scène*, or of Ned Broy (Stephen Rea) who actually lived to a ripe old age, are overripe fictions which highlight a general dilemma. The two-hour-plus epic must always select and compress history for its own purposes. On the detail Jordan has options, but in the general picture no choice. History and his story part company at key moments, not only in what they retell but what they do not tell. For those who know Irish history, the absences haunt. Thus the controversies raging over the Collins we never see, the politician negotiating painfully with British ministers or fruitlessly with Northern Unionists. Yet Jordan more than compensates by evoking the continuity of present-day Dublin and the city of Collins. It is an intuitive flair for the right setting and right location. The insulation serves the pattern of the picture, turning it into an epic weaving history after its own pattern. Alternating the O'Connell Street set with location shooting, Jordan's use of the living city is effervescent, both in the tight atmospheric use of dockland warehouses and in the use of Dublin Castle where, Jordan tells us, Mary Robinson interrupted the shoot of the handover of the Castle to Collin's forces to attend the Forum on Peace and Reconciliation.[22] His eye for the living detail is never clearer than in the attack on the Diehards holed up in the Four Courts Building, which Collins orders from across the River Liffey. The Four Courts are still there, the bridges across the river are still there, the guns fire on cue and as the camera pans right down the river as it flows out to sea, the Liffey skyline seems to span all of eighty years. Emptied of traffic for the duration of this shoot, the image has an uncanny durability. Time past has suddenly become time present and the Civil War, with its clear echo of the ongoing Troubles, becomes living tragedy.

Jordan has referred to *Michael Collins* as a film of 'elegaic realism' in which sudden bursts of violence would contrast with longer sequences both languorous and operatic.[23] As a result the montage is rhythmically the most satisfying of all his films. Reunited with cinematographer Chris Menges for the first time since *Angel*, he makes positive use of silhouette and available light, desaturating the image in post-production to create a slightly faded look that never degenerates into pastiche. This is the image of living history, not only in how things were but how things are. The look and style dovetail with a key element in Jordan's political vision. For the political films are governed by a key obsession, shared by many of his generation faced with an intermittent thirty-year war, and made manifest by the frailties of the 1998 Good Friday Agreement. That is the conceit of cessation. Both films have heroes who at a key moment have a specific courage. This is not only the agony of the decision to start the fight but the decision about whether to relinquish the fight because it is no longer fruitful to go on. The aspiration is clear. It is to spring the trap of instrumental terror, to limit the cost of sacrifice and actively will peace to break out. It is to know when to stop.

Both *Michael Collins* and *The Crying Game* stress the conditional triumph of a certain kind of reason, which can wager on terror of a limited kind and a limited duration. *Angel* and *The Butcher Boy* do the opposite. Their darkness raises the spectre of terror out of control, unlimited. There is surely a frisson at the end of *The Butcher Boy* when the adult Francie, played by Rea who had earlier played his father, first appears. His voice has the guttural, robotic edge of Danny's at the end of *Angel*, his face the same cowed look, the same downcast eyes. Both figures are numbed by their killing and can never, you suspect, recover their earlier selves, that pre-homicidal virginity of which Malraux once spoke with contempt, but which here is positively Edenic. They are, we might say, the vessels of a sacrificial unconscious in which they unwittingly sacrifice and are sacrificed at the same time, victims and perpetrators both. Though it could be argued that the sacrificial unconscious in our culture is at the basis of much recent cinema ranging from Tarkovsky to Greenaway, the Irish edge it assumes is surely that of Pearse's blood-sacrifice and its manifold legacies. At best, reason and goodness are born again out of the exhaustion of evil, but there is no surety that evil is exhausted, no guarantee that it will not be reborn. Evil, after all, begets evil and the chain is also a circle. This Jordan well knows.

*Chapter 6*

# THE REVIVAL OF THE CINEMATIC CITY

Many strategies for analysing the cinematic city go two different ways at once for inspiration, to the past for theories validating it and to the future for the *mise-en-scène* defining it. The past brings forth the usual suspects, among them Baudelaire, Simmel, Benjamin, Lefebvre, who have framed our socio-aesthetic of the metropolis. Since *2001*, or 1969, the date of its release, the future has brought forth science fiction. On this mountaintop an alien must land, down these mean streets a replicant must go. In one scenario, *flâneurs* stroll at their leisure. In another, terminators keep on coming. What is more, an architectural style (unknown to Lyotard when he wrote *The Postmodern Condition*) now defines many late twentieth-century films. Yet post-modern architecture seldom features in 'post-modern' films. In the canonical text of post-modernity, *Blade Runner*, Bukatman has pointed to the prevalence of modernist design and *mise-en-scène*, the use of styles such as Neo-Mayan or Art Deco which preceded the later standardisation of the Bauhaus and Le Corbusier.[1]

To see the cinematic city as hyper-modern is to stress a different point from the post-modernists. It is to highlight a series of iconic signs that implode with layered density and conceal a reflexive vision of the networked society. In an age of electronic reproduction, this sign-series forges a new structure of feeling we have termed coeval disconnection. It stands in counterpoint to the cult of 'TechGnosis', which now governs contrasting communication rhetorics, both the euphoric counter-cultures of cyberspace and the official discourse of the 'information superhighway'. Yet as the source of city's represented images for our time, the hyper-modern does even more. Its mutable vision fuses the city of atoms to the city of bits, the tangible to the intangible, the visible to the invisible, the real to the unreal. The new city on celluloid is both absent and present at the same time.

Among the changing post-modern rhetoric of the city, the closest link here may well be Lyotard's recent formula of post-modern fable. Lyotard sees such fables as imaginary stories of the real, which lack the emancipation or the finality of earlier meta-narratives, and thrive instead on reflexive melancholia.[2] His disavowal of Baudrillard's world of simulacra, and of the rhetorics of nostalgia and pastiche, leads to a stress on the constant mutation of post-modern discourse, spurred by the fragmentation of the real, which is an unending aesthetic challenge. This endorses a separation of the aesthetic from the social, dimensions which post-modernism often elides. The post-modern fable is in essence, Lyotard claims, a fable about *modernity*'s fate.[3] This rereading of modernity in a fabulist manner keys us in to one major consequence of the endless fragmentation of the real. The city itself can no longer be viewed as a tangible entity with distinct boundaries. Instead Lyotard speaks of the vast geopolitical zones of the megalopolis in which the barriers of city and suburb break down and the suburbs of different cities join up with one another, in which edge cities are both part of larger cities but also separate entities in their own right.[4] As cities spread out, physically extending their boundaries and often their populations, they also radiate outwards through networks connecting with each other across different time–space zones. The new life of the megalopolis is no less real than any of its predecessors. Yet its diverse operations cannot be grasped with any finality. The Lyotardian fable is a reflexive comment on its own weakness and resignation, its inevitable failure to tell the whole story.

The art of the cinematic city goes further than Lyotard's textual fable in a very specific way. Film as a visual form crosses over two vital dimensions of social space. It films on location the diverse way in which city space is designed and redesigned and at the same time the ways in which that space is directly lived in, used and inhabited. In filming that unbounded space in segments, the narrative camera represents it as a spatial imaginary rooted in the real, as a set of segmented spaces through which city-dwellers move independently before and after the film set itself. The film set of course transforms the scene. It can add its own design, houses built on vacant lots,

stylised actors and automobiles, buildings painted different colours or
adorned with different signs, interiors transformed. So the boundary
between designed and lived space is never fully clear. The architectural nature of film takes us back from Lyotard to Lefebvre. In his
terms we might say that 'representations of space' trigger the 'representational spaces' which film embellishes. On the one hand city
spaces are conceptualised by planners, designers and engineers. On
the other hand those spaces are directly lived in and experienced
through images and symbols permeating the culture.[5] Film at its best
raises the representational space to a fine art through its own concept
and design. It is both an accretion and a supplementary layer. Here
filmic renewal relies less on the studio city pioneered by Lang and
developed by Fellini, Scott and Besson. It relies more on the actual
city seen and filmed in segments and seen too by its audience in a
different light. In architecture, city space is socially transformed. In
film it is artistically transformed. Both are forms of renewal that play
off one another. Thus the renewal of the cinematic city is a transformation of ways of seeing. In critique the fusion of Lefebvre and Lyotard
announces the arrival of the hyper-modern.

I

Usually the rhetoric of the cinematic city starts and ends with Los
Angeles. Yet renewal takes place largely elsewhere. We can associate
places and names, Kieślowski with Warsaw and Geneva, Wong Kar-
Wai with Hong Kong and Buenos Aires, Edward Yang and Tsai
Ming-Liang with Taipei, Wenders and Fred Kelemen with Berlin,
"Beat" Takeshi and Imamura with Tokyo, E J-Yong with Seoul, Egoyan
and Cronenberg with Toronto and any number of cineastes with Paris.
The London of the 1990s has also been the epicentre of a new cinema,
with films by Loach, Jordan, Leigh, Oldman and others generating a
new cinema of the streets echoing that of 1920s Weimar. By contrast,
the great American city films are from the previous generation of Allen,
Scorsese, Coppola, Pakula and Cassavetes. Indeed many current Asian
and European cineastes have taken back Scorsese and Cassavetes into
their own cultural ambit, in the same way the Americans once took the
French New Wave into theirs. The fact remains that major American

cities now seem over-exposed on the global treadmill of the audiovisual image. Instead Hollywood has innovated through the dystopian city of the future. In *Demolition Man* or *Twelve Monkeys*, for example, city locations of the present are turned into dystopian venues of the future. Yet by and large, the sci-fi city is a studio city with location add-ons. Moreover, the city has now been abandoned by film noir, which is either future noir or country noir, a successor to the road movie of the 1970s.[6] Meanwhile American independents have often joined Hollywood in using city locations as little more than scenic backdrops for romantic comedies or thrillers. Yet there remain defining moments of exploration, San Francisco in *Fearless* or Las Vegas in Figgis's *Leaving Las Vegas*, the San Fernando valley in Todd Haynes's *Safe*, modernist Phoenix in *Suture* or black Brooklyn in *Do the Right Thing*, the eerie suburbs of virtual spectacle created by Tim Burton in *Edward Scissorhands* or Peter Weir in *The Truman Show*.

In Europe and the Pacific Rim we have also witnessed new narratives and new ways of seeing forged out of the city-as-found. Here social difference is not the false hope of outdated meta-narrative, but a living tissue of film and culture. We see, though, not simply a filmic topography of divide, bourgeois versus proletarian, black versus white, yuppie versus bohemian, but something more graduated and subtle, a register of the differential impact of risk. The Lyotardian fable needs to be modified here to incorporate risk into film narrative. For the prosperous, city risk is the effect of fragile cultural capital, an affluence without belonging, a portfolio of cultural riches without possession. For the disprivileged it is the danger of the streets, a promise-threat nourished by the vagaries of drift, of worklessness, of casual crime. Here film plays powerfully on the 'divide' of working class and underclass, a chimerical boundary which haunts the collective imagination of us all. To this can be added the familiar dialectic of country and city, the country boy who comes to town only to find that appearances are never what they seem, a trope used to great effect in Téchiné's *J'embrasse pas* or Jordan's *The Crying Game*. In both films sexuality comes decisively into play. It is neither secret nor revelation, but a source of perpetual ambivalence, an endless interplay of male and female, of transfer and rebound which is ever open and, in Lyotard's fabulist idiom, incomplete. In Egoyan's Toronto, megalopolis of the North and site of *Family Viewing*, *The Adjuster* and *Exotica*, the dialectic is one of suburb and centre, core and periphery where endless transfers of movement between disconnected places dissolve the core of sexual persona. Instead of the city as source of self-discovery, the site of a new sexuality, it acts as the opposite, an endless cycle of resolving and dissolving where discovery and loss become identical.

Here certain regularities stand out. Cinema is not fiction. Where the latter favours serious narratives of bourgeois intimacy, in cinema they are conspicuous by their absence except in France where they are conspicuous by their ubiquity. Yet the pull of cinema is generally in two directions. The privileged inhabit history, the disprivileged inhabit the present. The wealthy lived in country houses, the poor live in rundown districts of inner cities. The contemporary bourgeois spend most of their fictional lives on television where there are investigators, detectives, police inspectors, journalists, psychologists, doctors, surgeons or pathologists. What they investigate is murder, crime and scandal and the personal lives of other bourgeois where the lure of investigating leads, twenty-five minutes in, to side-supply sex and local scandal. Alternatively, they investigate villains who are not of their own kind, the monstrous other of the underclass as serial rapist or killer. In film nothing could be more different. Barring the ever-triumphant comedy of manners, in British and Irish cinema the bourgeoisie go strangely absent. North rather than southeast Dublin provides the setting for the films of Jim Sheridan and the film versions of Roddy Doyle's fiction. In London the city is a location setting for scarcely any serious film about the lure of privilege, the most memorable being *The Wings of the Dove*, which boldly brings forward James's tragic fiction into the Edwardian era. Yet in contemporary London serious money is not an issue in romantic comedies such as *Truly, Madly, Deeply, Four Weddings and a Funeral, Sliding Doors* or *Notting Hill*. It is either assumed or celebrated. Contrast for example the Underground sequence which opens *The Wings of the Dove* with the Underground sequence which starts *Sliding Doors*, the former tight, constrained, erotic, an interpolation of James which is impressively doom-laden, self-consciously noir, the latter a piece of whimsy which plays sentimentally on the modernist trope of alternating narratives and reduces it to wishful romance.

Only in French cinema, we are tempted to suggest, do the middle classes remain a serious force. Here two things combine: the durability of a cinephile culture and of Francophone funding which makes the serious bourgeois narrative part of a wider spectrum of filming, wide enough in scope to embrace all classes and races, and dissect the divides of city and country alike. In the 1990s that class divide is expressed in Francophone stardom. The first icon that springs to mind is Juliette Binoche, making the transition from eye-patch vagabond in Carax's *Les Amants du Pont-neuf,* to famous composer's spouse in Kieślowski's *Blue.* Yet there are others equally imposing. Only in Paris could Vincent Cassel double as madman Vinz in the rundown suburb of *La Haine* and as yuppie executive in *L'Appartement,* or Emmanuelle Béart as street hooker in *J'embrasse pas* and the successful violinist in *Un Cœur en hiver.* Let us first take the films by Kassovitz and Téchiné. Both show how the cinematic city operates at its most powerful and mythic. The constructive energies of film form are derived from the destructive energies of their street personae, characters that are open to the found location and move through it relentlessly while being tracked relentlessly by the following camera. Their tragic fate, that is to say, is inseparable from the living tissue of the city.

Let us now take the rather different features of Kieślowski and Sautet. They show something else – the city as an arena for the circulation of intimacies where the fabric of city life is cushioned by the two kinds of capital which count, money and culture. In *Blue* and *Un Cœur en hiver* one such vital culture, music, flows in and out of diegesis as a source of both risk and redemption. Binoche destroys and then rescues her dead spouse's orchestral composition. Béart's violin-playing rescues her from the catastrophe of her aborted affair with her spouse's violin-maker. Although characters circulate in a world of money and culture, which is in part assumed, beyond it is a quest for contentment that can never be learnt or bought, which exists neither in objects or taste. We know for sure when we start to watch these films we shall witness the drama of failed relationships and the ineffability of solitude. We see this, even with comic touches, in the Parisian films of Kieślowski, Rohmer and Rivette. All three have lone heroines whose sense of place becomes displaced, who circulate between city apartment and an elsewhere outside the city limits, whose identity is premised not only on who they are but where they are. Identity is inseparable not only from setting but also from movement and French cinema at its best springs from a dynamic topography which is deep and lateral, mental and spatial at the same time.

In British film the revival of the city has worked in tandem with changes in Western Europe but is distinctive in its own right. It brings a new focus on danger and the dispossessed, a new gloss on the Heideggerian fallenness of the risk location and risk narrative. Its scenarios are diverse, and to see this movement through the late 1980s and the 1990s as simply a realist revival is to miss the point. We can characterise it for sure as a British 'neo-realism' if we measure it against the early 1960s films of Reisz, Richardson and Anderson. It is less formulaic, more dispersed, more fragmented in narrative, and yet it hinges as they do upon the representational image and the located space – but more is at stake. Its renewal of the realist form, which makes us realise that Bazin never went away and never will, is framed against key structures of disconnection. Thus scenarios of want and constraint, bleak narratives of the solitary and exploited are replaced by scenarios of risk and dislocation within a different frame, a networked consumerism with no safety cushion for the excluded.

Take 1990s London. One of its starting points is Alan Clarke's *The Firm*, a television film with cinematic qualities that has stamped its imprint on the decade. The group of West Ham Casuals run by estate agent Gary Oldman uneasily overlaps class and racial boundaries, divisions stitched together by an amoral laddism of the smartly dressed which prides itself not on watching football but showing instant venom to other fans. Clarke's sweeping Steadicam shots are bold brush strokes which journey from Thamesmead into the heart of the city, a panorama of imperceptible gradations of status drowned by the weekend buzz of Oldman's speed tribe. Rumbles occur in places of transit, the non-places of Tube station, underground car park, motorway service station and finally the East End pub whose ambush the Steadicam tracking follows tight in, from outside to inside with a tragic finality. Clarke's effortless mastery of city spaces, his power to stage them as scenes of encounter which are nasty, brutish and short, infuses film with a new dynamism that is tactile and expansive. The *mise-en-scène* takes in so much that there is an acrid lyricism in its forms of disconnection, where disconnection within the frame, for example, is supplemented by the disconnecting leaps of montage. The narrative is both a way of experiencing and a way of filming. It is the lived world of his characters and, at the same time, the renewal of film style.

Clarke's innovating method has lead to crystalline transparencies of inside and outside in the films that succeeded him. In Loach's *Riff-Raff* Robert Carlyle is a Glaswegian incomer in the Smoke, a casual building worker who drifts into a dangerous job constructing luxury apartments with no safety standards while squatting in a derelict flat in a decaying tenement. Loach matches the images of the half-built apartment block with its scaffolding, timber and empty window frames to the rotting walls and broken furniture of the squat, the half-apartment and the half-ruin, images of constructing and destructing both porous and transient. In Mike Leigh's *Naked* Mancunian David Thewlis drifting his way through the drab streets of London, with his diseased stream of consciousness and his drive towards self-destruction, has two epiphanic moments of the street. In the first, he encounters Scot Ewen Bremner waiting on the corner for his girl and wailing into the night like a coyote howling at the wind. In a series of long takes and long-lens shots with no reverse angles the film frames them both tight against shop windows, hemmed in by oblivious traffic, dispensable beings. When the girl finally appears, all three talk and shout at cross-purposes in a fugue of lyrical disconnections. Later Thewlis alights at a brand new office block, still unoccupied, its windows illuminated and transparent, a prime target for the homeless. He cons his way inside, though the camera still films him from the outside, and, in the city of William Blake, regales the distraught security guard with psychotic tales of the apocalypse. Both epiphanies highlight strange encounters of motormouth lonely hearts, and that sense of deep disturbance prompts Leigh to show a visual inspiration lacking, for example, in the 'talking heads' scenario of *Secrets and Lies*. The office block encounter which stays in the memory long after the film has ended is framed unusually for Leigh in long wide-angle takes and imbued with the metaphysical stillness of Antonioni.

These are unusual films for Loach and Leigh because they are so visually memorable. Too often their primary function in British film has been to present alternating perspectives on the mundane and the ordinary. These, it has to be said, have become part of the staple diet of middle-brow consumption. For at his worst Loach evokes a watery compassion bordering on sentimentality while Leigh has a eye for human weakness which often borders on contempt. Here what saves them is the inventiveness of their ensemble directing, their talent for binding actors into a collective presence and re-inventing styles of acting. Yet the limits of their work are thrown into relief by Oldman's *Nil by Mouth*, which is a defining moment of British cinema in the 1990s. Oldman fuses the influence of Clarke with the style of Cassavetes in revealing once more the strength of the autobiographical city. The competition is indeed strong. Douglas in Edinburgh, Davies in Liverpool, MacKinnon and Ramsay in Glasgow have all produced different registers of recent time remembered, the past still effervescent and alive in the tissue of the present. Oldman, however, fuses the two in what he has called his 'blues' of life remembered in South London. Yet unlike the others, this is not memory film at all. The feel is instant, contemporary, not elegiac or reflective, and the result is explosive.

The South London council flat shared by Ray Winstone and Kathy Burke is framed as a makeshift home of glass partitions trading on the illusion of spatial depth. Oldman's telephoto lens, which captures them in differing degrees of close-up and blockage by domestic bric-à-brac, creates the intimacy of claustrophobic emotion through its fishbowl effect. Outside, the peripatetic rambling of Burke's junkie brother (Charlie Creed-Miles) through long winding corridors and balconies of nearby projects is dark and disordered, a hemming-in by ceilings, walls and grey skies. The launderette where Miles hangs out with his cronies again affords Oldman the chance of a reflecting outside window shot, as if the characters are constantly moving behind and in front of a transparent screen. Inside when Burke and Winstone look out through the glass partition into the adjacent room, we see at one point the reflection of a TV image at the side of the glass, *our* side, so that it is impossible to tell whether they are looking towards or away from the screen whose noise competes with their own talk. When Winstone and his pals drive up to Soho for a night out they are equally hemmed in by glass and neon, the camera squashed with them inside the car as they cruise. Though this is drug-fuelled male hedonism wearing its cliché on its lapel, the spectacle is both ugly and poetic at the same time. For such deformed sensibility knows neither bright daylight nor *Lebensraum*. This is the heart, the core of its asphalt pathos.

The rhythms are both diurnal and disintegrating. The buzz of booze and gear builds them up for the Soho foray and a set of half-cocked adventures which we know will later be transformed into the tall tales they constantly tell each other to fuel their appetite for more of the same. A cyclical pattern is set in train. The tall story in club and pub is the end and outcome of the 'adventure', but also the catalyst for its future repetition. Yet the venture skates on thin ice, becomes in a way a brittle illusion of control just as control is being lost and metabolism goes awry. The breakdown is also a building-up, in the case of Miles to the heroin fix which furthers the anxieties of addiction, the 'sixty pounds a day' habit his mother reluctantly pays for as connections are missed or go astray. In the case of Winstone the addiction is to the fist and boot as alternate means of control when the joke and the tale and the gear no longer suffice. Oldman gives us a parallel cutting that weaves separate narratives in and out of one another. Both men are separately on the skids but sunk by propinquity, their path crossing abrasively as they abuse their female kin and sink deeper into the mire. There is an indiscernible slowing of time here and for us a sense of entrapment. We are forced into an involuntary witnessing, like passers-by whose bodies feel uncomfortably close but whose minds are uneasily distant. That is to say, we start by feeling a distance we then question. The long-lens shot becomes the indispensable medium of this reluctant intimacy, reversing the deep-focus techniques of Bergman in addressing, generically, the same domestic predicament.

Let us return to Paris. *La Haine* and Yolande Zaubermann's *Clubbed to Death* take the ethnic equation further than any of the British movies of the period, whose main protagonists are mainly white and male. The film of Kassovitz, as indebted to Scorsese as Oldman is to Cassavetes, contrasts the suburb and the city as alternate places of danger and safety but then charts the overspill as his trio of misfits move from one to the other. He films the two locations differently, however, the first as a place of rapid swooping movement shot in wide angle, the latter through hand-held long-lens shots largely static to emphasise compression.[7] The visual contrast is clear, the freedom of belonging versus the constraint of intrusion. Thus the infraction of the law is in effect an infraction of territory with fatal consequences, that of being in the wrong place at the wrong time. In *Clubbed to Death* there is a different kind of play on the margin of the city, this time on a district which is literally at the end of the bus line for clubber

Elodie Bouchez. This is *La Haine* in reverse, the twenty-something hedonist from a comfortable *arrondissement* discovering the city limits where wasteland and clubland meet. Like the inter-ethnic bonding of the misfit trio of *La Haine*, Arab, Black and Jew, Bouchez's visit to the hidden rave scene is a rainbow experience, extending the multiracial trio of *La Haine* into a fleeting collective subject of great size. The club interior, a converted depot, is also an intermingling but is tightly hermetic. Thus the forgotten world of the metropolitan edge mirrors the subterranean world of the rave interior, and yet they are as day and night, the exterior cold, banal, transparent, the interior narcotic and exotic in its constant self-obsessed self-creation. The constant drug fixing reminds us that the mirror can be shattered. The interior also acts as a refuge from the exterior, and thrives on the illusion of surpassing it even though it never can.

There is a further defining feature of the world of the city in the information age. The city is the epicentre of a new communications empire in which many now participate in some degree and those who do not are deemed lost. We might rephrase this dystopically. Not only are those out of the loop hopelessly lost but also those within the loop are equally lost, yet in a different way. The chief metaphorical expression of this double bereavement was *Wings of Desire*. Wenders' self-styled 'vertical road movie' shows both angelic observers and their earth-bound subjects as lost souls. Berlin city-dwellers have muted nobility but cannot transcend their habitat. Damiel and Cassiel transcend it but cannot alter it. The angelic gaze with its swooping aerial shots and hazardous tracking over and through high buildings is countered by the film-within-a-film made by Peter Falk about the city's past below ground. The aerial view of the present is offset by subterranean pastiche of the city's flawed history, both forms of detachment – one searching for new truths, the other repeating stale myths. The pathos of the aerial view of the human comedy, however, where Wenders' angels see and hear but cannot intervene, is given substance by a single image, the Wall which divides the city and becomes a character in the film as much as the city itself. It is a real wall which Wenders films from the air and a built facsimile he films at ground level, but the setting of so many sequences, such as that in the State Library so close to the Wall, is a sign of his fascination with borders. The film seems a premonition less of 'the end of the world', the title of Wenders' next feature, as the end of the Wall. The Nietzschean 'Superlove' finale between Bruno Ganz and Solveig Dommartin is meant as ethereal transcending of the degradation in the Nick Cave club sequences. What better contrast than Fred Kelemen's on-the-hoof 16 mm *Fate*, where the hand-held camera clings limpet-like to his Russian migrants amidst the seedier sites/sights of Kreuzberg and seems not only to witness but to feel the very weight of their self-destructing. No transcendence here.

While Wenders monitors the Berlin Wall with a reflexive melancholy, Egoyan's *The Adjuster* and Cronenberg's *Crash* seem to search out an imaginary border at the edge of Toronto in the same vein, at the edge of a megalopolis where no border exists. Both films go boldly in their sexual politics, linking the pornography of homelessness to endless circularity. Egoyan's home movie-making couple make movies in other people's homes, then burn them down or else act out their own titillating charades in public places as if back on the other side of the camera. Cronenberg's car couples come together through the crashes which injure and disfigure them and celebrate by car-copulating at the prospect of further crashes or in celebration of the simulation of great car crashes in the past, hence the James Dean 'reconstruction'. The car as instrument of circulation assumes a different kind of circularity, an addiction to the link between Eros and death. Sex becomes an act of mechanical reproduction but not in the sense that nature intended. It is equally an act of mechanical reproduction in *The Adjuster*, where it is reproduced by the movie camera and ends up on the censor's screen watched by Arsinée Khanjian, who mechanically presses the buttons on her viewing chair which assign its graded degradations to different categories in the Board's rule book. In *Crash* James Spader's high-rise balcony loftily overlooks a Toronto expressway with double figure-lanes where signs of life are strictly confined to moving automobiles. The instrument which transports from A to B then takes on a life of its own, part of a movement in perpetuity that lifts Cronenberg's characters out of the greater terror of immobility in the lifeless apartment, even though their injuries reduce them to that very state. Car and driver's 'natural' resting-place, the motel, becomes an additional character in Egoyan's film, a highway-fronting Noah's Ark sheltering victims of fire at the behest of insurance adjuster Elias Koteas. Just as Egoyan's static framing contrasts with Cronenberg's travelling shots, so in *Crash* the site of sex is the car, and in *The Adjuster* the site of sex is the motel, a perfect pairing if ever there was one, of motion and rest, speed and immobility.

## II

The car often has its own obscenity, which is born somehow out of its technical innocence, its very lack of affect. In *Paris, Texas* the disoriented Travis encounters a deranged orator on a footbridge over an LA freeway prophesying the end of the world to the endless stream of automobiles cruising below, sleek, noisy, oblivious. Yet at speed the car is a lethal instrument. In Sean Penn's *The Crossing Guard*, the relationship of crime and guilt in LA is marked by a single moment of madness. Drunk driver David Morse has run down and killed Jack Nicholson's daughter on a crossing in a busy street. Once out of jail and still guilt-stricken, he must travel the city uncannily by bus as Nicholson indulges in his own bout of drunk driving while plotting to secure pointless revenge. If the right-eous indignation the car generates, the bad faith of endless circulation, leads Nicholson to imitate the crime he is trying to avenge, then Lynch makes the point even more disturbingly in the road-rage sequence from *Lost Highway*. In his slick black Mercedes 6.9, Mr Eddy is out testing the fuel injection with bodyguards and mechanic Pete Dayton along scenic Mulholland Drive, cruising within the speed limit when he is tailgated, then overtaken by a new T-Bird whose driver gestures at him triumphantly. The demonic power of German technology more than matches the sleekness of American design as Mr Eddy catches up and overtakes his unknown adversary.

His ensuing road-rage is an extended fugue, that Lynchian mixture of parody and terror, which should never work but nearly always does, and deftly illustrates the point. Mr Eddy beats and kicks his adversary to the tune of a righteous vindication and the look of a moral avenger from on high. Snarling and guttural recitation of the perils of dangerous driving act as aural counterpoint to the vicious blows we see raining down on the defenceless body beneath him. Mr Eddy's black Mercedes follows the demonic iconography of earlier LA films such as *American Gigolo* and *The Player*, which had marked out the cutting-edge German saloon as a sign of the sleek, efficient depravity of both owner and instrument, man and machine. The black Cadillac convertible, Mr Eddy's other favourite car, has a different resonance. It poses a more acceptable danger, the blonde Alice Wakefield sitting languidly in the front passenger seat. That monochrome image at the garage, blonde on black, is the true fatal attraction, a mix of things truly American which he cannot resist. In contrast, we can see the iconic force of Cronenberg. By featuring Vaughan in a black Lincoln Continental like Kennedy's, an American convertible par excellence, there is the knowing detachment of a Canadian perversity.

As a film *Crash* ultimately succumbs to its unconscious limits. Yet that is not at all clear on a first viewing where the cineaste's intentional line seems to win out. Early dialogue between Spader and Koteas clarifies Cronenberg's aim to go beyond the clichéd sci-fi trope of the technology remoulding the body, to something that for him, as for Ballard, was more fundamental, the machine as the future source and substance of all desire. Thus the film is set in the present with its simulations of the recent past through the big crash, not only Dean but Jayne Mansfield, yet sees its addictive mindset as a sign of the near-future, the bourgeoisie not overthrown along with their cars and capitalism à la Godard in *Week-End*, but integrated into the destructive rhythms of the machine itself. The car is, in this respect, a speed extension of bourgeois individualism, the source of privacy, free choice, comfort and pleasure, which finally traps all self-expression. The culture it taps into is more addictive perhaps than even Cronenberg realises. Just as narcotic addiction is the leitmotif of *Dead Ringers* and *Naked Lunch*, so the addiction here is autophallic. The car as speed, shape, movement and wreck is a source of masturbatory desire in which the other is an intermediary, a catalyst. While, on the surface, the wrecked speed machine is both site and source of a bisexual desire for the human body, something else happens in the film. Sexual desire punctuates and perpetuates the reign of the wrecked machine, which is celebrated by sacrificing the body of the lover to its material aura. Just as Cronenberg's disfigured lovers recover from their wounds to drive and have sex once more until all permutations of car and partner run out, so their wrecked machines rise from the scrapyard to be reclaimed as the icons of that desire. The lover starts out by desiring the disfigured body encased in the disfigured machine and ends up desiring the damaged machine that encloses the damaged body.

The film's cold detachment from its subject matter, a disembodied camera that is close and glacial at the same time, is only possible because it has, at bottom, a censoring gaze. It is a residual Puritanism, which casts all desire as a profane dance of death. There is no sense in this film of any form of desire that is not a harbinger of the grave. The glacial stillness of Deborah Unger's face suggests a mannequin locked purely into the postures of desire, a posture similar to Monica Vitti in *L'Eclisse* but radically different, since the anxious gaze of Vitti's petrified figure had still sought a difference between sex and love.[8] Here sex in the machine is the risk that can only end in death, and never in life. In the animal kingdom, the close relationship between copulation, conception and birth is often seasonal and sporadic. In the childless world of this film the circulation of sexual and car-borne traffic is just one form of networking among many others. Desire leads to a recycled sterility of humping bodies, scarred, marked, tattooed, disfigured, repeatedly acting out a pastiche of a ritual ceremony premised not on the sacred but the profane. Instead of ritual sacrifices to the deity, the sacrificial unconscious is harnessed to the worshipping of transient machines whose crashes mimic the disfigurement of the bodies within them. The taboo here consists not in any restraint upon the nature or variety of the sex act, even though there are multiple permutations of car and body to rile the censors. The real taboo to be broken is in actively thinking that any one of these acts can bring forth life. In the machine age the film decisively severs the connection of sex and procreation.

Cronenberg may well have been inspired to film Ballard's book by Baudrillard's notes on the novel's powers of simulation and if so, the Dean crash scenario which is not in the book may well be passing homage to the French maestro.[9] After all Baudrillard had said the book surpassed the normal sci-fi plot hinging on machine malfunction to create a state of total immersion in the network, where any alternative to the matrix of Eros, machine and death was now unthinkable. This is only made possible, however, because the filming of *Crash* testifies to a real world of suburban Toronto which at times seems to stretch beyond any horizon, and is so featureless it could be any like city in the Western world. This is Cronenberg's own territory and that in part must account for his sureness of touch. The territory is a dense fragmented layering of concrete landscapes, damaged machines and addictive desires, a world without end both real and artificial at the same time. Although he self-consciously uses simulation for the mythic re-enactment of the celebrity crash, to speak of the separation of the real from the simulated here, or the displacement of one by the other, has no genuine meaning. It is the filmic framing of a tactile territory that gives the simulated genuine conviction.

Kieślowski's use of Warsaw and Paris also provides defining contrasts of city life, of the polar opposites of fatality and freedom where the car is, at critical moments, a defining presence. *Blue* and *A Short Film about Killing* both have the distinctive look of Slawomir Idziak's cinematography and, prompted by Kieślowski, his decisive use of filters. Indeed the Warsaw film could well have been named 'a hundred colours green' as varying hues of sea and slime coat the lenses of the camera in charting the inferno of Jacek's drift into mayhem and disaster. One of the many accomplishments of the film is the perfect fusion of movement through space and time. Its duration is a day in the life of Warsaw and of three characters unknown to one another, whose fates intersect. As well as Jacek, the young drifter, there is the cynical cabbie he will brutally murder and Piotr, the moped-bound lawyer just accepted to the bar, who will later defend him in court. The lawyer makes unwitting contact with both of them before one murders the other. His moped pirouettes through traffic after his successful interview, prompting contempt from the nameless taxi-driver, while he later meets with his girlfriend in the café where Jacek brings comic relief to his desolate journey by pinging cream from his éclair at two girls watching him through the window.

Kieślowski gives us parallel subjectivities of motion in the city – foot, moped, cab – and captures in the movement of each the varying rhythms of the soul, naive optimism, cruel cynicism and pathological despair. The parallel cutting suggests three people partially enclosed in their own worlds, inaccessible to others yet sharing the same time-space circuit. Here the dense filters which govern Jacek's point of view always channel us towards the image at the centre of the frame, fore-shadowing the tunnel vision which Kieślowski uses to such effect in *Blue*. There seems in Jacek's case no difference between how he sees the city and how he would choose to see it. It is almost as if the city is seen for him by some irresistible force, which turns out to be a force of evil. In the instance where he looks over the bridge leading to the Old Town on to the road beneath, he frames the look through his crooked elbow. In a New Wave movie this might come across as a spontaneous impulse. Here it suggests something darker, a human gesture confirming something predetermined, which is above and beyond its control.

The taxi-driver, meanwhile, ignores the pleas of beleaguered city-dwellers to pick up the sociopath destined to strangle him in real time, all seven minutes of it, in the stillness of countryside outside city limits. He is pure victim and yet, without violating the law, he also already violated our sense of trust. Without knowing it, Jacek takes a vicious revenge on something that embodies the callous indifference he senses in city life. Kieślowski's film finds solitude and the absence of trust in a society officially governed by communalist rhetoric, yet this is not anti-Party polemic. It is rather an image of social solipsism suggesting impending breakdown. The sociopath lies outside the official domain of the 'socialised' community while, likewise, the taxi-driver has more feeling for his car than for his fellow-beings. The art of wonder which lies at the core of meta-modern film here breaks down, or rather crosses over towards the disconnections of the hyper-modern, Kieślowski at the cinematic frontier of East and West. Tarkovsky's legacy, strong throughout his Polish films, lies in the abiding sense of fate beyond the frame, but fate here is catastrophe at the edge of the abyss. All traces of wonder have evaporated as breakdown assumes a tragic form. There is something prophetic in this film made in 1988 under the weakening constraint of martial law, that heavy shadow of military politics cast across the Dekalog. It suggests with no obvious hint of politics a system that is crumbling beyond repair. The communal no longer exists, and the cab is a viral carrier of distrust before it becomes the site of a terrible crime.

In *Blue* things change. The colour of freedom was a highly conscious choice and it is Kieślowski's expert un-Western eye that beams in on freedom's difficulties. Unlike the camera style of *Nil by Mouth* with its blocking devices, its steady panning shots, its deep compression, that of *Blue* gives us the determination of the hand-held tracking shot to match the determination of Binoche's stride. This is the look of uncertain transformation, that jagged changing of identity forced by bereavement, linear rather than circular, the new *arrondissement*, the new address, the new life. At each stage Binoche has to make a decision about her life, to withdraw or return, to be connected or disconnected, to live or to die. Freedom counts, is weighted with every moment, far from the fatal timbre of *Killing* where blind chance is turned, in a single moment, into iron necessity. In *Red* chance takes on a different hue as the accident in which the dog is run down in the street by her car leads Jacob to the suburban house of Trintignant and to her witnessing of the telephonic voyeur, tapping into everyone's conversations in the neighbourhood. Thus Kieślowski integrates theme and style, story and look in matching Geneva, the city of atoms where cars run down dogs, to Geneva, the city of bits where intimate conversations passing through invisible cables are intercepted for the pleasure of the judge turned idle voyeur.

In the film text with no car fetish, a cinematic city without cars as obvious icons, movement is not necessarily more innocent, as Wong Kar-Wai proves in Hong Kong or Tran Anh Hung's *Cyclo* proves in Saigon. The city as a tragic site is rarely engaged but it is here on the margins between ideological systems, Saigon in Tran's film where its other name is Ho Chi Minh City. We could say that in Tran's Vietnamese films there is a reverse mirroring of Kieślowski's frontier between East and West on the other side of the globe, in that same aura of the art of wonder which turns tragic and disintegrates. Like *Crash*, both *Killing* and *Cyclo* take the circulation of traffic, noisy, monotonous, banal, as a source of impending death. The cyclo-cab and the taxi become metonyms of catastrophe for their young riders. In *Cyclo*, as in the films of Wong Kar-Wai, there lurks a menacing sense of space compressed, peopled by bodies moving at all angles in all directions, and of no clear boundaries between interior and exterior. In *ChungKing Express* and *Fallen Angels* space is inside and outside at the same time and Western conceptions of privacy seem inapplicable. Wong's aesthetic also points to something more fundamental which links him back to Egoyan and Kieślowski: lived city experience as pure coeval disconnection. His dynamic use of step-printing and film speed, where the action of close-in characters can speed up or slow down like a narcotic reflex against a background shot in real time, matches lived experience to spatial dislocation. This is the city moving from real time to narcotic time, and disoriented space adjusting accordingly.

The metonymic rush of the hand-held camera perfected here by Chris Doyle has its low-budget echoes in the European city too. We can think of *Last Of England* and, ten years on, of Kelemen's *Fate* and Nikolas Winding Refn's *Pusher,* in which the camera is both travelling witness but also at times disoriented junkie, too much in a rush to notice its surroundings. *Pusher* stands in contrast to much of Dogme '95 in one respect. It is a film of the living city. Apart from the incisive opening of Thomas Vinterberg's *The Greatest Heroes*, Copenhagen is, to date, largely absent from its body of work. Refn's film, on the fringe of the Dogme movement, more than atones. It is a hand-held location shoot using available light, and edited in the medium in which it is filmed. Its small-time gangster ambience may echo Scorsese and *Mean Streets*. Yet its sense of fatality has more in common with *Killing, Cyclo* or *See How They Fall*. Frank, a small-time dealer in the Vesterbro district, blows a deal and owes to a Balkan gangster who applies to him the same terror he in turn has applied to all his small-time users – cyclical journeys, rotation, constant doubling, cyclical fate. This picaresque yet stoic odyssey of no exit creates its own sense of city time as brutal duration quickening with the pulse of doom.

Wong's aesthetic holds here too, where speed can be a form of oblivion, a space-time compression in which you have no time to gauge where you are or indeed care and perspective is lost in the blur of deranged subjectivities which are none the less outer not inner experiences, uncannily real and not fantastic. Here the trope of alien-ation seems somehow too old-fashioned to critique what is happening, because too much is happening and the filmic city-dweller is at the centre of its excess. Moreover that other form of presence that is not spatial sends excess into overdrive. Spatial presence has to battle with telepresence in everything, from daily routine to secret desire. The communications revolution of the information age accelerates this sense of solitude rather than alleviating it – think of the dislocating role of the telephone in *Red* or *L'Appartement* or the use of the moving image in *Family Viewing*. Irony here is not cool à la Tarantino but melancholic and cues in the materialism of solitude as modernity's current fate in the city.

*Chapter 7*

# FRENCH OR AMERICAN?
# THE TIME-IMAGE IN THE 1990s

———⟶⟵———

In the 1990s French film and American film have formed a fascinating contrast in the adventures of the time-image, which comes, so to speak, full circle. For Deleuze had seen the primal source of the time-image in two key figures of the neo-modern era, Welles and Resnais, both forging over forty years ago the landmark narrative forms which remain with us. These, of course, were not the only cinematic possibilities. We have already seen how the time narratives of *Mirror* or *Ulysses' Gaze* work in the cinema of wonder, how Tarkovsky's aesthetic of 'sculpting in time' stresses the duration of time in the shot and the sequence as a key to cinematic rhythm as such. Yet in his use of editing, Resnais is closer to Welles than to Tarkovsky. That affinity is part of the Atlantic alliance of the Gallic and the American, and while it is weaker now than in the 1960s, key continuities remain. The *Cahiers* critics have always enthused over American directors from Hitchcock, Hawks and Ford in the 1950s to Ferrara, De Palma and Tarantino in the 1990s. Conversely the creative flow has often gone in the other direction. From the New Wave onwards, American cinema has borrowed quite extensively from French film, from its depth and variety of theme, its power of innovation and its virtuoso variations in style.

The French connection is also fascinating because of deep differences in the two cinemas. Earlier, we set the time-image of Resnais's *Providence* against the streamlined time-travel of Hollywood science fiction. We might now recall another source of genre time-travelling, Chris Marker's short film of 1962, a photomontage entitled *La Jetée*.

Not only does it echo Resnais's vision of temporality in its meditation
on the ruins of war. The still images charting the aftermath of nuclear
war are haunting for a deeper reason. They chart the pathos of irreversible time. The hero, an experiment-victim of a new totalitarian
regime, has an exceptional memory and through it is projected back
to seek out the beautiful woman he had watched as a child at Orly
airport. Thrust back into the past, he tries in vain to change the terrifying future still to come. Terry Gilliam acknowledges *La Jetée* as a
key source of *Twelve Monkeys*, where the climactic airport sequence
shows Bruce Willis trying, and failing, to alter future catastrophe. The
pathos of Marker's time-trope is equally present in films as diverse
as *The Terminator* and *Contact*. Yet the stillness at the centre of Marker's
images is lost in the hyper-modern melodrama of the spectacle-image.

Here the streamlined time-travel of Hollywood obliterates the
pattern of Resnais and Marker. To use Deleuze's terminology to reverse
Deleuze, it subordinates the time-image to the action-image. The
quest to reverse time, as in the Terminator films, may start out as the
pathos of the impossible task. Yet it soon becomes a launch pad for
prolonged action sequences, restoring to narrative the sensory-motor
functions which, Deleuze insists, the 'pure optical and sound situation'
of the time-image had disconnected.[1] The glitter of hardware replaces
the uncanny image of time suspended. The alternating fear and thrill
of disaster replace the puzzle of time passing. Reflexively, the sci-fi
plot (heroic) to save the world, which follows from the apocalyptic
plot (evil) to destroy it, becomes in the process a plot easily followed
by a mass audience, a ploy to entice them by transforming time back
into impact, metaphysics back into suspense. In this respect its new
hybrid form is not the action-image of classical Hollywood film but
something new, a spectacle-image providing the narrative drive of
horror and science fiction.

This, then, is the dilemma. The spectacle-image takes convenient
short cuts. It replaces the fallible human with the infallible machine. The
metaphysics of time and mortality at one level are unthinkable, for how
can human time be reversed? The answer is by drafting them into the
spectacular event, for which special effects, morphing and cyborg motifs
are all *de rigueur*. Train of thought, in this formula, is overtaken by the
speed of the event. By saving the world from extinction, the cyborg saves
the mind from the unthinkable, the nature of time itself. The Deleuzian

movement from classical to modern, from action-image to time-image, is not so much reversed, since no one can go back again. Rather, time narrative is absorbed into the spectacle-image by an 'impact aesthetic' of imaginary futures and imaginary planets. Time is time future, terrestrial space is always determined elsewhere. Yet as we have also seen, the spectacle-image can apply to the immediate past, as it does in *JFK*. Stone turns a form of tragic public spectacle into a sustained spectacle-image. Every narrative flashback ordained by Costner's voice keys in a display of virtuoso montage, aspiring to be fact but addicted to impact. For impact, in Stone as in Cameron, is the mythic underlay of truth.

Outside of Hollywood things have been very different, and the cineastic exploration of time is often inseparable from the frail, half-formed nature of identity. In the 1990s, key films by figures as diverse as Kieślowski, Egoyan, Almodóvar and Wong Kar-Wai testify to this fractured match between figures searching for a future self and spiralling backwards as they do so into a past they have still to discover. In *The Sweet Hereafter* Egoyan blends past and present so seamlessly that often the flashback appears as a forward movement, a continuity montage seeming to resemble duration yet signifying time reversing. In Almodóvar's *Live Flesh* the recent past comes full circle through the miracle of childbirth on a transit bus. In the metropolitan struggle of line and circle, which re-appears in the Parisian time-image of Rivette's *Secret Défense*, the adult Victor (Liberto Rabal), born on the Franco bus twenty years ago, now travels Madrid's circle line in a mock repetition of his unorthodox origin.[2] Politics crystallises in the twenty-year flash-forward as he changes from crying infant into raw adult. The bustling streets of the 1990s replace the silent streets of the 1970s as a democratic Madrid throws into relief its grim Francoist past. Yet if Victor repeats the past, he also outlives it. For Almodóvar, the tragedy of the present is the tragedy of a particular form of freedom, in which people can ruin by chance the lives of others, and have to live with the consequences. At the same time, in moving forwards they have the freedom to make their own decisions and enact psychodramas the world of dictatorship had denied to the previous generation. Almodóvar's tone here blends the active and contemplative in a form of dynamic meditation.

Just as Egoyan's time-meditations in *The Adjuster* and *Exotica* are Canadian deconstructions of Hollywood narrative, so *Live Flesh*, one of the major Spanish films of the late century, has a key adjacency to the French time-image. During the French New Wave, the double formation of the time-image had separated out in the work of Resnais and Rivette. In Resnais's films, the key trope is time-as-past or how time returns. In Rivette's films it is time as duration, or how time unfolds. Both are indispensable elements in neo-modern narrative yet stylistically Resnais and Rivette inhabit different worlds. The power of Almodóvar's film lies in its capacity to blend these worlds so seamlessly together. The double flash-forward, Victor as bus baby to Victor as unwitting gunman and thence to Victor as ex-con, creates a superb tension of ellipsis, of time-as-return. Time as duration, on the other hand, is embodied, literally, in the fate of his main protagonist. Javier Bardem plays Victor's cop victim, David, who is disabled and made paraplegic by the accidental bullet. Bardem, whose archetypical machismo had been mocked and celebrated in Luna's *Jamón! Jamón!*, gives an extraordinary performance of wheelchair endeavour, not only in playing basketball but in the sheer tenacity of putting his rival's love-life under surveillance. As he negotiates the ramp up to Victor's makeshift apartment or manoeuvres himself out of chair into car, time slows into real time so that its impact becomes visceral in the mundane activities normally taken for granted by able-bodied spectators. Almodóvar moves fluently across the wide spectrum of the time-image, and in doing so seems to encapsulate an epoch of Spanish history.

In American noir of the 1990s, the vision of the past also changes. It goes beyond its organic 1940s role as a formulaic flashback of passionate conspiracy to become more visceral, enigmatic, unfinished. If sexuality is more explicit and gender roles change, the past becomes more mysterious, more oblique than ever. The legacy of Welles and Hitchcock is revered by being transformed. We can see the strong influence of Hitchcock at work in the time-inflected passions of *Kill me Again* or *Liebestraum*, that of Welles in the temporal ambiguities of *One False Move* and *The Usual Suspects*. Situated action of course dominates these films but the relationship of the action-image and time-image is reordered in the diegesis. For it is the past which moves the present forwards, galvanises it, interrupts it and gives it the urgency of its tragic rush towards violence and destruction.

The filmic renewal of the time-image lies precisely in this exploration of the radical uncertainty which exists within the cultural fabric of the age. There is nothing pathological in this. The 'JFK' scenario unwittingly demonstrated that often the more we investigate, the more we find that we do not know. Accordingly, the power of the filmic image to represent is called into question, because the mapping of the plot linking disparate layers of time is always suspect. In Bryan Singer's *The Usual Suspects*, brilliantly scripted by Christopher McQuarrie, time is suspect because motive is suspect. Indeed Singer's 'usual suspects' prove to be highly unusual. Not only do they cast a question mark over plot and action – who did what, when, where and how? They also cast a shadow over character, prompting not only the leading question, 'Who is Keyser Soze?', but also the wider question, 'Who, exactly, are any of these characters we have seen on screen over the last two hours?' How much or little of what Kevin Spacey says are we entitled to believe? Lynch's *Lost Highway* poses the same questions with a different emphasis. What 'characters' are Bill Pullman, Patricia Arquette and Balthazar Getty actually playing? Is Dick Laurent also Mr Eddy? When did the intercom voice, which starts and ends the film with its grisly utterance, 'Dick Laurent is dead,' take effect? Viewers and reviewers have come up with very different answers or with no answers at all. One thing is for sure. The lack of clear answers means that solution and resolution vanish into the void. Neither of these films is a recognisable Hollywood picture. In the elusive figures of Keyser Soze and Verbal Kint, Fred Madison and Dick Laurent, one recalls instead the shadowy figure of Welles's Gregory Arkadin.

Lynch's career provides a practical variant on the French connection. His producer is the French independent, CiBy 2000, who also produces Wenders and Almodóvar, and while Americans scratched their heads over the most puzzling film in Lynch's repertoire, *Le Monde* and many French critics proclaimed it a masterpiece. The perverse pattern echoes that of *Touch of Evil* in 1958, American rejection followed by French adulation. A few years earlier, the project of *The Usual Suspects* seemed headed at pre-production stage for the same fate of American indifference. The story had been pitched around Hollywood for over two years to meet a similar blank response, and the film's eventual triumph under the Polygram label went against all odds. It had the surety of the gangster genre, but even there it went into deeper territories of incertitude than either Scorsese or Tarantino had done before it. Though both directors play ingeniously and triumphantly with the time-image, they both invent knowable worlds to frame its appearance and its destiny. For Scorsese the gangster play is existential and the multiple voice-overs in *Goodfellas* and *Casino* help us recover segments of the American past, like the multiple voice-overs of *Kane*. They do so with that flair for lyrical detail that has become Scorsese's trademark. For Tarantino, time looping is a neat way of matching suspense to deadpan irony, its payback the knowable product of a repetition that reveals all. *Pulp Fiction* ingeniously meanders, pretends to lose the plot and to be in danger of eluding its audience, but finally delivers by returning to its point of origin, in vindication of its strategy of narrative cool. *Lost Highway* and *Suspects* offer no such consolation. The surety of the world is ever-vulnerable, prone at all times to that nuclear core of the Wellesian time-image, the powers of the false, where certainty in a land founded on the rhetoric of truth and discovery evaporates.

The renewed time-image in these two films fuses the powers of the false with that other hyper-modern structure of feeling, coeval disconnection. Different sheets of time and space are co-present on the same diurnal plane. Not only do they cue the experience of information overload but, more profoundly, experience of the void of knowledge within the vortex of that overload. Coeval disconnection fractures the empirical continuities of time, creating discontinuities experienced within the screen by the bemused protagonist and outside the screen by the uncertain viewer. A poetic unity proceeds from this *fin de siècle* fracturing, an elevation of time-sequence in Deleuzian terms on to a higher plane of image-consciousness. This same unity is to be found in three French films of the 1990s that renew the time-image by challenging our view of the past – *L'Appartement, Regarde les Hommes Tomber (See How They Fall)* and *Secret Défense*. The key to their success lies here in matching time present and its tactile world to the quandaries of time past. Their narratives play to our sense that the past which matters most to us will also elude us, for which reason we try all the harder to resurrect it, to bring it to the present as truth mummified, preserved and frozen in time. At key narrative moments, we experience a vertigo that comes from not knowing which tense we are in, or which world we inhabit. While the American speciality has often been the power of the false fusing of time with action, the French speciality often lies in the memory-spiral linking imitation to desire. Interestingly, the 1995 thriller of Quebec director Robert LePage, *Le Confessional*, lies at the cultural intersection of these two time-images. It remakes Hitchcock's *I Confess* as part of its own story, which integrates the time and place of Hitchcock's film, 1952 Quebec, with that of its own, 1989 Quebec, crossing culture and language as it crosses generations, creating a darker mood for the corruptions of its own age than for the hypocrisies of the previous one.

Canadian cineaste LePage clearly shows his Francophone heritage. For the French memory-spiral launches itself on a rampant cinephilia risking all and triumphs only by the thinnest of margins. Self-conscious homage and transcendence of Hitchcock are equally apparent in *L'Appartement*, Gilles Mimouni's first feature shot in Paris. Here we can trace a myriad of cinephile images. There is a double-edged homage to Hitchcock in which Mimouni recreates the three women of *Vertigo*, Madeleine, Judy and Midge, as Lisa, Alice and Muriel, two of them also doubles, from whom Max (Vincent Cassel) must choose. Cassel's piercing blue eyes are dead ringers for Stewart's in *Vertigo* and in *Rear Window*, whose courtyard is also evoked in the first spying sequence where Max watches Lisa (Monica Bellucci) from an opposite apartment. The film has the romantic feel and surge of early Truffaut, echoed in the impromptu dance to Charles Aznavour's haunting, apposite 'Le Temps', a song played twice over in different time frames. The swift forward track and zoom of the camera to meet its subject's advance, and to reverse-angle the lover's gaze, is a style-echo of Bertolucci's great Parisian film *The Conformist*. If that was not enough, the melding of Art Nouveau and Art Deco interiors with Gaudiesque touches recalls the poetic realism of Alexander Trauner's designs for Marcel Carné. The narrative backrush of time is indebted to Resnais while the moral densities of desire echo those of Rohmer, whose *Full Moon in Paris* also plays on the doubling of apartments. The film echoes a recent rival, Claude Sautet's *Un Cœur en hiver*, in its dissection of a passion shadowed by the same-sex friendships of its two lovers.

In *Secret Défense* Rivette has absorbed filmic echo more seamlessly into his narrative. Research scientist Sylvie Rousseau (Sandrine Bonnaire) recalls the solitary Parisian women of Rohmer, Godard and Kieślowski, not to say the terror faced by Bridget Fonda, heroine of *Single White Female*, the New York thriller of Rivette's ex-colleague,

Barbet Schroeder. Bonnaire's firm striding into a set of circular journeys recalls the martyred drifter she had played in Agnès Varda's *Vagabonde*, while her martyrdom is a perfect match for the historic martyrdom she had shown in Rivette's previous film *Jeanne la Pucelle*. Her gaunt face and virtuous stalking of arms industrialist Walser (Jerzy Radziwilowicz) also recall Krystyna Janda's hyperactive quest after the same actor in Andrzej Wajda's *Man of Marble*, but with a knowing difference. In Wajda's Polish masterpiece, Radziwilowicz had played Birkut, a fresh-faced hero of labour. Here as the German Walser, he is a devious proprietor of missile technology. Indeed the referencing seems effortless and infinite. The cool whites and blues of office and laboratory echo the clinical hygiene of Antonioni's design for *The Red Desert*. Hitchcock's middle period is also present in the clear plot-echoes of *Dial M for Murder* and *Strangers on a Train*, while the look-alike sisters in *Psycho*, Janet Leigh and Vera Miles, are signified by the doubling of sisters Véronique and Ludivine. That in turn appears as Rivette's knowing version of 'the double life of Véronique', a nod to Kieślowski with more sinister intent.

If the two films are full of film history as a form of time past, they are even more full of time as duration within narrative itself. The present does not stand still long enough for us to recapture the past and yet those past secrets, which the present reveals to us, turn out to be the seeds of destruction. Time is not the great healer but the great destroyer, a volcanic eruption threatening to send all movement into reverse. Yet as the present always moves on, so the eruption sets up a contrapuntal movement out of which tragedy is born. In Jacques Audiard's *See How They Fall*, this movement is one of adjacency. Audiard's first feature, made in 1993, about a contract killing and a stake-out gone wrong, starts with a reverse similar to the one used two years earlier by Tarantino in *Reservoir Dogs*. Tarantino's gangster film about a heist gone wrong had begun with its violent ending then cut back to its very beginning. In contrast, *See How They Fall* runs a parallel montage between the overlapping stories of failing salesman Simon Hirsch (Jean Yanne) and no-hope drifters Marx (Jean-Louis Trintignant) and Frédéric (Matthieu Kassovitz) until their paths finally cross. The novelty is the use of parallel tales within different time-planes. Yanne is tracking down the two killers of a cop acquaintance. Their story, *prior* to the actual killing, is told in conjunction with his own as he searches for them, vengefully, in time present. Each of the narratives is weighted and spaced as if they are happening in the same time frame, and we experience them as coeval. In fact they are sequential. As a result the narrative moment as their paths first cross entails continuity in one story, that of Yanne, but time-ellipsis in the other, that of Trintignant. Yanne's tale is linear and moves the present forwards whereas Trintignant's tale suddenly jumps from the past into the future and moves him inexorably towards his own death.

*See How They Fall* and *L'Appartement* share the same challenge to viewing as their characters face on screen. Just as they struggle to find out what has happened in the past, so do we as spectators, but we undergo that process by a different route. We are forced to keep in mind each detail of what has previously happened while taking in what is currently happening. This is not so much the effortless pleasure of the invisible narrative, more the forcible concentration upon the elusive mystery. Unlike *See How they Fall*, Mimouni's film does not signal in advance the coming darkness it contains at its core. It cues us into a romantic comedy of errors and becomes, in the spirit of Renoir, a breathless love-farce ending on a tragic note. Even its mishaps of passion have their own comic enchantment, Max when he recalls rescuing his first date with Lisa after all seemed lost, or later when he rescues Alice (Romaine Bohringer) from a fall at the apartment window, thinking her to be Lisa. Yet the main theme is one, like Resnais's *Marienbad*, that matches Hitchcock to Proust, time to suspense, remembrance to mystery. Instead of Resnais's cerebral metaphor of seduction-as-knowledge, however, Mimouni reverts to source, the Hitchcockian pathos of seduction-as-image. Thus in his quest to recapture time-as-passion, Max feels time receding and redoubles his efforts to resurrect lost love, only for it to slip through his fingers once more.

Mimouni remakes *Vertigo* with a Francophile slant. As the hapless, hyperactive Max, Cassel's curse is his double infatuation, first with the image of Bellucci, which he sees on videotape, and then with Bohringer, the real-life copy who imitates her best friend to gain his attention. Mimouni gives us in Bellucci and Bohringer separate body images whose appearances briefly intersect. Like Hitchcock's Stewart, Cassel is aroused by substitutes only because he mistakes them for the original. As a result the time-image of the original woman cannot match the look and flesh of her imitator, who by convention is less beautiful. His distraction by one woman in his search for another proves to be fatal. When Lisa perishes through fire, it is by the caprice of chance, but only because he fails to turn up for the meeting for which he had worked so feverishly. As the plot moves forwards it scrolls backwards, showing us that Alice, who unwittingly brought Max and Lisa together, had always prefaced their movements. It is she who has brought the damaged video of Lisa into Max's shop with the hope of ensnaring him. In the sequence of events, the format is set in stone. Max has already seen the copy (Alice) and the image (video clip) of the original before he sees the original herself.

If image and copy precede the original in a pure delirium à la Baudrillard, the film's title is also a doubling device. To which apartment does it refer? Mimouni doubles the original apartment of the past affair with the apartment of the present, the former cramped and full of life, the latter spacious and empty. The shift is also a move from modest to affluent, from casual to elegant. The current apartment is stylish, the present Lisa sophisticated, the present Max yuppified, the present Alice glamorous. Yet the flashbacks create, paradoxically, a world of greater substance. The film's narrative is a paradox. For its characters have more presence in the past and in memory than they do in the present and in contingency. They have grown into the images of the beautiful people they aspired to become, but are the emptier for it. The new apartment with its sumptuous interiors is more Spanish than French in style and reminiscent of the interior décor of Almodóvar, who also doubles apartments, one seedy, one sumptuous, in that other erotic parable of time, *Live Flesh*. In both films, the apartment can be a place of disorienting, a non-place which human presence fails to fill out. Yet both compare well in this doubled form to the sparse desolation of *Lost Highway*'s suburban home or Bonnaire's apartment in *Secret Défense*, which has the cold look of immense solitude. In these two dwellings, resonating as emotional non-places, the occupiers are not only threatened by voyeurism and the uncanny arrangement of space. The non-place interpolates the uncertainties of time past and time future, and becomes a staging post to disaster.

*See How They Fall* shares the same themes of emulation and desire as *L'Appartement* but lacks its abstract and formal design, which converts the symmetries of desire into rational delirium. Instead of the pattern of social ascent marking off the present from the past, it uses a subtler device of transverse crossover. In present time we follow the descent of Jean Yanne from respectable salesman to maverick investigator to homeless drifter. In past time we witness the ascent of drifters Trintignant and Kassovitz into well-heeled assassins. The film is arguably the most powerful reading of the contract killer in French film since *Le Samourai*, in part because it upsets the noir conventions it uses so well. We are clearly meant to see the male bonding of Marx and Frédéric as homoerotic, but something more is at stake. Kassovitz plays the part of Frédéric as a slack-jawed innocent in a corrupt world, yet his ambiguous role in the plot marks him out as a wide-eyed corrupter, who will enact with Yanne the charade of passion that results in Trintignant's murder. The killer of the lover is a substitute for the lover, who is also a killer, as now is the beloved. The circles of homicidal and homoerotic desire are simultaneously closed.

In Mimouni's regress we accept the convention of the flashback because it turns on the struggle between conflicting points of view, male and female. *The Usual Suspects* presents us with something different: the flashbacks of an unreliable suspect which spiral back into the dark void. The present provides the evidence of disaster, the shattered deck of the blazing ship at San Pedro harbour, on which so many lose their lives. Indeed the gutted hulk is like a floating Xanadu awaiting the story of how it all started. But the dying Keaton (Gabriel Byrne), crooked ex-cop, is not a dying Kane, an enigma to be cross-checked by multiple narratives. His story, or lack of one, is told by Verbal Kint (Kevin Spacey), the gang's sole survivor, and suggests a different version of events. Kint may or may not be Keyser Soze, the monster he narrates as the orchestrator of the bloodbath. Under interrogation by customs agent Kujan (Chazz Palminteri) a cat-and-mouse game ensues in which Kint's story zigzags back towards the present from its elusive starting point, the line-up in New York. The film uses the interrogation device to subordinate the action-image, which is bountiful, to the time-image, which retains its mystery. The time-image of the flashback brings forth body count abundance, terror and revenge killings, casual murder and final slaughter, but how much of it is true we do not know. At the end, as Kujan looks at the names and places Kint has taken from the police notice board and woven fictitiously into his tall tale, we sense the extent of his duplicity but also, after two hours, our own ignorance. For we can never know the ratio of fact to fiction, what is true or what is false. Kint, the narrator, is also the cineaste's double, manipulating Kujan in the way that the director tries to shift around the audience, every so often taking the ground from beneath their feet. The mayhem recounted by Kint is inseparable from the mayhem recounted by Singer himself. The tall tale after all is the director's licence to kill.

The encounter of Kint and Kujan recalls that of Arkadin and Van Stratten in Welles's 1955 film *Mr Arkadin (Confidential Report)*. There are even minor details which McQuarrie and Singer have used – the opening flashback of the assassin who limps like Kint, and whose victim on the Naples quayside suffers the knife in the back like the one which does for McManus (Stephen Baldwin) on the boat in *Suspects*. With his dying breath the unknown victim whispers the name of 'Arkadin', just as the Hungarian sailor burnt to a frazzle and fast expiring in *Suspects* utters the name of 'Keyser Soze'. Like Van Stratten, whom the 'amnesiac' Arkadin hires to investigate his own 'forgotten' past, Kujan must piece together something bearing no official existence. Arkadin's shadowy past is one precedent for the shadowy past of Soze, who may also, however, be Kint. Just as Arkadin confronts the absurd by having someone investigate something he knows only too well, Kujan may be forcing Kint under interrogation to talk about himself, also absurdly, as if he were someone else. Arkadin wants Van Stratten to rediscover the cronies who know about his tainted past in order that he can eliminate them one by one and so preserve his new persona. Likewise, in liquidating the other suspects who form the police line-up and the crew of the burning boat, Soze may well be doing the same thing. Just as Arkadin refuses to be photographed to avoid visual trace, so Soze extinguishes those who may recognise him for the same reason. As Rohmer noted in his brilliant review of *Arkadin* for *Cahiers du Cinéma*, the desperation of this quest to bury recognition is a violation of the past, a rape of time itself.[3] For those who know Arkadin's past have, ironically, no wish to remember it any more while Van Stratten and Arkadin are both obsessed by it. In the same way, the actual reasons for Soze's wish to dispose of the 'usual suspects', how they might have crossed or double-crossed him, are at best red herrings to distract Kujan. They are killed because they threaten the legend.

*Suspects* is at once more radical and more restrained than *Arkadin*. Its police interrogation room maps out a clear point of departure and return for the viewer. The present moves into the past through flashback and is then restored to its known *mise-en-scène*, the tight, windowless office where Kujan and Kint eye each other warily. Thus anchored, the noir overlay lies elsewhere. Most mystery comes from the dark infill of the eerie flashback image, that which cannot be fully seen as it lurks in the shadow, but Kint 'recalls' each episode as a segment in a linear story with a discrete punch line. Here the viewer must piece all the episodes together. True or false, we cannot of course know but evidence of some sort is assembled. In *Arkadin* Welles had done almost the opposite. He lets his wide-angle lens induce distortion and delirium in the enquiring image. The camera stumbles around in the same fog of frenzy as the naive investigator it films, and Wellesian *découpage* allows no resting-place for the battered eye. Constantly altering the angle of the shot through the cut, nearly every shot becomes a disestablishing shot. There are few eye-level matches and no sanctuary from dazzling low-angle distortions for the bemused spectator's gaze. On the other hand the story's climax makes some sense of its complex charade and ends in bittersweet finality. By contrast *Suspects* chances more in its deconstructive ending. It is stylistically contained, genre-centred but narratively bolder. We are then led to a central affinity. Soze and Arkadin are transcontinental legends of gangster capitalism for different generations. The global abyss that Welles had invoked, tough for any audience to take, is replaced here by the image of the all-American wise guy. We know where we are with the iconography of the line-up, even more so with a title taken from *Casablanca*. With the central protagonist the reverse is the case. Where Arkadin has a presence always looming out of the shadows, Soze never leaves them. He is the ultimate unknown, no more and no less than Kint, who has been given mysterious immunity by the DA's office, makes of him in the two hours of interrogation allotted to Kujan. In that sense what we see as viewers is what Kujan gets out of him as investigator.

Both films invoke what Deleuze sees as the essence of modern as opposed to classical cinema, 'the powers of the false'. Yet this is even more complex than he seems to think. Falsehood in our culture works at two different levels, that of ethics and epistemology, which then become hopelessly tangled. Most of the time it is a violation of both the true and the good, but we never know what is absolutely true or what is absolutely right, or how they are related to each other. The time-image is beyond good and evil in Nietzsche's sense, but is also the filmic offspring of Bergson's *durée*. In the French philosopher's theory of duration, time continually challenges the perceptual evidence of the senses so that morality finds itself on shifting sands. Beyond this, however, an implicit value judgement is made by Deleuze, one that separates him from Tarkovsky who, as we have seen, regards the time-image as source of moral strength. In the Western time-image, however, morality is not merely subverted by passage of time, it is more directly challenged through the powers of human deception, a deception of others and of oneself.

Deception is made easier through time passing, but the ontological dilemma remains, since time passing does not explain deception in the first place. To make matters more complex, the cinematic difficulty is also reflexive. It lies both in the nature of film itself, on which both these films reflect, and in a human nature which remains equally opaque. Evil is often intangible in the fabric of the life-world, and so the evidence of the senses is undermined. Yet because time erodes the evidence of the senses, evil becomes more intangible. For Resnais, the dilemma revolves around present judgement of the evils of the past which time makes more elusive. Is the subject who was there and remembers, responsible or complicit? These were the key questions in *Hiroshima mon amour* and *La Guerre est finie*. For Welles, however, the subject is not stained or compromised by being present, or by merely witnessing, but by acting wrongly and knowing it. Welles's subjects are, as he once said of his Joseph K in *The Trial*, guilty from the start. His films explore the nature of that guilt, its murky clandestine depths, as a mix of good and bad, righteousness and evil. Hitchcock, intriguingly, occupies the middle ground. His subjects stand in the shadow between complicity and enactment so that guilt is always ambiguous.

Close affinities between French and American time-images thus remain but shade off at a vital juncture. We can explore intriguing overlaps between Mimouni and Singer, or Lynch and Rivette, buried affiliations of style and theme. Yet we can also detect two different structures of feeling. Rivette, Audiard and Mimouni follow Resnais on the question of the right and the just. Lynch, Tarantino and Singer follow Welles. Max Mayer, Simon Hirsch and Sylvie Rousseau resurrect the past and become complicit in the present. Fred Madison, Verbal Kint and Tarantino's colour-coded 'reservoir dogs' are already living in what Welles once called 'a bright, guilty world'. For the French protagonist, reclaiming the past has tragic consequences. For the American, the past is a web of deception and self-deception, which can yet trigger the escape from present guilt and also from justice itself. In the American time-image, we could say, there are merely degrees of guilt. In the French time-image there are still varying degrees of innocence in the midst of complicity.

The films of Rivette and Lynch both relentlessly track the claustrophobic mindscreen of their main protagonist. Yet their respective styles are as day and night. In Lynch the images springing out of Bill Pullman's gaze are subjective, tight, hallucinatory, psychogenic. In Rivette the image is objectified. The camera, ever a companion to Sandrine Bonnaire's curiosity, none the less observes her with a studious, clinical eye. Each film deals with a common predicament of solitude and suspicion, but in a different way. Pullman finds his predicament turbulent, disorienting, a source of derangement and terror. Bonnaire, as Sylvie Rousseau, finds hers equally intangible but still on the perilous verge of that reason and virtue whose legend her surname embodies. Here we have national differences in the vision of bourgeois malaise. Lynch's southern Californian angst nails down a mindset of paranoid entrapment spiralling into fears of cuckoldry and betrayal, imagining a deadly web of pornographic corruption that is in the air, in the culture, in the bland party networks of LA cocktails and glittering couples. Rivette's Parisian angst, filtered through the scientific reason of Bonnaire, is fed by the lure of curiosity, the regress into dark family secrets contrasting with the hygienic brightness of her laboratory. In both these spaces and in Bonnaire's apartment there are dark corners which seem to evade the rational will, which invite the uncanny disturbance of the sudden and unexpected caller.

In Lynch the intrusion is invisible, a voice with no source on the entryphone, an untitled videotape at the door with no messenger, a zoom through the skylight with no cameraman which shows the couple in the intimate privacy of their own bedroom. Outside is merely the partial vision through slatted windows of a deserted suburban street.

Lynch's desolation is visceral and disturbing. Rivette's solitude is subtle and disquieting. Instead of the lone couple who are also disconnected from each other, we have a lone woman whose independence has banned everyone including her ex-lover from her apartment's lonely interior. Every banal ring on the bell, every ordinary visit, which Rivette naturalises with the same precision that Lynch turns into psychodrama, seems an affront, a moment of uncertainty in a world officially governed by technical expertise and rational certainty.

For both cineastes, the telephone is monstrous. Lynch demonises the instrument while Rivette endows it with a naturalistic terror. Lynch's *coup de grâce* is the figure of the Mystery Man (Robert Blake) in the celebrated scene at Andy's party, who having assured Pullman that they 'met before', advises the distraught sax player to call him on his mobile at Pullman's home. When Pullman obliges, it is as if he were speaking to Satan's double through the miracle of the latest technology. When we later see the Mystery Man with a video camera plugged to one eye by a single hand, the other eye in fanatic gleaming, we have something even more disturbing. The video, like the phone, is a form of techno-rape. For Rivette the telephone is a source of unwanted surprises, the answerphone a source of unwanted obstruction. On the surface it is an active agent of communication allowing Bonnaire to be decisive, to act and place herself within the world. In actuality it is out of her control. She cannot reach people when it is necessary to her but only, it seems, when it is necessary to them. They, on the other hand, tend to call her up when she is least expecting it for reasons she can never quite fathom.

The pattern of chance Rivette sets up is antithetical to any normal distribution of the predictable and the indeterminate. Yet the world created is as nightmarish in its own way as that of Lynch. Lynch's earthquake-rumbling soundtrack, his Baconian blood colours, his segmented Bergmanesque close-ups and apocalyptic techno-rock cue us in to a scenario of metaphysical horror. Rivette's soundtrack, by contrast, seems empty, a brief scattering of natural sounds. No close-ups disrupt a sequence of long shots drenched in Bazinian ontology. This is the daily world to the middle-distant observer with few reverse-angles. Yet it still registers an insidious terror of the unknown, and because the unknown is rooted in Bonnaire's family past, it is something that in the rational scheme of things should be brought into the light of day. The opposite happens. Every current event is a lure to her curiosity about the unfinished past, provoking it, teasing and finally bringing it to breaking point.

Pullman's and Bonnaire's journeys are imagined journeys of vengeance, the former to kill his wife's lover, the second to murder her father's killer. As such they are journeys into the past, journeys to the source of a transgression still shrouded in mystery. They demonstrate the extreme polarities of the time-image. Bonnaire's trip is sane, naturalistic and morally driven. Pullman's hallucinatory 'psychogenic fugue' of an altered state of mind is fittingly cued on the soundtrack by David Bowie's 'I'm Deranged'. In the topography of both films, there is a centre and a periphery, Paris and the country house at Chagny near Dijon, suburban LA and the Mystery Man's shack in the desert. Both subjects journey from one to another in two radically opposed versions of a 'lost highway'. Bonnaire hopes to recover history, Pullman to rewrite it on the verge of execution. In this respect the TGV train out of whose window the perturbed Bonnaire gazes is a naturalistic match for the noirish flicker of the broken dividing line of the desert highway caught in the glow of Pullman's headlamps.

Both films hold and nourish key images of line and circle. Rivette locates his in the mundane train journeys of *aller et retour* which he cunningly turns into a series of circular images overriding the linear route. Each outward journey is a return home. Each return journey to Paris takes Bonnaire back to where she now lives. As Pullman is chased out into the desert by the cops at the end of Lynch's film, he traverses the route he has already taken. The line signifies purpose, resolve, intention. The circle and the return cue in the nightmare from which the subject cannot awake. In both cases, style and context are different. In *Lost Highway* we are at the suburban home one moment and in the desert the next. The space-in-between, of looping freeways and concrete megalopolis, does not exist. The time-space jump is oneiric, a dream-leap into the desert as the non-place of civilisation, the unknown. *Secret Défense*, by contrast, charts different segments of a fateful journey, the changing of trains and stations and the *durée* of the journey itself. It is real time masquerading as dead time, deceptively mundane but in fact the time of resolution when Bonnaire must firm up her decision to kill, and to renew the Electra myth in the ironic form Rivette adopts to subvert the pattern of the classical plot.

Ironically it is Rivette's avenger who is the more existential, who must decide there is no going back. Lynch's narrative has all the compulsion of classical tragedy in which choice no longer seems to exist.

Both films follow Hitchcock as the model for the female double. From *Psycho* Rivette takes on the theme of one sister tracking the mystery disappearance of the other, both played by Laure Marsac. For Lynch's doubling of Patricia Arquette as the dark-haired Renee and the blonde-haired Alice, the model is surely *Vertigo*. Curiously, there are completely different takes on the character by actress and director. Arquette saw herself as playing two different women, whereas Lynch has implied that the two women are the same.[4] A similar ambiguity can be found in Rivette's sisters, Véronique and Ludivine. While Lynch's film oscillates between alternate meanings neither of which crystallises, Rivette's does the opposite. It gives us one reading, obvious and apparent, and another that is subtly buried in his cinematic style. Yet these strategies converge, for both cineastes use filmic doubling to baffle their audience and incite an active spectatorship. In Lynch's doubling of Pullman and Getty, the twenty-four-year-old Pete Dayton replaces the thirty-two-year Fred Madison, surnames courtesy of mid-west cities, and takes his place in the condemned cell without explanation. Later, after lovemaking in the desert, Pete is metamorphosed back into Fred as Alice disappears, naked, into the night. One reading of Lynch's narrative is dreamed transformation, the wish of the condemned man to escape prison through the persona of a youthful lover of his murdered spouse, a project of rejuvenation familiar in the Lynch canon. While Getty is the young lover who gives Alice the sexual satisfaction Pullman has failed to give Renee, the iconic drive of the film goes in the opposite direction. As the haunted cuckold, Pullman's screen presence has a riveting power, which Getty, as the gauche young lover, lacks. As a result it allows Arquette, who is magnificent in both roles, to command the film's middle section as the blonde Alice.

The transformation of Pullman into Getty remains troubling. How can we read 'the wrong guy in the cell', as Lynch puts it, except as supernatural horror? We can pose, as Marina Warner does, the idea of voodoo possession and the spirit world, where in the realm of parallel lives one being takes over another.[5] Alternatively, we can reduce it to derangement, even if the psychic becomes mythical. As a projective fantasy of a man's literal desire for reincarnation in a younger virile body, the doomed Pullman's resurrection call seems to echo the crucified corpse in the Gospels that vanished from the cave. This 'heavenly ascent' into a younger body is, however, doomed by the looping of time before which mere nostalgia for youth is helpless. If Getty is both innocent and virile, he in turn undergoes a change that will bring him to the point of breakdown Pullman has already reached. He can only grow, that is, into damnation and derangement. There is a constant tension here between dream and narrative, which goes to the heart of film itself. Dream freezes in time at the moment of desire but narrative projects it forwards to the point at which time betrays desire.

Rivette's film also raises the question of contrary readings, but with a mere hint rather than a fanfare. The upfront reading is itself complex. It is an existential twist on the classical plot of Electra's revenge. Instead of avenging her father and sister by killing Walser, Sylvie shoots his secretary, Véro, by accident in the struggle for her gun. Starting out to perpetrate one form of destiny, Sylvie ends up as the victim of another. Walser later tells her the source of her father's murder lay not in business envy but in his abuse of her teenage sister, selling her, according to Walser, for sexual favours to a client in order to clinch an arms contract. Bonnaire appears to miscalculate twice over, failing to find the reason for her father's murder and her sister's suicide, and then compounding her error through accidental killing. Rivette's measured irony here replaces one form of fate, classical and determined, by another, existential and modern. Sylvie, notably, fails to live up to her name Rousseau, the name of her father that she wishes to avenge, since her 'authentic virtue' tragically mistranslates into the actual world of justice.

For any knowing cinephile, however, Rivette's prehistory is even more loaded than that of Lynch. The American plays on a straight preference for the virile innocence of the young male, James Dean-style, against the corrupt ways of his deranged seniors, Kyle MacLachlan against Dennis Hopper or Nicolas Cage against Willem Dafoe and Crispin Glover. Rivette's prehistory points us in a rather different direction. The puzzling instance of the clash of actorly styles in *Secret Défense* becomes clearer if we remember the force of illusion running through *Paris nous appartient*, *Céline et Julie* and the start of *La Belle Noiseuse*. Here endless rehearsal, charade and the house of

illusions dissolve Bazinian ontology, which often appears second
nature in his *mise-en-scène*. The killings of the two women in Le
Domaine seem like theatrical events, staged happenings that contrast
with Parisian transparency. It is not only a tale of two places, city and
country, but also a tale of two styles. The city is Bazinian, le Domaine
at Chagny filmed in the low-key lighting of 1940s melodrama. While
Bonnaire's performance is a naturalised version of the rational investigator driven by curiosity about events in her own past, Walser's
secretary seems at times to be acting out a role under Walser's
prompting, a ploy Rivette keys obliquely into the respective nicknames
of the two sisters, Véro and Ludi, 'truth' and 'play'. More than once
Sylvie accuses Walser of playing games, of toying with her, and more
than once Walser comes across as a ludic impresario, effortless in his
mastery of the game he does not even acknowledge. Here we leave
the world of fate in its Greek sense and enter the modern world of
paranoia and conspiracy. Is Walser, the German industrialist, an
update of Lang's sinister Mabuse, forging diabolical plots but without
appearing to do so?

   This reading, which takes in the game-playing nature of Walser and
theatrical ploys of Véro and Ludi, launches us on a real paranoia curve.
As played by Marsac, are the two 'sisters' really the same woman,
Walser's lover and confederate? Fearing Sylvie's probe into the murky
past, has Walser staged Véro's 'death' and unseen disposal of the
body and then 'replaced' her with Ludi to prey on Sylvie's guilt and
destroy her? There are faint clues, the ease with which Walser, first
confronted by Ludivino, shows her a secret laboratory in his arms
plant (*secret défense*), invites her to Le Domaine where her sister has
been 'killed' and seduces her, first having introduced her to Sylvie
with sadistic flair. In a telling shot he places her in the shadow of the
hallway and then has her move her head to act out the ploy of
the returning ghost for the bewildered Sylvie. This spectatorship-
paranoia clearly has a logic that enters into the nightmare zone. On
the surface there is a kind of linear country-house plotting comforting
to readers of Agatha Christie or viewers of *Inspector Morse*. In truth
there is no way out of the Rivettian labyrinth. Everything works in
terms of a deceptive timing: Véro's early appearance at Sylvie's apartment before the older woman has decided on her plan of revenge,
Walser's equally sudden appearance there much later to confess to

murder, or near the end, the 'coincidental' meeting with her mother at Dijon station. How much of this is play-acting, the staging of a psychodrama of entrapment, the placing of bait that lures Sylvie deeper into nightmare and finally to her own death? At this stage the paranoia curve goes off the scale. Yet there may be a third reading afoot, somewhere between the two. Walser's flair for improvising allows him to turn the sudden appearance of Véro's sister to his own advantage, to use her, as he uses all the others, as a pawn in his elaborate game to tighten the noose around Sylvie's neck. Ludi is indeed playing games but without her knowledge. Like Verbal Kint, Walser is the mirror-image maestro of the director, reflecting the desire of his maker to pull all the strings at the right moment.

In the fascinating documentary on Rivette made by Claire Denis, his lengthy discussions with Serge Daney reveal many things, and three of clear interest to this film. The first is his deep awareness of the transformation of film time since Antonioni and Deleuze's theorising of it; the second is his fascination with the etymological overlap between the English 'plot' and the French 'complot'; while the third is the sense we get of a solitary Parisian fascinated by the passengers and the movement of trains. Co-written with Pascal Bonitzer and Emmanuelle Cuau, *Secret Défense* brings all three things into play. At each stage there is a rational explanation to allay the fears of the solitary investigator, more vulnerable because female. Yet behind this façade there are always nuances of timing, suggesting a diabolic conspiracy afoot to bring about her destruction. The rules of the science laboratory do not apply to the investigation of family affairs or the nature of power. Where Lynch delivers tangible and screeching villainy, forcing us to bear witness to evil, Rivette focuses on how evidence of crime is concealed, guilt evaded, ambiguity given full dominion. Walser's persona is thus the opposite of Lynch's doubled villain Laurent/Mr Eddy, and in terms of performance Radziwilowicz stands far above the one-dimensional Robert Loggia. Loggia, it is true, comes up with a brilliant road-rage epiphany, but as a whole his character is on a single plane. The persona of Walser has several layers, and Radziwilowicz acts out the part of a natural-born stoic, prepared for any eventuality or accusation that life can throw at him – but he is quite ruthless. Walser's strategy wins because he escapes death, whereas in the immortal words of *Lost Highway*, 'Dick Laurent is dead.'

Deleuze asserted that the conspiratorial atmosphere of Rivette's earlier work may be an apt reflection on the commercial nature of the industry out of which his films are born, a landmark on the Francophone atoll surrounded by a sea of American domination. 'The cinema as art', he wrote, 'now lives in a direct relation with a permanent plot (complot), an international conspiracy which conditions it from within, as the most intimate and indispensable enemy. This conspiracy is that of money; what defines industrial art is not mechanical reproduction, but the internalised relation with money.'[6] This has already been glossed openly by European cineastes with one eye on the American threat, Wenders in *The State of Things* and Godard in *Passion*, but here things are less obvious, more discreet. Part of that lies for Rivette in the discretion of money-power, always adept at concealing its hand, and not just American. Whereas Michel Piccoli in *La Belle Noiseuse* is the cheating artist playing games with his life-model, Walser is the cheating industrialist, cheating to a different scale and design. Piccoli lures his subject into a portrait eventually to be buried in a wall, and an ersatz portrait almost financially worthless to his hapless agent. Walser however deals in real power and real money. *Secret Défense* describes not only the concealed nature of his arms production empire but the methods he employs to maximise its power. While Piccoli and Béart engage in an unequal tug-of-war at the heart of art, Bonnaire and Radziwilowicz act out the unequal tug-of-war in the domain of science. The missile industry wins out over cancer research.

*Lost Highway* uses the same atmosphere of conspiracy but is more direct, if we return to Deleuze, in glossing the hidden source by merely taking a step sideways. The porn industry after all is an offshoot of the movie industry, an ancillary Hollywood with its unofficial mega-buck industry of crooks, hustlers, failed actors and opportunists, now reputedly one-fifth of all film production in Los Angeles. In Lynch's film the ubiquity of porn is in the air, an invisible part of ambience, reeking corruption. It contains an oblique vision of the 'Other Hollywood' in the San Fernando Valley where pornography has become a billion-dollar industry.[7] Loggia is its demonic incarnation. Pullman's be-bop saxophone may well be the strident plea of the ignored artist in a world where the corruptions of the flesh are the more sellable product. Lynch sees only too clearly his filmic project in these terms, the figure on the fringe, out of the loop. Here both films also join forces with *The Usual Suspects*. We have three films disconnecting time from plot but then linking it back to *complot*, to conspiracy. The conspiracy, which comes out of the 'internalised relation with money', produces the resistances that challenge it, a defiance that feeds back, fruitfully, into the art of film itself.

# ENDNOTES

## FOREWORD   THE UNCERTAINTY PRINCIPLE

1. 'Kiarostami's Uncertainty Principle', *Sight and Sound*, June 1998. See also Fergus Daly, 'The Mirror of Possible Worlds', *Film West*, no. 32, 34–8; 'Near and Far: Kiarostami in Interview with Nassia Hamid', *Sight and Sound*, February 1997.

## CHAPTER 1   THE RISE OF HYPER-MODERN FILM

1. John Orr, *Cinema and Modernity*, Cambridge: Polity, 1993, 2–10, 15–28.
2. Marc Augé, *Non-Places: an Introduction to the Anthropology of Supermodernity*, London: Verso, 1995, 116–20. See also Manuel Castells, *The Rise of the Network Society*, Oxford: Basil Blackwell, 1996, 1–29.
3. Fredric Jameson, *Postmodernism, or the Cultural Logic of Late-Capitalism*, London: Verso, 1991, 289–98.
4. For the development of Brazilian Cinema Novo and the Japanese New Wave see, respectively, Randal Johnson and Robert Stern (eds), *Brazilian Cinema*, New York: Columbia University Press, 1982, pt 1 53–81, pt 2 115–234; and David Desser, *Eros plus Massacre: an Introduction to the Japanese New Wave Cinema*, Bloomington: Indiana University Press, 1988, 13–39, 76–108.
5. Gilles Deleuze *Cinema 1: the Movement-Image*, London: Athlone, 1986, 3–24.
6. On the device of remarriage in classical narrative see Stanley Cavell *Pursuits of Happiness: the Hollywood Comedy of Remarriage*, Cambridge, MA: Harvard University Press, 1981.

7.  Peter Cowie, *Annie Hall*, London: British Film Institute, 1996, 23, 26, 48.
8.  Ivone Margulies, 'John Cassavetes: Amateur Director' in Jon Lewis (ed), *The New American Cinema*, Durham, NC: Duke University Press, 1998, 292–4. See also Art Carney, *The Films of John Cassavetes*, Cambridge: Cambridge University Press, 1994, 176–80.
9.  Jacques Aumont, *The Image* (translated by Claire Pajackowska), London: British Film Institute, 1997, 117–18.
10. Angela Delle Vacche, *Cinema and Painting*, London: Athlone, 1996, 66–7, 126–7.
11. The term 'mindscreen' is used and explained by Bruce Kawin in *Mindscreen: Bergman, Godard and First-Person Film*, Princeton: Princeton University Press, 1978, Chapter 1.
12. See Cronenberg's remarks on 'disconnected' sex in *Crash* in Chris Rodley (ed), *Cronenberg on Cronenberg*, London: Faber, 1998, 198–9.
13. For the role of the sublime in science fiction, see Scott Bukatman 'The Artificial Infinite' in Lynne Cooke and Peter Wollen (eds), *Visual Display*, Seattle: Bay, 1995, 266–83; also John Orr, *Contemporary Cinema*, Edinburgh: Edinburgh University Press, 1998, 202–4.
14. Paul Virilio, *Open Sky* (translated by Julie Rose), London: Verso, 1996, 38–45.
15. Geoff Andrew, *The Three Colours Trilogy*, London: British Film Institute, 1998, 55–62.
16. Jean-Marc Lalanne, 'Images from the Inside' in *Wong Kar-Wai*, Paris: Dis Voir, 1998, 19–27.
17. *Signatures of the Visible*, London: Routledge, 1991, 194.
18. See William J Mitchell, *City of Bits: Space, Place and the Infobahn*, Cambridge, MA: MIT Press, 1996, 6–36; Nicholas Negroponte, *Being Digital*, Cambridge, MA: MIT Press, 1995.

CHAPTER 2   HOLLYWOOD AND THE POLITICS OF
VIRTUAL SPECTACLE

1.  For this virtual war of the worlds, see Michael Rogin, *Independence Day*, London: British Film institute, 1998, 73–7.
2.  Mike Davis, *The Ecology of Fear: Los Angeles and the Imagination of Disaster*, London: Picador, 1998, 392–8.
3.  Jon Lewis, 'Money Matters: Hollywood in the Corporate Era' in Lewis (ed), *The New American Cinema*, Durham, NC: Duke University Press, 1998, 98–100.

4. See *My Dark Places: An L.A. Crime Memoir*, London: Arrow, 1997, 292–5.
5. Mike Davis, *The Ecology of Fear*, 3–57.
6. See John Gregory Dunne, 'Law and Disorder', *New York Review of Books*, 10 October 1991; Mike Davis, *City of Quartz*, London: Verso, 1990, 267–77.
7. Mann's script notes for the key meeting between protagonists Pacino and De Niro stress 'cocoon closeness: feeling of pal-ship and intimacy'. 'Bob and Al in the Coffee Shop', *Sight and Sound*, March 1996.
8. Manuel Castells, *The Rise of the Network Society*, Oxford: Basil Blackwell, 1996, 327–76.
9. 'Apocalypse Now' in *Simulacra and Simulation* (trans. Sheila Faria Glaser), Ann Arbor: University of Michigan Press, 1994, 59–61.
10. *Open Sky* (translated by Julie Rose), London: Verso, 1996, 23–4, 131.
11. Paul Edwards, *The Closed World: Computers and the Politics of Discourse in Cold-War America*, Cambridge, MA: MIT Press, 1996, 279.
12. Ibid. 147
13. See Peter Wollen, 'Cinema and Technology' in *Readings and Writings: Semiotic Counter-Strategies*, London: Verso, 1982, 169–77.
14. Walter Murch discusses the sound in *Projections 9*, London: Faber & Faber, 1998; Vittorio Storaro discusses the cinematography in Dennis Schaefer and Larry Salvato (eds), *Masters of Light*, Berkeley: University of California Press, 1984; Dean Tavoularis discusses the production design in 'Setting the Stage', *Cineaste*, Vol. XXIII, no. 4, 1998, 20–4.
15. See Robert Kolker, *The Altering Eye*, New York: Oxford University Press, 1986, 40–65.
16. John Orr, *Contemporary Cinema*, Edinburgh: Edinburgh University Press, 1998, 194–8.
17. For a discussion of impact aesthetics, see Robin Baker, 'Computer Technology and Special Effects in Contemporary Cinema' in Philip Hayward and Tana Wollen (eds), *Future Visions: Key Technologies of the Screen*, London: British Film Institute, 1993, 39–42.
18. Highly prevalent in writings for *Screen* in the 1970s, this critique is best summarised in Colin MacCabe, 'Theory and Film: Principles of Realism and Pleasure' in *Theoretical Essays: Film, Linguistics, Literature*, Manchester: Manchester University Press, 1985, 58–81.
19. Janet Abrams, 'Escape from Gravity', *Sight and Sound*, May 1995.
20. 'Zooming Out: the End of Offscreen Space' in Lewis, *The New American Cinema*, 253.
21. Ibid. 267.
22. Elaine Showalter, *Hystories: Hysterical Epidemics and Modern Culture*, London: Picador, 1997, 189–202.

23. Thomas Disch, *The Dreams Our Stuff is Made of: How Science Fiction Conquered the World*, London: Free Press, 1998, 78–97.

24. Peter Wollen, 'Theme Parks and Variations', *Sight and Sound*, July 1993.

25. Gilles Deleuze, *Cinema 2: the Time-Image*, London: Athlone, 1989, 205–6, 265.

26. Ibid. 207–9.

27. Noel Carroll, *The Philosophy of Horror*, London: Routledge, 1990, 12–42.

28. Klaus Thewelheit, *Male Fantasies 2: Male Bodies: Psychoanalysing the White Terror* (translated by Chris Turner and Erica Carter), Cambridge: Polity Press, 1989, 162–8; also Scott Bukatman, *Terminal Identity: the Virtual Subject in Post-modern Science Fiction*, Durham, NC: Duke University Press, 1993, 302–11.

29. Philip Hayward, 'Situating Cyberspace: the Popularisation of Virtual Reality' in Hayward and Wollen, *Future Visions*, 193–8.

30. On the links between 1960s psychedelia and 1980s Silicon Valley, see Erik Davis, *TechGnosis: Myth, Magic and Mysticism in the Age of Information*, London: Serpent's Tail, 1999, 148–56.

31. Denis Duclos, *The Werewolf Complex: America's Fascination with Violence*, Oxford: Berg, 1998, 169–71.

32. Ibid. 153–67.

33. Erik Davis, *TechGnosis*, 77–8, 93–101.

34. Ibid. 170.

35. Ibid. 235.

36. Zygmunt Bauman analyses the 'new poor' of the information society in *Globalisation: the Human Consequences*, Cambridge: Polity, 1998, 12–16, 96–7.

CHAPTER 3   THE COLD WAR AND THE CINEMA OF
WONDER

1. The bible of global convergence theory in the early 1990s was Francis Fukuyama's *The End of History and the Last Man*, London: Penguin, 1992.

2. Fredric Jameson argues for the existence of a global cinematic system in *The Geopolitical Aesthetic: Cinema and Space in the World System*, London: British Film Institute, 1992. For a critique of the limits of Jameson's theory, see Michael Walsh, 'Jameson and "Global Aesthetics"' in David Bordwell and Noel Carroll (eds), *Post-Theory: Reconstructing Film Studies*, Madison: University of Wisconsin Press, 1996, 481–501.

3. Samuel P Huntingdon, *The Clash of Civilisations and the Remaking of World Order*, London: Touchstone, 1998, 19–39.

4. Philip Fisher, *Wonder, the Rainbow and the Aesthetics of Rare Experiences*, Cambridge, MA: Harvard University Press, 1998, 17–22.

5. Kracauer's discussion of 'special modes of reality' is in *Theory of Film: the Redemption of Physical Reality*, Princeton: Princeton University Press, 1977, 46–59.

6. For this unique fusion of Orthodox iconography and classical myth in the work of the Greek director, see Andrew Horton, *The Films of Theo Angeloupolos: a Cinema of Contemplation*, Princeton: Princeton University Press, 1997, 26–36.

7. John Orr, *Contemporary Cinema*, Edinburgh: Edinburgh University Press, 1998, 140.

8. David Bordwell analyses Jancsó's use of cinematic space through the 1969 film *The Confrontation* in *Narration in the Fiction Film*, London: Methuen, 1986, 130–147. For a brief overview of Jancsó's work, see Robert Kolker, *The Altering Eye*, New York: Oxford University Press, 1986, 311–19.

9. On this theme, Rey Chow discusses Chen's filmic rendering of Daoist aesthetics in *Yellow Earth* in *Primitive Passions: Visuality, Sexuality, Ethnography and Contemporary Chinese Cinema*, New York: Columbia University Press, 1995, 87–107.

10. Andrei Tarkovsky, *Time Within Time: The Diaries* (translated by Kitty Hunter-Blair), Calcutta: Seagull, 1991, 100.

11. *Sculpting in Time: Reflections on the Cinema*, London: Bodley Head, 1987, 57.

12. Ibid. 166–7.

13. Mark Le Fanu analyses the intensive use of the sequence-shot in Tarkovsky's last film, *The Sacrifice*, in *The Cinema of Andrei Tarkovsky*, London: British Film Institute, 1987, 124–38.

14. Tarkovsky, *Sculpting in Time*, 123.

15. Tarkovsky, *Time Within Time*, 5–6.

16. For Tokyo as a cinematic city, see Peter Conrad, *Modern Times, Modern Places: Life and Art in the Twentieth Century*, London: Thames & Hudson, 1998, 675–81.

17. A detailed critique of these themes in Sokurov can be found in Ian Christie, 'Returning to Zero', *Sight and Sound*, April 1998; and Mikhail Iampolski, 'Representation–Mimicry–Death: the latest films of Alexander Sokurov' in Brigit Beumers (ed), *Russia on Reels: the Russian Idea in Post-Soviet Cinema*, London: IB Tauris, 1999, 127–44.

18. David Bordwell, 'Modernism, Minimalism, Melancholy: Angelopoulos

and Visual Style' in Andrew Horton (ed), *The Last Modernist: the Films of Theo Angelopoulos*, Trowbridge: Flick, 1997, 17–22.

19. Bordwell, *Narration in the Fiction Film*.
20. See Jonathan Romney's interview with Angelopoulos in 'Make it Yellow', *Sight and Sound*, May 1999.

CHAPTER 4   CONSPIRACY THEORY: *JFK* AND THE
NIGHTMARE ON ELM STREET REVISITED

1. On the political connections between the Waco and Oklahoma massacres, see Damien Thompson, *The End of Time: Fear and Faith in the Shadow of the Millennium*, London: Vintage, 1999, 278–305.
2. On the vexed question of Kennedy's knowledge of the Castro plot, see Thomas Powers, 'The Spook of Spooks' in *New York Review of Books*, 1 December 1994.
3. On illegal surveillance and burglary during the Johnson and Nixon administrations, see David Wise, *The American Police State: the Government against the People*, New York: Random House, 1976; on FBI surveillance of Martin Luther King, see David J Garrow, *Bearing the Cross: Martin Luther King and the Southern Christian Leadership Conference*, New York: William Morrow, 1986; and Anthony Summers, *Official and Confidential: the Life of J. Edgar Hoover*, London: Corgi Books, 1994.
4. 'Simulacra and Simulation' in Mark Poster (ed), *Selected Writings of Jean Baudrillard*, Cambridge; Polity, 1988, 174.
5. Brian Pendreigh reports that according to Jim Lesar, the lawyer who runs the Assassinations Archive and Research Centre in Washington, the CIA had 'hung onto some really juicy stuff'. See 'Shots in the Dark', *The Scotsman,*12 November 1994.
6. Anthony and Robin Summers, 'The Ghosts of November', *Vanity Fair*, December 1994.
7. See the interview with Stone in *Cineaste*, vol. XIX, no. 1. On the tangled issue of Shaw, fascism and homophobia, see the exchange between Zachary Sklar, co-writer of the *JFK* screenplay, and David Ehrenstein, 'Getting the Facts Straight: an Interview with Zachary Sklar', *Cineaste*, vol. XIX, no. 1 and Ehrenstein's letter 'Jim Garrison as Gaybasher?' with a reply by Sklar in *Cineaste*, vol. XIX, 2–3. Christopher Sharrett has pointed out that Garrison suppressed all reference to the homosexuality of Shaw and Ferrie in the hearings and the trial. See 'Conspiracy Theory and Political Murder in America:

Oliver Stone's *JFK* and the Facts of the Matter' in Jon Lewis (ed), *The New American Cinema*, Durham, NC: Duke University Press, 1998, 225–6.

8. On the circumstances of de Mohrenschildt's death, see Gerald Posner, *Case Closed: Lee Harvey Oswald and the Assassination of JFK*, London: Warner, 1993; and Norman Mailer, *Oswald's Tale: an American Mystery*, London: Abacus, 1996, 440–6.

9. Paul Boyer claims that the film's parody sequence captures the conspiracy thinking endemic in American 'Prophecy Belief' in the post-war period. See *When Time Shall Be No More: Prophecy Belief in Modern American Culture*, Cambridge, MA: Harvard University Press, 1992, 271.

10. According to Ostrovsky, Mossad showed their own film on the training course, 'A President on the Crosshairs', and did simulation exercises of the shooting by using every film and photograph ever taken of the assassination; see Victor Ostrovsky and Claire Hoy, *By Way of Deception: the Making and Unmaking of a Mossad Officer*, New York: St Martins, 1990, 41–3.

11. This was used by CBS in its *48 Hours* programme, 'JFK', 5 February 1992, and further developed by Failure Analysis Associates (FAA) using 3-D scale generations of Dealey Plaza. See Posner, *Case Closed*, 317–18. The FAA programme was used by the prosecution team for a mock trial of Oswald conducted by the American Bar Association, where the jurors voted 7–5 in favour of conviction. See Summers and Summers, 'The Ghosts of November', 43.

12. Bonar Meinunger, *Mortal Error: the Shot that Killed JFK*, London: Sidgewick & Jackson, 1992, 139–81.

13. *Libra*, Harmondsworth: Penguin, 1989, 400.

14. Summers and Summers, The Chosts of November, 38, 43.

15. *Constructing Post-Modernism*, London: Routledge, 1992, 83–5.

16. *The Kennedy Conspiracy* (2nd edn), London: Sphere, 1992, 293–5.

17. Posner, *Case Closed*, 140–1.

18. Posner, *Case Closed*, 173; Summers, *The Kennedy Conspiracy*, 96.

19. Posner, *Case Closed*, 97; Summers, *The Kennedy Conspiracy*, 84–6.

20. Summers' two witnesses were Acquila Clemons, who claimed there were two men at the murder scene escaping on foot in different directions, and Frank Wright, who never publicly testified but claimed to Columbia University researchers that there was only one killer who got into an old grey coupé and drove away. Summers, *The Kennedy Conspiracy*, 487–8.

21. Novelist Robert Stone has dismissed his namesake's claim to be a maker of counter-myths, arguing that Stone was a great simplifier

of moral issues in *Salvador, The Doors* and *JFK,* and instead a creator of complacent liberal myths: 'to the Hollywood official history of the American intervention in Central America and the Hollywood official history of Sixties music, Stone added the Hollywood official history of the Kennedy assassination.' *New York Review of Books,* 17 February 1994. In contrast Robert Hughes slates Stone as a mendacious fabricator of counter-myths. See *Culture of Complaint,* London: Harvill, 1994, 5.

22. Franco Moretti, *Signs Taken for Wonders,* London: Verso, 1988, 135–5.
23. Ibid. 137.
24. *The Crying of Lot 49,* London: Picador, 1966, 128.
25. Paul Coates, *The Gorgon's Gaze,* Cambridge: Cambridge University Press, 1991, 5.
26. Summers, *The Kennedy Conspiracy,* 524–7; Posner, *Case Closed,* 468.
27. For a somewhat cruel gloss on Garrison's paranoia, before and after the trial, see Posner, *Case Closed,* 448–9.
28. Native American leader Dennis Banks, defended by Lane in his 1973 trial after the occupation of Wounded Knee, said that he was a 'good investigator but too conspiracist. He's trying to hook together pieces of evidence whether they fit or not.' Cited in Peter Mathieson, *In the Spirit of Crazy Horse,* London: Harvill, 1992, 88–9.
29. The fictional character of Branch echoes two real-life cases in particular. The first is Fletcher Prouty, a loose model for Donald Sutherland's 'Deep Throat' in *JFK* and adviser on the film. The second is conspiracy buff John Newman, a former major in US army intelligence, who liaised with the National Security Agency. See Sharrett, in Lewis, *The New American Cinema,* 221, 230; Summers and Summers, The Ghosts of November, 62–3.
30. Colson's novel *Kingdoms in Conflict* (1987) is a fundamentalist fiction in which a future US president, a composite of Jerry Falwell and Pat Robertson, arranges the secret demolition of the Dome of the Rock in Jerusalem to make way for the rebuilding of the Jerusalem Temple. See Boyer, *When Time Shall Be No More,* 141–2.
31. DeLillo, *Libra* 300–1.
32. Mailer, *Oswald's Tale,* 617–33, 734–78.
33. On the importance of Capra for Stone, and its effect on creating a persona for Costner very different from the real-life Garrison, see Sharrett, in Lewis, *The New American Cinema,* 235.
34. The essence and curse of ambiguity, which the assassination highlights, is best analysed by Ron Rosenbaum in 'Oswald's Ghost', reprinted in his journalistic essays, *Travels with Dr Death,* London:

Papermac, 1999. In 1983, Rosenbaum discussed Kennedy with conspiracy buff Josiah Thompson, ex-philosophy don and biographer of Nietzsche turned private eye, and concluded 'the JFK case is a lesson in the limits of reason, in the impossibility of ever knowing anything with absolute certainty, Godel's proof and Heisenberg's Uncertainty Principle all wrapped into one' (ibid. 89).

## CHAPTER 5   THE ART OF IDENTITY: GREENAWAY, JARMAN, JORDAN

1. For an analysis of recent British heritage film including Merchant-Ivory productions, see Andrew Higson, 'Re-presenting the National Past: Nostalgia and Pastiche in the Heritage Film' in Lester Friedman (ed), *British Cinema and Thatcherism*, London: UCL Press, 1996, 109–30.
2. Adorno theorises the impersonal nature of the artwork in *Aesthetic Theory* (translated by C Lenhardt), London: Routledge, 1984, 251–68.
3. Details of Channel Four commissioning and transmission, including the films of Greenaway and Jarman, can be found in John Pym, *Film on Four: a Survey 1982–1991*, London: British Film Institute, 1992.
4. Hobbs discusses his ingenious techniques for cut-price design in 'Film Architecture: the Imagination of Lies' in François Penz and Maureen Thomas (eds), *Cinema and Architecture: Meliès, Mallet-Stevens, Multimedia*, London: British Film Institute, 1997, 67–171.
5. Michael O'Pray, *Derek Jarman: Dreams of England*, London: British Film Institute, 1996, 42–6.
6. David Pascoe, *Peter Greenaway: Museums and Moving Images*, London; Reaktion, 1997, 42–6.
7. Bond's dramaturgy is analysed by Jenny Shaw in *Dramatic Strategies in the Plays of Edward Bond*, Cambridge: Cambridge University Press, 1992.
8. On the contributions of Burch and Bonitzer to the discourse of spatial framing, see Jacques Aumont, *The Image* (translated by Claire Pajackowska), London: British Film Institute, 1997, 99–111, 160–73.
9. See his key essay 'The Concept and Tragedy of Culture' in David Frisby and Mike Featherstone (eds), *Simmel on Culture*, London: Sage, 1997, 55–75.
10. Adorno, *Aesthetic Theory*, 337–41.
11. Colin MacCabe, 'A Post-National European Cinema: Derek Jarman's *The Tempest* and *Edward II*' in Duncan Petrie (ed), *Screening Europe*, London: British Film Institute, 1992, 12–14.

12. Jarman discusses these aspects of his childhood in *Kicking the Pricks*, London: Vintage, 1996, 107–9, 115–22.

13. See Terry Eagleton, *Heathcliff and the Great Hunger*, London: Verso, 1995, 305–8.

14. See 'Interview with Neil Jordan' in Brian McIlroy (ed), *World Cinema 4: Ireland*, Trowbridge: Flicks, 117–18.

15. For an analysis of mute male hysteria, and its lack of recognition in the public domain, see Elaine Showalter, *Hystories: Hysterical Epidemics and Modern Cultures*, London: Picador, 1997, 62–80.

16. 'The Cinema of Poetry' in Pier Paolo Pasolini, *Heretical Empiricism*, (translated by Ben Lawton and Louise Barnett), Bloomington: Indiana University Press, 1988, 170–82; also Naomi Greene, *Pier Paolo Pasolini: Cinema as Heresy*, Princeton: Princeton University Press, 1993, 92–127.

17. Martin McLoone, 'The Abused Child of History: Neil Jordan's *The Butcher Boy*', *Cineaste*, vol. XXIII, no. 4, 1998, 32–8.

18. Duncan Petrie, *Creativity and Constraint in the British Film Industry*, Basingstoke: Macmillan Press, 1991, 59–60.

19. Neil Jordan, *The Crying Game*, London: Vintage, 1993, xiii.

20. Jane Giles, *The Crying Game*, London: British Film Institute, 1997, 28–30.

21. Neil Jordan, *Michael Collins: Film Diary and Screenplay*, London: Vintage, 1996, 58–9.

22. Ibid. 37.

23. 'Neil Jordan in Interview with Seamus McSwiney', *Film West*, no. 26, Autumn 1996.

CHAPTER 6   THE REVIVAL OF THE CINEMATIC CITY

1. *Blade Runner*, London: British Film Institute, 1997, 59–63.

2. *Postmodern Fables* (translated by Georges van den Abbeele), Minneapolis: University of Minnesota Press, 1997, 100–1.

3. Ibid. 96–7.

4. Ibid. 26–31.

5. Henri Lefebvre, *The Production of Space*, Oxford: Blackwell, 1991, 28–42.

6. John Orr, *Contemporary Cinema*, Edinburgh: Edinburgh University Press, 1998, 210–21.

7. 'Matthieu Kassovitz: *La Haine*' in Michael Ciment and Noel Herpe, *Projections 9: French Film-makers on Film-making*, London: Faber & Faber, 1999, 188.

8. Iain Sinclair also likens Unger to a 'blonde Ava Gardner, or one of Hitchcock's ice women' and suggests she 'has the presence of a computer-generated simulacrum of a star from the great days of the studios'. *Crash*, London: British Film Institute, 1999, 59.
9. 'Crash' in *Simulacra and Simulation* (translated by Sheila Faria Glaser), Ann Arbor: University of Michigan Press, 1994, 111–21.


CHAPTER 7   FRENCH OR AMERICAN?
THE TIME-IMAGE IN THE 1990s

1. Gilles Deleuze, *Cinema 2: the Time-Image*, London: Athlone, 1989, 41–2.
2. On Almodóvar's circular structures, see Paul Julian Smith, 'Absolute Certainty', *Sight and Sound*, April 1998.
3. Eric Rohmer, 'A Twentieth Century Tale: Orson Welles's *Mr Arkadin*' in *The Taste for Beauty* (translated by Carol Volk), Cambridge: Cambridge University Press, 1989, 135–40.
4. Chris Rodley, 'Funny How Secrets Travel: an Interview with David Lynch' in David Lynch and Barry Gifford, *Lost Highway*, London: Faber & Faber, 1997, xiv–xv.
5. Marina Warner, 'Voodoo Road', *Sight and Sound*, April 1997.
6. Deleuze, *Cinema 2: the Time-Image*, 77.
7. See Edward Helmore, 'Porn Waxes as Movies Wane', *Observer*, 16 September 1999.

# SELECT BIBLIOGRAPHY

Andrew, Geoff, *The Three Colours Trilogy*, London: British Film Institute, 1998

Augé, Marc, *Non-Places: an Introduction to the Anthropology of Super-modernity*, London: Verso, 1995

Aumont, Jacques, *The Image* (translated by Claire Pajackowska), London: British Film Institute, 1997

Bersani, Leo & Dutoit, Ulysses, *Caravaggio*, London: British Film Institute, 1999

Bordwell, David, *Narration in the Fiction Film*, London: Methuen, 1987

Bukatman, Scott, *Blade Runner*, London: British Film Institute, 1997
    *Terminal Identity: the Virtual Subject in Postmodern Science Fiction*, Durham, NC: Duke University Press, 1993

Carney, Art, *The Films of John Cassavetes*, Cambridge: Cambridge University Press, 1994

Carroll, Noel, *The Philosophy of Horror*, London: Routledge, 1990

Castells, Manuel, *The Rise of the Network Society*, Oxford: Basil Blackwell, 1996

Chow, Rey, *Primitive Passions: Visuality, Sexuality, Ethnography and Contemporary Chinese Cinema*, New York: Columbia University Press, 1995

Ciment, Michael & Herpe, Noel, *Projections 9: French Film-makers on Film-making*, London: Faber & Faber, 1999

Conrad, Peter, *Modern Times, Modern Places: Life and Art in the Twentieth Century*, London: Thames & Hudson, 1998

Cowie, Peter, *Annie Hall*, London: British Film Institute, 1996

Davis, Erik, *TechGnosis: Myth, Magic and Mysticism in the Age of Information*, London: Serpent's Tail, 1999

Davis, Mike, *The Ecology of Fear: Los Angeles and the Imagination of Disaster*, London: Picador, 1998

Deleuze, Gilles, *Cinema 1: the Movement-Image*, London: Athlone, 1986
    *Cinema 2: the Time-Image*, London: Athlone, 1989

Delle Vacche, Angela, *Cinema and Painting*, London: Athlone, 1996

Desser, David, *Eros plus Massacre: an Introduction to the Japanese New Wave Cinema*, Bloomington: Indiana University Press, 1988

Duclos, Denis, *The Werewolf Complex: America's Fascination with Violence*, Oxford: Berg, 1998

Edwards, Paul, *The Closed World: Computers and the Politics of Discourse in Cold-War America*, Cambridge, MA: MIT Press, 1996

Elliott, Bridget & Purdy, Anthony, *Peter Greenaway: Architecture and Allegory*, London: Academy, 1997

Fisher, Philip, *Wonder, the Rainbow and the Aesthetics of Rare Experiences*, Cambridge, MA: Harvard University Press, 1998

Giles, Jane, *The Crying Game*, London: British Film Institute, 1997

Hayward, Philip & Wollen, Tana (eds), *Future Visions: Key Technologies of the Screen*, London: British Film Institute, 1993

Higson, Andrew, 'Re-presenting the National Past: Nostalgia and Pastiche in the Heritage Film' in Lester Friedman (ed), *British Cinema and Thatcherism*, London: UCL Press, 1996

Horton, Andrew, *The Films of Theo Angelopoulos: a Cinema of Contemplation*, Princeton: Princeton University Press, 1997

Horton, Andrew (ed), *The Last Modernist: the Films of Theo Angelopoulos*, Trowbridge: Flicks, 1997

Iampolski, Mikhail, 'Representation–Mimicry–Death: the latest films of Alexander Sokurov' in Brigit Beumers (ed), *Russia on Reels: The Russian Idea in Post-Soviet Cinema*, London: IB Tauris, 1999

Jameson, Fredric, *The Geopolitical Aesthetic: Cinema and Space in the World-System*, London: British Film Institute, 1992
*Postmodernism, or the Cultural Logic of Late-Capitalism*, London: Verso, 1991
*Signatures of the Visible*, London: Routledge, 1991

Jarman, Derek, *Kicking the Pricks*, London: Vintage, 1996

Johnson, Randal & Stern, Robert (eds), *Brazilian Cinema*, New York: Columbia University Press, 1982

Jordan, Neil, *The Crying Game*, London: Vintage, 1993
*Michael Collins: Film Diary and Screenplay*, London: Vintage, 1996

Kawin, Bruce, *Mindscreen: Bergman, Godard and First-Person Film*, Princeton: Princeton University Press, 1978

Kolker, Robert, *The Altering Eye*, New York: Oxford University Press, 1986

Kracauer, Siegfried, *Theory of Film: the Redemption of Physical Reality*, Princeton: Princeton University Press, 1977

Lalanne, Jean-Marc (et al.), *Wong Kar-Wai*, Paris: Dis Voir, 1998

Le Fanu, Mark, *The Cinema of Andrei Tarkovsky*, London: British Film Institute, 1987

Lefebvre, Henri, *The Production of Space*, Oxford: Blackwell, 1991

Lewis, Jon (ed), *The New American Cinema*, Durham, NC: Duke University Press, 1998

Lippard, Chris (ed), *By Angels Driven: the Films of Derek Jarman*, Westport: Greenwood, 1996

Lyotard, Jean-François, *Postmodern Fables* (translated by Georges van den Abbeele), Minneapolis: University of Minnesota Press, 1997

MacCabe, Colin, 'A Post-National European Cinema: Derek Jarman's *The Tempest* and *Edward II*' in Duncan Petrie (ed), *Screening Europe*, London: British Film Institute, 1998

'Theory and Film: Principles of Realism and Pleasure' in *Theoretical Essays: Film, Linguistics, Literature*, Manchester: Manchester University Press, 1985

McLoone, Martin, 'The Abused Child of History: Neil Jordan's *The Butcher Boy*' *Cineaste*, vol. XXIII, no. 4, 1998, 32–8

Mailer, Norman, *Oswald's Tale: an American Mystery*, London: Abacus, 1996

Mitchell, William J, *City of Bits: Space, Place and the Infobahn*, Cambridge, MA: MIT Press, 1996

Mulvey, Laura, 'Kiarostami's Uncertainty Principle', *Sight and Sound*, June 1998

Negroponte, Nicholas, *Being Digital*, Cambridge, MA: MIT Press, 1995

Orr, John, *Cinema and Modernity*, Cambridge: Polity, 1993

*Contemporary Cinema*, Edinburgh: Edinburgh University Press, 1998

Palley, Marcia, 'Order vs. Chaos: the Films of Peter Greenaway', *Cineaste*, vol. XVII, no. 3, 1991

Pascoe, David, *Peter Greenaway: Museums and Moving Images*, London: Reaktion, 1997

Pasolini, Pier Paolo, *Heretical Empiricism* (translated by Ben Lawton and Louise Barnett), Bloomington: Indiana University Press, 1988

Penz, François & Thomas, Maureen (eds), *Cinema and Architecture*, London: British Film Institute, 1997

Petrie, Duncan, *Creativity and Constraint in the British Film Industry*, Basingstoke: Macmillan, 1991

Posner, Gerald, *Case Closed: Lee Harvey Oswald and the Assassination of JFK*, London: Warner, 1993

Rodley, Chris (ed), *Cronenberg on Cronenberg*, London: Faber, 1998

'Funny How Secrets Travel: an Interview with David Lynch' in David Lynch & Barry Gifford, *Lost Highway*, London: Faber & Faber, 1997

Rogin, Michael, *Independence Day*, London: British Film Institute, 1998

Rohmer, Eric, 'A Twentieth Century Tale: Orson Welles's *Mr. Arkadin*' in *The Taste for Beauty* (translated by Carol Volk), Cambridge: Cambridge University Press, 1989

Rosenbaum, Ron, *Travels with Dr Death*, London: Papermac, 1999

Showalter, Elaine, *Hystories: Hysterical Epidemics and Modern Culture*, London: Picador, 1997

Summers, Anthony, *The Kennedy Conspiracy* (2nd edn), London: Sphere, 1992

Tarkovsky, Andrei, *Sculpting in Time: Reflections on the Cinema*, London: Bodley Head, 1987

Tarkovsky, Andrei, *Time Within Time: the Diaries* (translated by Kitty Hunter-Blair), Calcutta: Seagull, 1991

Thewelheit, Klaus, *Male Fantasies 2: Male Bodies: Psychoanalysing the White Terror* (translated by Chris Turner and Erica Carter), Cambridge: Polity, 1989

Virilio, Paul, *Open Sky* (translated by Julie Rose), London: Verso, 1996

Walsh, Michael, 'Jameson and "Global Aesthetics"' in David Bordwell and Noel Carroll (eds) *Post-Theory: Reconstructing Film Studies*, Madison: University of Wisconsin Press, 1996

Wollen, Peter, 'Cinema and Technology' in *Readings and Writings: Semiotic Counter-Strategies*, London: Verso, 1982

'The Last New Wave: Modernism in the British Films of the Thatcher Era' in Lester Friedman, *British Cinema and Thatcherism*, London: UCL Press, 1993

Woods, Alan, *Being Naked, Playing Dead: the Art of Peter Greenaway*, Manchester: Manchester University Press, 1996

# INDEX